# Constitutional Law in Bulgaria

# Constitutional Law in Bulgaria

**Martin Belov**

This book was originally published as a monograph in the International Encyclopaedia of Laws/Constitutional Law.

Founding Editor: Roger Blanpain
General Editor: Frank Hendrickx
Volume Editors: André Alen & David Haljan

Wolters Kluwer

*Published by:*
Kluwer Law International B.V.
PO Box 316
2400 AH Alphen aan den Rijn
The Netherlands
E-mail: international-sales@wolterskluwer.com
Website: lrus.wolterskluwer.com

*Sold and distributed in North, Central and South America by:*
Wolters Kluwer Legal & Regulatory U.S.
7201 McKinney Circle
Frederick, MD 21704
United States of America
Email: customer.service@wolterskluwer.com

*Sold and distributed in all other countries by:*
Air Business Subscriptions
Rockwood House
Haywards Heath
West Sussex
RH16 3DH
United Kingdom
Email: international-customerservice@wolterskluwer.com



ISBN 978-94-035-1735-3

e-Book: ISBN 978-94-035-1782-7
web-PDF: ISBN 978-94-035-1830-5

# The Author

Dr Martin Belov has a Master's (2004) and PhD (2009) in Law from the University of Sofia 'St. Kliment Ohridski', Bulgaria. He is an associate professor of Constitutional Law, Comparative Constitutional Law, European Constitutional Law and Supranational Constitutionalism at the University of Sofia 'St. Kliment Ohridski', Bulgaria. Martin Belov is vice dean of the University of Sofia 'St. Kliment Ohridski', Faculty of Law (since 2019). He has been a guest lecturer and a visiting professor at the University Paris II Pantheon-Assas, France (2019), University Roma Tre, Italy (2019), LUISS 'Guido Carli', Rome, Italy (2019), 'Goethe' University, Frankfurt am Main, Germany (2019), the European Academy of Legal Theory (2019), University of Girona, Spain (2019), Europa-University Viadrina, Frankfurt/Oder, Germany (2017 and 2018), Masaryk University, Brno, Czech Republic (2018), European Law and Governance School, Athens, Greece (2017),, University of Södertorn, Stockholm, Sweden, (2017), Scuolla Superiore Sant'Anna, Pisa, Italy (2016), Berufsakademie Sachsen, Staatlichen Studienakademie, Bautzen (Germany), University of Warsaw, Poland (2015), University of Lisbon, Portugal (2012), State University of Milan, Italy (2011) and University of Cologne, Germany (2007–2009). Martin Belov has delivered public lectures at the University of Oxford, UK (2018), 'Goethe' University, Frankfurt am Main, Germany, 'Sigmund Freud' University, Vienna, Austria (2018), LUISS 'Guido Carli', Rome, Italy (2016) and University of Lodz, Poland (2015).

Martin Belov has been a project researcher at the Max-Planck Institute for European Legal History, Frankfurt am Main, Germany (2010–2012) and a visiting researcher at the Institute for Federalism, Fribourg, Switzerland (2014). He has specialized at the University of Oxford, UK (2017), Max-Planck Institute for Comparative Public Law and International Law, Heidelberg, Germany (2009), Technical University of Dresden, Germany (2006), University of Gent, Belgium (2004), University of Strasbourg 'Robert Schumann', France (2003), University of Hamburg, Germany (2002–2003), European Academy for Legal Theory, Brussels, Belgium (2001) and the University of Vienna, Austria (2001).

Martin Belov has published fourteen books and more than eighty scientific papers. Martin Belov is a member of the European Group of Public Law and International Association of Legislation. He is a member of the Advisory Board of the Central

**The Author**

and Eastern European Forum of the Young Legal, Political and Social Theorists. Prof. Belov can be contacted on his e-mail: martinbelov@yahoo.com

# Table of Contents

# List of Abbreviations

| | |
|---|---|
| CETA | EU-Canada Comprehensive Economic and Trade Agreement |
| CFREU | Charter of Fundamental Rights of the EU |
| CoE | Council of Europe |
| ECJ | Court of Justice of the European Union |
| EU | European Union |
| EConvHR | European Convention of Human Rights and Fundamental Freedoms |
| ECtHR | European Court of Human Rights |
| ICCPR | International Covenant on Civil and Political Rights |
| ICESCR | International Covenant of Economic, Social and Cultural Rights |
| ILO | International Labour Organization |
| MEP | Member of the European Parliament |
| MP | Member of Parliament |
| NATO | North Atlantic Treaty Organization |
| SG | State Gazette (the Official Journal of the Republic of Bulgaria) |
| UN | United Nations |
| UNESCO | United Nations Educational, Scientific and Cultural Organization |
| UDHR | Universal Declaration of Human Rights |

## List of Abbreviations

# General Introduction

## §1. An Outline of Bulgarian Constitutional History

*1.* Bulgaria has had four constitutions adopted in 1879, 1947, 1971 and 1991. The first Bulgarian Constitution is the Tarnovo Constitution which was adopted by the Constituent Assembly on 16 April 1879 in the medieval Bulgarian capital city of Tarnovo (currently Veliko Tarnovo). It is a version of the 1831 Belgian Constitution which had been transplanted[1] to Bulgaria both directly and via its Balkan versions – the 1864 Greek Constitution, the 1866 Romanian Constitution and the 1869 Serbian Constitution.[2]

*2.* Consequently, the Tarnovo Constitution, together with the other abovementioned Balkan constitutions of the 1860s, is actually a result of a broader geopolitical decision that has two main elements. The first element is that the Balkans must and will be part of Europe, and they will belong to the European constitutional and political civilization. The second is that the constitutional monarchy, which is a compromise between monarchical and democratic constitutionalism and between monarchism and parliamentarism that spread throughout most parts of Europe in the second half of the nineteenth century, will be implemented and imposed also on the Balkans.

*3.* The Tarnovo Constitution provides for constitutional monarchy with elements of parliamentary monarchy. Its constitutional monarchical features comprise the following main elements. There is a separation of powers scheme enshrined in a written constitution with supremacy in the domestic sources of law. The constitutional model for the separation of powers provides for the central place of the monarch who possesses key competences in all state powers with the partial exception of the judicial power where he has a more symbolic presence. The monarch has the right to introduce legislation and to exercise a veto. He hires and fires the Prime Minister, government Ministers, military officers, diplomats and the office holders

1. Alan Watson, *Legal Transplants: An Approach to Comparative Law,* 21–31 (University of Georgia Press, 1974).
2. More about the sources of influence for the 1879 Tarnovo Constitution *see* Stefan Kirov, *Bulgarian Constitutional Law*, part I, 28 et seq. (T. Chipev, 1938) (in Bulgarian).

of the most important administrative offices. The monarch can dissolve the Parliament, suspend its sessions and approve its Chairman. The monarch determines the strategical priorities and sets the tactical guidelines for the executive power in both internal and external policy.

*4.* On the contrary, there are specifics of the institutional design provided by the Tarnovo Constitution which could have led to the development of parliamentarism and the establishment of parliamentary instead of constitutional monarchy in Bulgaria. The Tarnovo Constitution provides for a wide range of political rights, such as census-free universal electoral suffrage, freedom of assembly and freedom of speech. Hence the legal prerequisites for the emergence of deliberative and participatory democracy and for active civic society have been enshrined in the Tarnovo Constitution. The National Assembly is the unicameral Parliament. There is no second chamber which could have eventually served as an ally of the monarch in the legislative, budgetary and other decision-making processes. The Parliament possesses a constitutionally granted system of instruments for parliamentary control. There is individual and collective political responsibility of Ministers and the government before Parliament provided by Article 153 of the Tarnovo Constitution.

*5.* However, several factors have prevented the development of the parliamentary and democratic potential of the first Bulgarian Constitution. The lack of necessary social preconditions, such as an autonomous and developed civic society, real ideology-based non-clientelistic political parties, an independent media, free elections and so on, impeded the emergence of enhanced parliamentarism in Bulgaria. The constitutionally proclaimed free and universal suffrage was drastically infringed by legislation which provided only for male suffrage (with some exceptions introduced in 1937). The elections were typically compromised and unfair.

*6.* Moreover, capitalism is an important prerequisite for the emergence of both bourgeoisie and middle class. Thus capitalism is also a fundamental precondition for liberal democracy, although not all capitalist systems were and are capable of developing and maintaining democracy. Hence capitalism is a basic but insufficient prerequisite of representative government and liberal democracy. The Bulgarian society in the period from the Liberation of Bulgaria in 1878 until the establishment of the Soviet-type political regime in the country in 1947 was rather egalitarian–agrarian society with only emergent capitalist structure, weak bourgeoisie and middle class. That is why the monarch was able to make the system function as a constitutional instead of parliamentary monarchy, relying on the support of the military as functional equivalent of the missing Bulgarian aristocracy and clearly dominating the political discourse despite the checks on his power provided by the Tarnovo Constitution.

*7.* Thus Bulgaria was ruled predominantly as an authoritarian regime masqueraded as a constitutional monarchy. It took different shapes: an unconstitutional monarchical dictatorship under the regime of plenary powers of Knjaz Alexander I Battenberg (1881–1883), the personal regime of Tzar Ferdinand I Saxe-Coburg-Gotha (at the beginning of the twentieth century), the authoritarian regime of Tzar

Boris III Saxe-Coburg-Gotha (1935–1943), the dictatorships of Prime Ministers Stefan Stambolov (1886–1894) and Alexander Stamboliyski (1919–1923) and the shared authoritarian rule of the monarch and the Prime Minister under Tzar Boris and Prime Ministers Alexander Tzankov (1923–1925) and Kimon Georgiev (1934–1935).

*8.* That is why Bulgaria has been governed in a relatively democratic manner in short periods of time at the end of the nineteenth century and the beginning of the twentieth century under Prime Ministers Konstantin Stoilov and Petko Karavelov and from 1926 to 1934 under Prime Ministers Andrey Lyapchev, Alexander Malinov and Nikola Mushanov. The lack of a developed civic society, the sociopolitical catastrophes caused by lost wars and the rise of authoritarian tendencies in Europe were among the main reasons for the impossibility to establish effective and functional democracy in the interwar period despite the fact that Bulgaria, in contrast to the other Balkan states, preserved its liberal and democratic constitution until 1947. In fact the Tarnovo Constitution has been the most liberal constitution on the Balkans at that time.

*9.* In the post-Liberation period, the political spectrum in Bulgaria has been artificially structured in liberal and conservative camps which were lacking the sociopolitical preconditions for their existence and were masquerading leadership parties. This 'liberal–conservative' cleavage, rather artificial in an egalitarian peasant society, was transplanted from Romania which itself had copied it from the French political life used as a prototype for social and political modernization. In the Interwar period this artificial cleavage and the plethora of quasi-liberal and quasi-conservative parties have been replaced by fierce clash between radical left (agrarian and communist) and radical right (nationalist) parties, followed by the prohibition of political pluralism and political parties in 1934 paving the way for the personal regime of Tzar Boris III.

*10.* In 1947, a new communist constitution was adopted and then replaced in 1971 by a second communist constitution of Bulgaria. Both constitutions were inspired by the Soviet constitutional model. They proclaimed the unity of state power, the supremacy of the national representative body and the election of the magistrates either by the people or by the representative bodies. They abolished representative democracy and political pluralism and established a planned economy with a clear predominance of, or even the exclusive existence of, state-owned property. Typical for both the 1947 and the 1971 constitutions are the separate chapters on the socio-economic principles of the state and the society. They are a result of the Marxist theoretical stipulation of the political role of the economy and thus of the predetermination of the state and politics by the economy.

*11.* Despite the general transplantation of the Soviet model, the 1947 and the 1971 constitutions also preserved some elements of the Bulgarian national constitutional design. The most important deviation from the Soviet constitutions was the preservation of the National Assembly, which served the function of the supreme council. Formally, all civic rights and most of the political rights had also been proclaimed. However, in the context of the party dictatorship of the Bulgarian Communist Party (with the nominal and formal collaboration of the Bulgarian Agricultural Peoples Union), political rights lost their function as instruments for active and autonomous civic participation in politics and were turned instead to serve as instruments for mass mobilization.

*12.* Among the most important institutional novelties introduced by the 1947 and the 1971 constitutions was the Presidium of the National Assembly, to be later replaced in 1971 by the State Council. These institutions served simultaneously the functions of collective head of state, legislative and decision-making bodies. Formally, the supreme power of the state and the people was vested in the National Assembly which was also the legislative body. In practice, the National Assembly was composed of non-professional Members of Parliament (MPs). They were summoned for limited periods of time in order to rubber-stamp the political decisions and the legislative acts which were already either predetermined or directly adopted by the Presidium of the National Assembly (later the State Council) and the Council of Ministers.

*13.* The 1947 Constitution was initially intended to have a compromising character, that is establishing an economy dominated by state paternalism and enhanced solidarity and limiting but not fully abolishing political pluralism. Especially in its draft version, it was a constitution capable of framing capitalist society and pluralist political discourse with enhanced role of solidarism and with a mixture of *etatism* and paternalism. The 1947 Constitution in its initial version was a mixture of the 1946 Italian Constitution and the Soviet constitutions. It did not explicitly prohibit private property, market economy and political parties. However, after the fall of the 'iron curtain' and the geopolitical decision that Bulgaria will be allocated entirely in the Soviet sphere of influence, the constitutional text was adjusted to this trend. What is more important is that despite the moderate illiberal tone of the constitutional text, the political practice was dominated by drastic violations of human rights culminating in nationalization of private property and massive radical repressions over political opponents to the new communist regime.

*14.* The 1971 Constitution is much more radical than the 1947 Constitution in providing Soviet-type features and in establishing the dictatorship of the Bulgarian Communist Party and the planned economy. Its Article 1 declares the leading role of the Bulgarian Communist Party. Moreover, the 1971 Constitution prohibits private property which has economic functions and replaces it with 'personal property'. That is, private property that has only consumer and no productive function. The 1971 Constitution additionally strengthens the Soviet-type institutional design by reinforcing the emphasis on the unity of state power.

*15.* It is interesting to note that both the 1947 and 1971 Constitutions have been part of the two waves of adoption of communist Soviet-type constitutions in Central and Eastern Europe. Thus they are the result of coordinated constitution-making process encompassing the states belonging to the Soviet geopolitical sphere of influence.

*16.* The fall of the Berlin wall in 1989 triggered a geopolitical reorientation in all Central and East European states. In Bulgaria, the communist leader Todor Jivkov was replaced by a velvet revolution inside the Bulgarian Communist Party on 10 November 1989. This revolution was a result of the political bargaining between the USSR leader Mikhail Gorbachev and the US President Ronald Reagan related to the future of the world in general and of Central and Eastern Europe in particular. In 1990, some of the key provisions of the 1971 Constitution, such as the leading role of the Bulgarian Communist Party, were abolished in order to allow for the elections to the Grand National Assembly. In 1990, the VII Grand National Assembly was elected. On 12 July 1991, it adopted the current Bulgarian Constitution which was the first entirely new post-communist constitution in Europe.

## §2. Characteristics of the Bulgarian State

### I. Parliamentary Republic

*17.* The republican tradition was established in Bulgaria with the abolition of the monarchy via national referendum held in 1946. Despite that fact during the communist period (1944–1989) it was impossible to combine the republican with parliamentary and democratic forms of government.

*18.* The republican tradition has two main dimensions. The first concerns the republican form of government. The second consists in the existence of civic activism and engagement and the democratic awareness of a large part of the population. Bulgaria has a deeply and firmly established republican tradition with regard to that first aspect concerning the form of government. Three out of four Bulgarian constitutions have been republican. Up to 2018 Bulgaria was governed as a monarchy for sixty-seven years and as a republic for seventy-two years. Moreover, the republican period encompasses precisely these past seventy-two years.

*19.* However, the second aspect of the republican tradition consisting in the existence of civic activism and critical political engagement is traditionally rather weak. This is due to many reasons: centuries of foreign domination, specifics of the political culture and the constitutional anthropology, decades of inexistent or very weak civil society during both the period of constitutional monarchy and the communist period, and so on.

*20.* The 1991 Constitution provides for most of the features of the parliamentary form of government. These are the flexible separation of powers, the parliamentary origin and investiture of the government, the genetic and functional interdependence between National Assembly and Council of Ministers[3] and the developed forms of parliamentary control and imposition and ascription of political responsibility on the government by the Parliament.[4]

*21.* The Bulgarian parliamentary model possesses also some specifics and deviations from the pure parliamentary republican model. The most important among them are the direct election of the President of the Republic by the people, the moderate but in some cases important competences of the head of state, the lack of competence of the government to dissolve the Parliament, the lack of delegated legislation and the incompatibility of the position as an MP with the office as member of the government.[5]

*22.* This is the reason why some authors define Bulgaria as a hybrid parliamentary,[6] or even as semi-presidential, republic.[7] Indeed Bulgaria is a hybrid parliamentary republic due to the predominance of the parliamentary features of the system despite the above-mentioned deviations. These deviations are predominantly borrowings from the semi-presidential republic, but in some cases (e.g., the lack of delegated legislation and the lack of competence of the government to dissolve the Parliament) are also reflection of issues and problems which have emerged in the Bulgarian constitutional history. However, they do not change the predominantly parliamentary outlook of the institutional design. The direct election of the President of the Republic and his position as a limited but not nominal head of state still do not permit the classification of Bulgaria as a semi-presidential republic. Any conclusion which might be focused on them overemphasizes the importance of the direct election of a head of state and does not take into account the definitely much more restricted functions and competences of the Bulgarian President in comparison to the Presidents of the semi-presidential republics.

## II. Unitary State with Local Self-Government

*23.* Bulgaria has always been a unitary state and only nominally and for very short periods of time was the local self-government replaced by the government of appointed, unelected state officials. Thus the unitary form of the territorial structure of public power as well as the local self-government may be perceived as durable and central elements of the Bulgarian constitutional tradition.

---

3. Georgi Bliznashki, *Parliamentary Law*, 47–48 ('St. Kliment Ohridski' University Press, 2015).
4. Plamen Kirov, *The President in the Bulgarian Constitutional Model*, 112 et seq. (Sibi, 2004) (in Bulgarian); Georgi Bliznashki, *The Parliamentary Government in Bulgaria*, 21 et seq. ('St. Kliment Ohridski' University Press, 2009) (in Bulgarian); Vasil Kirov, *The Public Power*, 151 et seq. (Ciela, 2004) (in Bulgarian).
5. Plamen Kirov, *supra* n. 4, 113 et seq., Georgi Bliznashki, *supra* n. 4, 21 et seq.
6. Georgi Bliznashki, *supra* n. 4, 22.
7. Vasil Kirov, *supra* n. 4, 225 et seq.

*24.* The self-government of the Bulgarian municipalities has been largely practised during the period of constitutional monarchy and the Tarnovo Constitution. No Bulgarian government has been either able or really willing to infringe in an enduring way on the self-government of the Bulgarian municipalities and local informal sociopolitical communities.

*25.* During the communist period, the institutions for local self-government were fully dependent on and controlled by the Bulgarian Communist Party. However, the same and even greater degree of party control was also accomplished at the national level. This control did not target the limitation of local self-government as such, but rather the establishment and the safeguarding of the total control of society by the state ruled by the Bulgarian Communist Party. Hence the limitation of local self-government has been based not on reasons related to the constitutionally provided form of territorial distribution of power but on party political grounds.

*26.* In the post-communist period, local self-government has been reinforced and additionally legally safeguarded. Since the constitutional reforms in 2006, municipalities have even received increased tax autonomy. However, the main problem for local self-government since 1991 is the existence of nepotistic and clientelistic practices and the dependence of municipal councils and the mayors on both national and local elites.

*27.* The Bulgarian Constitutional Court has a rather ambiguous stance on the effects of the EU membership and EU integration on the form of territorial distribution of power in general and on the unitary state in the particular Bulgarian case. In its seminal Decision No. 3 of 2004, the Constitutional Court provides that the EU is not a federation and the Bulgarian EU membership does not have any repercussions on the unitary character of its form of territorial distribution of power. That is why the introduction of the EU integration clause of Article 4, paragraph 3 of the Constitution could have been accomplished in 2005 by the Parliament and not by a special constituent assembly – the Grand National Assembly.

*28.* However, in the motives to its Decision No. 7 of 2018, the Constitutional Court stipulates that the integration clause of the Bulgarian Constitution provided in its Article 4, paragraph 3 is 'new basic principle and one of the fundamental principles of the established constitutional order in the country … belonging to the value core of the Bulgarian Constitution. This is the reason why the integration clause is systematically allocated in Chapter I of the Constitution 'Basic Principles'. According to the Constitutional Court, the provision of the integration clause is both norm-principle and norm-framework: 'In its capacity as norm-principle it introduces the European dimension of the Bulgarian statehood. The EU law and the domestic law form together legal space in which the public power jointly and simultaneously participates in the creation of the Union law and develops the national legal order taking into account the values and principles of the EU as well as the national interests. The integration clause is a framework which frames the transfer of state competences towards the EU – a process which is not unrestrained'. The Constitutional Court believes that by emphasizing the role of the

Republic of Bulgaria for the construction and development of the EU the constitutional legislator preserves the Bulgarian constitutional identity.

*29.* The rather bold and activist conclusion of the Constitutional Court that the Bulgarian integration in the EU is new power dimension added to the Bulgarian statehood and at the same time new constitutional principle triggers plethora of questions instead of providing for answers and solutions to problems. Among the most important questions are whether the 'new European dimension' added by the participation of Bulgaria in the construction and development of the EU concerns the form of territorial distribution of power since it constitutes, according to the Constitutional Court, both new constitutional principle and new power reality – the European dimension of the Bulgarian statehood. If this is the case, then Decision No. 7 of 2018 is a clear departure from the previous case law of the Constitutional Court (more precisely Decision No. 3 of 2004) according to which the EU integration of Bulgaria does not result in change of the form of territorial distribution of power and thus does not require the summoning of Grand National Assembly for approval of the Bulgarian membership in the EU.

*30.* Indeed it will not be fair to define Decision No. 7 of 2018 in such activist terms changing at once the system of constitutional principles and the form of territorial distribution of powers. The aim of the Constitutional Court was to provide for EU-friendly solution to a particular issue, namely the standing of the mixed international agreements in the Bulgarian legal order and the procedure for their ratification. However, Decision No. 7 of 2018 is evidence of the fuzzy practice of the Bulgarian Constitutional Court on the nature of the Bulgarian membership in the EU.

## III. Popular Sovereignty and Democracy

*31.* The principle of popular sovereignty has been explicitly proclaimed by the last three Bulgarian constitutions. The Tarnovo Constitution proclaims explicitly neither popular, nor national nor monarchical sovereignty. Implicitly it provides for a kind of shared sovereignty. The systematic interpretation of its provisions leads to the conclusion that neither the monarch nor the people can take fundamental constitutional decisions without achieving consensus on them.[8]

*32.* Hence sovereignty of the people is a persistent and fundamental characteristic of the Bulgarian constitutional tradition. It is not only proclaimed but is also further developed via institutions for amending the constitution and via political rights reflecting the presumed centrality of the people as a sovereign factor in the

8. For a critical analysis of the concept of dual sovereignty in Bulgaria under the Tarnovo Constitution *see* Stefan Kirov, *Parliamentary or Personal Regime*, 137 et seq. ('St. Kliment Ohridski' University Press, 2011) (in Bulgarian).

system. The 1991 Constitution explicitly proclaims the principle of popular sovereignty in its Article 1, paragraph 2. Popular sovereignty is further developed by different constitutional provisions related to democracy and political rights as well as by the constitutional legislation.

*33.* Democracy is part of the Bulgarian constitutional heritage due to its explicit proclamation as a constitutional principle or the provision of its most important aspects and elements by the Bulgarian constitutions. But democracy did not possess deep roots in sociopolitical relations despite the fact that all four Bulgarian constitutions did have explicit and extensive references to it, albeit investing quite different and even controversial content in the concept of democracy.

*34.* Thus Bulgaria did not have a fully-fledged democratic tradition until the adoption of the 1991 Constitution. Indeed the Tarnovo Constitution is deservedly praised as one of the most democratic constitutions of its epoch[9] due to the wide-ranging political rights and the political equality it provides as well as due to the elements of its institutional design (unicameral Parliament, parliamentary control over the government, etc.). However, political practice has been marked by the alteration of different authoritarian regimes with short periods of attempts at developing real democratic government.

*35.* The preamble of the 1991 Constitution explicitly proclaims the principle of democracy. The 1991 Constitution provides for the system of institutions of representative democracy. The Bulgarian representative democracy is shaped as a parliamentary party democracy. In addition, the 1991 Constitution provides for wide-ranging political rights capable of serving as a legal basis for the development of deliberative, participatory and direct democracy functioning as a supplement, and not as an alternative, to the representative democracy.

## IV. The Separation of Powers

*36.* The Tarnovo Constitution provides for a model for an asymmetrical separation of powers which is typical for the constitutional monarchies of the second half of the nineteenth century. The asymmetry is produced by the centrality of the monarch in the institutional design. The Tarnovo Constitution allocates to the monarch all state powers and defines the Parliament, the Council of Ministers and the courts as his partners in the legislative, executive and judicial power.

*37.* The 1947 and 1971 communist constitutions abolished the separation of powers. They replaced it with the unity of state power based on the presumption that

---

9. Lubomir Vladikin *History of the Tarnovo Constitution*, 1–283 (Narodna kultura, 1994) (in Bulgarian); Georgi Bliznashki Constitutionalism and Democracy, 72 ('St. Kliment Ohridski' University Press, 2009) (in Bulgarian).

in a class-free egalitarian society the sovereignty belongs to the people and should be vested in the National Assembly enjoying supremacy in the system of state institutions.

*38.* The 1991 Constitution reinstalls the principle of the separation of powers. The model for the separation of powers enshrined in the current Bulgarian Constitution is that of a parliamentary republic with a reinforced status of the President, thus being very different from the model of separation of powers provided by the Tarnovo Constitution. Hence the reintroduction of the principle of separation of powers in the Bulgarian constitutionalism in 1991 is not a reproduction of the previous constitutional model but constitutes a novelty in the Bulgarian constitutional tradition.

*39.* Article 8 of the 1991 Constitution provides that state power is divided into legislative, executive and judicial. This rather declaratory provision is actually inaccurate for two main reasons. First, if read in isolation from the other constitutional provisions, it might lead to the wrong conclusion that there is a rigid separation of powers in Bulgaria, which is typical for presidential republics and some forms of constitutional monarchies. However, the 1991 Constitution provides for a parliamentary form of government based on flexible separation of powers. Second, the differentiation of the state powers at the end of the twentieth century and the beginning of the twenty-first has led to a proliferation of the branches of state power. In other words, the classical trio of 'legislative-executive-judicial' based on the theory of Montesquieu seems not able to grasp the current complexity of state power. It does not provide for an explanatory framework for the competences of state institutions for representing the state in international relations and in the emerging supranational constitutionalism, in public finance management and in the accomplishment of the personal and the symbolic policy of the state. Moreover, it does not reflect the widespread understanding in the Bulgarian theory that the President of the Republic is not part of any of these powers but accomplishes 'neutral power'.[10]

*40.* Consequently, the traditional and rigid outlook of Article 8 of the 1991 Constitution is a result of two reasons and can be explained with a view to two factors. First, it is a provision which clearly demonstrates the reaction of the 1991 Constitution to the 1947 and the 1971 constitutions. The VII Grand National Assembly which adopted the 1991 post-communist Bulgarian Constitution aimed at demonstrating a clear departure from the principle of the unity of state power which was typical for the Soviet-type communist constitutional model. Second, Article 8 of the 1991 Constitution proves that the theory of separation of powers of Montesquieu

10. For the theory of the President of the Republic of Bulgaria as 'neutral power' *see* Georgi Bliznashki, *Parliamentary Law*, 120 ('St. Kliment Ohridski' University Press, 2015); Georgi Bliznashki, *The Parliamentary Government in Bulgaria*, 59 et seq. ('St. Kliment Ohridski' University Press, 2009) (in Bulgarian).

has been implicitly chosen as the normative ideology[11] and thus as a source of inspiration for the positive constitutional law encoded in the ideal constitution.[12]

*41.* The allocation of constitutional functions and competences among the state institutions will be subject to further in-depth analysis throughout many chapters of the book. Thus the model for the separation of powers enshrined in the 1991 Constitution will not be studied here in any further detail.

## V. Rechtsstaat, Constitutionalism and the Rule of Law

*42.* The Tarnovo Constitution does not explicitly declare the principle of rule of law. However, it provides for many of its elements. The 1947 and the 1971 constitutions replace the rule of law with the principle of 'socialist legality'. The principle of the rule of law is restored by the 1991 Constitution.

*43.* Article 4, paragraph 1 of the 1991 Constitution provides that the Republic of Bulgaria is a Rechtsstaat (**правова държава**). The 1991 Constitution not only proclaims the rule of law by explicitly referring to its continental version – the Rechtsstaat, but it also provides for all typical elements which are necessarily part of it. The 1991 Constitution provides for a wide-ranging catalogue of personal rights of man and citizen, a hierarchy of sources of law, the supremacy of the constitution, the primacy of international treaties over sub-constitutional Bulgarian legislation, the primacy of the acts of the Parliament over the acts of government and a prohibition on extraordinary legislation. It establishes institutional safeguards for human rights and rule of law such as the Constitutional Court, the administrative justice and the ombudsman. The principles of the judicial power such as due process of law, right to fair trial, right to defence, right to appeal, prohibition of retroactive justice, double sentencing and extraordinary courts, provision of public hearings are all granted by the 1991 Constitution.

*44.* The 1991 Constitution complies with international and supranational legal standards of rule of law. The Constitution has been adapted to the human rights' standards of the Council of Europe (CoE) and the United Nations (UN). This is because Bulgaria is a member of the UN since 1953, and it became a member of the CoE in 1992 – just several months after the adoption of its last constitution. Moreover, the 1991 Constitution has been amended several times in the course of Bulgarian EU integration in order to match the *acquis communautaire* in the field of the rule of law.[13]

---

11. For the concept of normative ideology, *see* Martin Belov, *The Ideological Heritage of Magna Charta and Its Reception in the Bulgarian Constitutionalism*, 453 et seq. ('St. Kliment Ohridski' University Press, 2017) (in Bulgarian).
12. For the concept of ideal constitution *see* Evgeni Tanchev, *Introduction in Constitutional Law*, 122 et seq. (Sibi, 2003) (in Bulgarian), as well as the literature which is cited there.
13. Evgeni Tanchev and Martin Belov *Constitutional Gradualism: Adapting to EU Membership and Improving the Judiciary in the Bulgarian Constitution*, 8(1) European Public Law, 3–19 (2008).

### VI. Welfare State

*45.* During the debates in the VII Grand National Assembly, the welfare state was the object of a superficial and a very ideological discussion. Some of the MPs insisted that the welfare state is part of the constitutional axiology of post-World War II West European constitutionalism. Others believed that it resembles too much the socialist state and is a version of socialism. As a result the welfare state has not been enshrined directly in the text of the 1991 Constitution but rather in its preamble. However, the preamble also has normative force even if it does not contain legal provisions structured as the main constitutional text.[14] In addition all components of the welfare state – economic, social and cultural rights, as well as principles of the economic constitution such as consumer protection, social security protection, protection of persons at high social risk of exclusion and so on – have been explicitly provided for by the 1991 Constitution.

*46.* Hence a conclusion can be drawn that the welfare state was proclaimed and provided for in Bulgarian constitutionalism for the first time by the 1991 Constitution. Indeed the 1947 and the 1971 constitutions contained detailed and elaborate provisions on the social, economic and cultural rights and on the role of the state as a safeguard for social security and the socio-economic prosperity of the citizens. However, these provisions were part of a rather different constitutional ideology and model. The Tarnovo Constitution provided for the right to free primary school education, but this is insufficient to believe that it implicitly also proclaimed substantial elements of the welfare state.

*47.* Thus the reintroduction of market economy and capitalism into Bulgaria after the fall of the communist regime has been done on the basis of a socio-liberal model of the constitutional principle of the welfare state. It differs from both the liberal model of a socially unrestrained market economy provided by the Tarnovo Constitution and the communist model of the planned economy enshrined in the 1947 and the 1971 constitutions.

## §3. State Territory, Population and Demographics

*48.* The territory of the Republic of Bulgaria encompasses 110,994 square kilometres since 1940.

*49.* Article 2 of the 1991 Constitution proclaims the unitary nature of the state, the indivisibility of the territory and prohibits the establishment of territorial autonomies. Threats to territorial integrity serve as a limitation on some political rights

14. Martin Belov, *The Preamble of the Constitution in the European Constitutionalism*, 20 Revista General de Derecho Romano (2013); Iustel & Martin Belov, *Functions of the Constitutional Preamble*, in Law, Governance and Media in XXI Century. Blagoevgrad: South-Western University Neofit Rilski Press, 2012 (in Bulgarian).

such as freedom of assembly and freedom of association. According to Article 9, paragraph 1 the territorial integrity of Bulgaria is safeguarded by its military forces.

*50.* The Bulgarian territory is divided into administrative–territorial units structured on two levels. The first level is the level of the regional government. On that level, the territory is divided into twenty-eight regions. The second level is the level of local self-government comprising the municipalities as the main administrative–territorial units and the '*rayons*' and '*mayorships*' as composite administrative–territorial units.

*51.* Minor changes in the Bulgarian territory resulting in its incremental adjustment can be accomplished by the National Assembly. Major territorial changes consisting in the cession or the acquisition of territory can be done only by the Grand National Assembly which must be elected especially for that purpose.

*52.* The population of the Republic of Bulgaria in 2015, according to the National Statistics Office,[15] comprises some 7,153,784 citizens. The male population amounts to 3,477,177 citizens and the female population, 3,676,607 citizens. Some 5,227,182 people live in cities whereas 1,926,602 people live in villages. According to the last official population census in 2011, citizens of Bulgarian origin are 5,664,624 (76.91% of the population), citizens of Turkish origin are 588,318 (7.98% of the population) and citizens of Roma origin, 325,343 (4.41% of the population). There are also some other minor groups of population.

15. National Statistics Institute http://www.nsi.bg, (accessed 17 July 2017).

# Part I. Sources of Constitutional Law

## Chapter 1. The Constitution

### §1. CHARACTERISTICS

*53.* The 1991 Constitution is the fourth constitution in the history of Bulgaria. It has been preceded by the 1879 Tarnovo Constitution and the 1947 and the 1971 communist constitutions. The 1991 Constitution has been adopted in the context of the post-communist reorientation of Bulgaria towards the Western constitutionalism. The 1991 Bulgarian Constitution may be defined as a compromise and mixture between liberalism, social democracy and welfare state and between nationalism, Europeanism and globalism. It balances the *étatist* with the human rights' dimension and establishes the constitutional foundations for the development of the civil society in Bulgaria.

*54.* Bulgaria has opted for the choice which has been made by most of the post-communist countries in Central and Eastern Europe apart from Poland and Hungary consisting in the adoption of a brand new constitution at the very beginning of the transition towards democracy, rule of law and market economy. It is interesting to note that the 1991 Bulgarian Constitution has been the first entirely new constitution adopted by European post-communist state although Poland and Hungary have already made substantial changes in their old Soviet-type constitutions. Although the 1991 Constitution has been adopted in order to establish the constitutional framework of democracy in transition, it is a permanent constitution. It has been properly adapted to the challenges of the shifting sociolegal context while serving as reliable and durable framework of the political process.

*55.* Moreover, the 1991 Bulgarian Constitution has served as an example for constitutional reform for some European states, e.g., in the Western Balkans. Thus the 1991 Constitution is the only Bulgarian Constitution which has asserted also some influence towards foreign states. This is due to the fact that many of the new democracies in Central and Eastern Europe have opted for hybrid parliamentarism in their new constitutions after the fall of communism, and Bulgaria was the first post-communist country in the region that has adopted the constitution of hybrid parliamentary republic (parliamentary republic with elements of semi-presidentialism). Moreover, being an EU Member State, Bulgaria has been a model for the Western Balkans, which has relatively similar social and historical development and sociolegal context.

*56.* The 1991 Constitution is the only Bulgarian Constitution that implicitly provides for the principle of the open statehood[16] and for the participation of the state in multilevel constitutional systems[17] and in the emerging global constitutionalism[18] and constitutional pluralism.[19] The 1991 Constitution served as a basis for the integration of Bulgaria in forms of institutionalized supranational and international cooperation of the Western civilization such as the CoE, the EU and the North Atlantic Treaty Organization (NATO). It is a constitution of the globalization and the Europeanization optimism born in the late Westphalian epoch thus providing for both safeguards for the state sovereignty and for the opening of the statehood towards the emerging supranational constitutionalism.

*57.* The 1991 Constitution is written and codified. In fact, all Bulgarian constitutions have been written and codified. The 1991 Constitution is reflexive and reactive constitution. It is adopted as rejection of the previous regime of the communist dictatorship (1947–1989) which has taken the form of people's democracy. At the same time, the current Bulgarian Constitution is also a deliberate alternative to the constitutional monarchy which has been the form of government under the Tarnovo Constitution from 1879 to 1947. In fact, all thirteen constitutional projects introduced for consideration by the Grand National Assembly in 1990–1991 have been republican.

*58.* Hence the 1991 Constitution can be viewed as rejection of both the Soviet type of people's democracy and of the constitutional monarchy. The 1991 Constitution is reactive[20] not only to the form of government of all previous Bulgarian constitutions but also to their constitutional axiology consisting in the constitutionally enshrined values and principles. The 1991 Constitution departs from the shared sovereignty between the monarch and the people implicitly provided by the Tarnovo Constitution by proclaiming the principle of people's sovereignty. It rejects also most of the principles of the 1947 and the 1971 constitutions.

*59.* In addition, the 1991 Constitution is not only reactive but also reflexive since it not only rejects important elements of the previous constitutional design but also

---

16. For the principle of the open statehood *see* Stefan Hobe, *Statehood at the End of the 20th Century – The Model of the 'Open State': A German Perspective*, 12 Austrian Review of International and European Law, 127–154 (1996).
17. For the concept and theory of multilevel constitutionalism, *see* Neil Walker, *Multilevel Constitutionalism: Looking Beyond the German Debate*, 8 LSE 'Europe in Question' Discussion Paper Series (2009) and Ingolf Pernice, *The Global Dimension of Multilevel Constitutionalism. A Legal Response to the Challenges of Globalization*, in Völkerrecht als Wertordnung. Festschrift für Christian Tomuschat, 973 et seq. (Engel Verlag, 2006).
18. For the concept of global constitutionalism *see* Anne Peters, *Global Constitutionalism*, in *The Encyclopedia of Political Thought* (M. Gibbons ed., Wiley, 2015).
19. For the concept of constitutional pluralism *see* Matej Avbelj and Jan Komarek (eds), *Constitutional Pluralism in the European Union and Beyond*, 1–452 (Hart Publishing, 2012).
20. For the reactive constitutions *see* Evgeni Tanchev, *Introduction in Constitutional Law*, 198 (Sibi, 2003) (in Bulgarian).

tries to remodel it creatively in order to avoid the re-emergence of negative phenomena experienced in the past.[21] Examples of both reactivity and reflexivity of the 1991 Constitution are the prohibition of delegated and extraordinary legislation and the non-provision of the right of the head of state or the government to dissolve the Parliament. This is because the Bulgarian monarchs misused these two competences thus biasing the constitutional monarchy provided by the Tarnovo Constitution in authoritarian direction.

*60.* Moreover, the 1991 Constitution proclaims the principle of political pluralism. This principle has been made obsolete during the last decades of the constitutional monarchy and more precisely since the prohibition of the political parties after the 19 May 1934 coup d'etat. It has been explicitly prohibited during the communist period especially with the 1971 Constitution which proclaimed the leading role of the communist party.

*61.* At the same time, the 1991 Constitution is also consolidating with regard to some aspects of the Bulgarian constitutional tradition established by the previous three constitutions. The most important elements of constitutional continuity are the unitary form of territorial distribution of state power, the unicameral structure of the Parliament, the non-composite structure of the government consisting in the lack of any substructures of the Council of Ministers as well as the provision of civil and political rights. However, it has to be underlined that the political rights and some of the civil rights have been systematically violated during the period of the constitutional monarchy (1879–1947) and have been fictitious although constitutionally proclaimed during the communist period (1947–1989). It is also interesting to note that the right to education has been proclaimed by all Bulgarian constitutions. This is to some extent a result of the fact that the ideology of the European Enlightenment has served as important formative factor for the modern Bulgarian constitutional culture.

*62.* The 1991 Constitution is the only Bulgarian Constitution which is not a direct transplant from concrete foreign constitutional model. The members of the VII Grand National Assembly that has adopted the current Bulgarian Constitution have used different sources of inspiration. Some of them were important acts of the emerging global constitutionalism such as the European Convention of Human Rights and Fundamental Freedoms (EConvHR), the Universal Declaration of Human Rights (UDHR), the International Covenant on Civil and Political Rights (ICCPR) and International Covenant of Economic, Social and Cultural Rights (ICESCR). They have massively influenced the constitutional preamble: Chapter I is devoted to the basic constitutional principles and especially Chapter II contains human rights provided by the Bulgarian Constitution. This is because during the time of adoption of the 1991 Constitution Bulgaria has been a member of the UN since 1953. Moreover, Bulgaria became a member of the CE in 1992 which is less than one year after the entering into force of the new constitution.

---

21. I owe the concepts of 'reflexive constitution' and 'reflexivity of the constitution' to Prof. Mark Ahrenhöfel.

*63.* The most important group of sources of inspiration for the creation of the 1991 Constitution are the constitutional models of some European states. The form of government has been inspired by the creative mixture of parliamentarism borrowed from the 1946 Italian, the 1978 Spanish and the 1975 Greek constitutions and semi-presidentialism taken from the Austrian, the 1958 French and the 1976 Portuguese constitutions. The model for constitutional control has been borrowed from the 1946 Italian and the 1978 Spanish Constitution whereas the model for administration of the judiciary has been massively influenced by the 1946 Italian and the 1958 French constitutions.

*64.* The constitutional legislator has tried to follow the example of countries that have accomplished successful transition from totalitarianism and authoritarianism to democracy. Other factors for the choice of the models for reception are the presumed cultural, anthropological and sociolegal proximity and the prestige of the borrowed constitutional models. In fact, the constitutional models of the South European states adopted during the second half of the twentieth century have been the predominant prototype that has been followed by the VII Grand National Assembly. Thus the post-authoritarian Mediterranean constitutional tradition as well as the institutional design provided by some Central European constitutions can be defined as a leading source of inspiration for the establishment of the current Bulgarian constitutional model.

*65.* Last but not least, the Bulgarian constitutional tradition has also served as determinant and source of inspiration for the founding fathers and mothers of the 1991 Constitution. It has already been mentioned that despite its predominant reactive character, the last Bulgarian Constitution also builds upon some persistent threats of the Bulgarian constitutional tradition.

## §2. Amending the Constitution

### I. A Two-Track Procedure

*66.* The 1991 Bulgarian Constitution is semi-rigid. This is because it can be amended by a two-track procedure. The most important constitutional amendments according to the view of the constitutional legislator as well as the adoption of new constitution can be accomplished only by a special covenant called 'Grand National Assembly'. The constitutional provisions reserved for the Grand National Assembly are enlisted in the catalogue of Article 158 of the Constitution and can be defined as an entrenched clause. The rest of the constitutional provisions can be amended by the National Assembly via qualified legislative procedure requiring additional readings and qualified majorities. Hence the 1991 Constitution is rigid due to the existence of the entrenched clause and the Grand National Assembly and flexible because the issues which do not fall into the scope of Article 158 of the Constitution can be amended by the ordinary Parliament.

*67.* The procedure for adoption of constitutional laws – laws by virtue of which constitutional amendment is accomplished – by the National Assembly differs from the ordinary legislative procedure for the adoption of acts of Parliament in three aspects. First, the constitutional laws may be initiated by a group of MPs and by the President whereas initiative for the acts of the Parliament belongs to a single MP and to the Council of Ministers. Second, the constitutional laws are adopted on three readings whereas the acts of the Parliament are adopted in two readings. Third, the constitutional laws require qualified majority amounting to three-fourths or in some instances two-thirds of all MPs whereas the acts of the Parliament can be adopted by absolute majority of all MPs.

*68.* Even greater are the differences between the constitutional laws adopted by the Grand National Assembly and the acts of the Parliament. In addition to the already-mentioned differences in the initiative subject, the number of the readings and the majorities required, it must be underlined that a fourth and most important difference exists. This is the institutional difference which consists in the fact that the constitutional laws on issues falling into the scope of the entrenched clause of Article 158 are adopted not by the Parliament but by a special covenant – the Grand National Assembly.

*69.* The right to initiate constitutional amendment belongs alternatively to a quota of the MPs in the National Assembly and to the President of the Republic. The proposal for the adoption of a new constitution or for the amendment of the provisions reserved for the Grand National Assembly can be made by one-half of the MPs in the National Assembly whereas the constitutional amendments which do not concern competences of the Grand National Assembly can be introduced on proposal of one-fourth of the MPs in the National Assembly.

*70.* The granting of right to constitutional initiative to the President of the Republic and not to the Council of Ministers as in the case of legislative initiative aims at introducing distinct and independent source of ideas for constitutional reform which might be an alternative to the governing majority. This is because the Bulgarian President is directly elected by the people and not by the Parliament, and Bulgaria is a parliamentary system in which the will of the government and the parliamentary majority usually coincide. The constitutional initiative is granted to the quota of the MPs and not to a single MP, which is the case with the legislative initiative. This is due to the need to safeguard that only sufficiently representative ideas for constitutional reform might be introduced for further consideration.

*71.* The proposal of one-fourth of the MPs or the President for amendment of the Constitution is considered not earlier than one and not later than three months after its introduction and registration in the National Assembly. The aim of the first term is to safeguard sufficient time for the MPs to get acquainted with the content and the consequences of the proposed constitutional amendment. The purpose of the latter term is to allow for sufficiently swift reaction of the Parliament to the initiative of the MPs or the President.

*72.* The National Assembly adopts the constitutional amendments in three readings which must be accomplished on three different days. The draft act for amendment of the Constitution must receive at least three-fourths of the votes of all MPs in order to be adopted. If the proposal receives the support of less than three-fourths but more than two-thirds of all MPs, then it can be scheduled for new consideration and voting not earlier than two and not later than five months since the last vote. The proposed constitutional amendment is adopted if it is supported by the positive vote of at least two-thirds of all MPs in the new voting.

*73.* The Grand National Assembly can be summoned on the initiative of the President and one-half of the MPs of the National Assembly only on the basis of a draft act for amendment of the constitution. However, the National Assembly is the only institution that can make a decision for the summoning of the Grand National Assembly. The National Assembly considers the proposal of the President or the MPs for the summoning of the Grand National Assembly not earlier than two and not later than five months of its introduction. This period is supposed to guarantee the opportunities for reasonable and informed debate in the Parliament and in the society as well as for timely accomplishment of elections for the Grand National Assembly, if so decided by the National Assembly. The National Assembly makes the decision for the accomplishment of elections for the Grand National Assembly with two-thirds majority of all MPs. The President fixes the concrete date for these elections within three months after the adoption of the parliamentary decision thus having no real discretion regarding the timing.

*74.* The National Assembly is dismissed as of the day of the elections for the Grand National Assembly. Hence the parallel existence of the National Assembly and the Grand National Assembly is constitutionally prohibited. In case of emergency, the Grand National Assembly, by way of exception, could accomplish also the functions of the National Assembly. Although adopted for practical reason to compensate the temporary lack of a functioning Parliament, this solution is rather problematic with a view to the fact that it allows the Grand National Assembly to merge and accomplish in parallel functions of constituent and constituted (in this case legislative) power. Thus it endangers the separation between the constituent and the constituted powers and creates opportunities for huge concentration and potentially for misuse of power by the Grand National Assembly which may start to function as a convent.

*75.* A potential safeguard against such risk for misuse of power is the provision of Article 162, paragraph 1, according to which the Grand National Assembly may discuss and make decisions only on the issues for which it has been elected. In other words, the scope of the mandate of the Grand National Assembly is predetermined by the previous Parliament and cannot be extended by this institution of the constituent power. For example, if the Grand National Assembly is elected in order to change the form of government, it cannot decide to adopt amendments also in the form of territorial distribution of power.

*76.* Moreover, the Grand National Assembly is not allowed to interfere in the sphere of competence of the National Assembly by adopting amendments falling outside the scope of Article 158. However, it will be very difficult to establish whether the sphere of competences of the Parliament to act as constitutional legislator has been really infringed by the Grand National Assembly. This is due to the fact that it is not sufficiently clear in advance where the borderline is between the competences of the National Assembly and the Grand National Assembly because the change in the form of government and in the form of territorial distribution of power usually would be introduced not via declarative proclamation but through amendments in the constitutional design and in the inter-institutional relations. Hence it is not always easy to identify which amendments in the constitutional status, functions and competences of the state institutions are fundamental and lead to change in the form of government and in the form of territorial distribution of power and which of them are just adjustments in the institutional design of secondary importance.

## II. The Role of the Constitutional Court in Delimiting the Competences Between the Grand National Assembly and the National Assembly

*77.* The vagueness and the openness of the concepts of form of government and form of territorial distribution of power as well as of some of the other elements of the constitutional design reserved for amendment by the Grand National Assembly have led to the adoption of three decisions of the Constitutional Court.[22] The need for interpretation of the provisions of Article 158 of the Constitution by the Constitutional Court was predetermined by the necessity to amend the Constitution in the context of the EU accession of Bulgaria. Thus the Constitutional Court through its rather activist jurisprudence based on extensive interpretation of the constitutional texts has turned to be a key player on the border between the constituent and the constituted powers. The Constitutional Court has even shifted and redefined this border in the context of the constitutional amendments needed for the EU integration of Bulgaria.

*78.* The first decision of the Constitutional Court – Decision No. 3 of 2003 – was aimed at giving a definition for the form of government and the form of territorial distribution of power. This was deemed necessary in order to determine whether several reforms of the institutional design triggered by the prospective Bulgarian EU membership can be made by the National Assembly or whether the summoning of the Grand National Assembly was inevitable.

*79.* Decision No. 3 of 2003 of the Constitutional Court can be criticized in several aspects. First, it is formal, superficial and declarative. It does not analyse the issue in detail by using comparative, theoretical and historical arguments but just stipulates presupposed solutions which are not proven by any substantial motives.

---

22. *See also* Evgeni Tanchev and Martin Belov, *supra* n. 13, 6–9 and Martin Belov, *The Bulgarian Constitutional Identity*, 173–195 (Sibi, 2017) (in Bulgarian).

Second, it excessively broadens the scope of the form of government and the form of territorial distribution of powers thus widening the competence of the Grand National Assembly and making impossible almost any amendment of the Constitution by the National Assembly. Third, the Constitutional Court constructs in a rather activist way the form of government and the form of territorial distribution of power as almost all-encompassing concepts.

*80.* Hence the constitutional amendments which were necessary for the EU accession of Bulgaria have been blocked by Decision No. 3 of 2003 of the Constitutional Court. This is the reason why just a year later the Constitutional Court had adopted a new Decision No. 3 of 2004 by virtue of which it has radically changed its practice. Thus Decision No. 3 of 2004 was a necessary precondition for the accomplishment of constitutional reform aiming at opening the way to the EU membership of Bulgaria. However, it is an example of questionable judicial activism. Moreover, it challenges the predictability of the jurisprudence of the Constitutional Court and consequently the principle of legal certainty which is a central element of the rule of law.

*81.* According to Decision No. 3 of 2004, the primacy and the direct effect of the EU law, the right of EU citizens to acquire land in Bulgaria, the provision of EU citizenship, the accomplishment of representative functions of Bulgarian office holders in the EU institutions, the preliminary control of the National Assembly on draft EU legislative acts, the permission of the extradition of Bulgarian citizens to international courts or to foreign countries as well as the provision of additional characteristics of equality stemming out of the Charter of Fundamental Rights of the EU (CFREU) do not concern the form of government and the form of territorial distribution of powers and consequently can be adopted, if constitutional amendment is needed, by the National Assembly. In fact, the Constitutional Court not only changed its previous decision less than a year after its adoption but also did not take into consideration the fact that some of these amendments may concern other issues reserved as exclusive competence of the Grand National Assembly.

*82.* For example, it is very doubtful whether the primacy and the direct effect of the EU law do not concern the supremacy of the Bulgarian Constitution. The Constitutional Court does not take explicit stance on the hierarchical place of the EU law in the Bulgarian legal order in any of its decisions. However, in the motives to Decision No. 3 of 2004, it subsumes the EU law under the category of 'international treaties' thus giving absolute supremacy of the Bulgarian Constitution over it. Moreover, in the motives to Decision No. 3 of 2012, the Constitutional Court discusses the primacy and the direct effect of the secondary EU law. The Constitutional Court provides that the regulations and the directives have absolute and immediate primacy over the Bulgarian legislation in accordance with Article 5, paragraph 4 of the Constitution. Hence the Constitutional Court equalizes the hierarchical ranking of the secondary EU law with the international treaties. Again, the main problem of such approach is that it subsumes EU law under the category of traditional international treaties which neither reflect the case law of the Court of Justice of the European Union (ECJ) nor take into account the substantial difference between primary EU law, secondary EU law and international treaties. The Constitutional Court refrains from engaging in direct judicial dialogue with the ECJ on that issue. In addition, the pronouncements of the Constitutional Court on the hierarchical standing of the EU law are contained in the motives and not in the dispositive part of the decision. Thus they do not have direct binding force but rather serve as sources of argumentation. Decision No. 7 of 2018 of the Constitutional Court does not explicitly subsume the EU law under the category of international law. It contains direct pronouncement only on the status of the mixed international agreements concluded between the EU and the Member States with third parties.

*83.* Moreover, the removal of the absolute ban on extradition of Bulgarian citizens infringes the irrevocability of human rights according to Article 57, paragraph 1 of the 1991 Constitution, and it should have been introduced by the Grand National Assembly. However, this constitutional amendment has been accomplished by the National Assembly on the basis of Decision No. 3 of 2004 of the Constitutional Court.

*84.* Finally, Decision No. 8 of 2005 opens the way for the accomplishment of constitutional reform of the judiciary. Such reform was deemed necessary in order for Bulgaria to meet the rule-of-law standards required for its EU membership.

*85.* In conclusion, these three decisions demonstrate that the Constitutional Court has functioned as a mediator between the constituent and the constituted power. The constitutional amendments introduced in the period prior to the EU accession of Bulgaria have been preceded by interpretative activism of the Constitutional Court. In its EU accession-related case law, the Constitutional Court has redrawn on several occasions the borderline between the constituent and the constituted power and between the competences of the National Assembly and the Grand National Assembly to amend the Constitution. The four constitutional amendments accomplished in the period 2003–2007 are to some extent a result of inter-institutional dialogue between the institutions that have initiated the cases in front of the Constitutional Court (the State Prosecutor General, the President of the Republic and the Supreme Court of Cassation), the Constitutional Court and the National Assembly which has adopted the subsequent constitutional reforms.

## III. Constitutional Amendment by Forms of Direct Democracy

*86.* The 1991 Constitution is rather unclear on the issue whether constitutional amendments may be introduced via forms of direct democracy such as the constitutional people's initiative and the constitutional referendum. On the one hand, it provides for the principle of popular sovereignty. According to Article 1, paragraph 2 of the Constitution, all state power stems out of the people and it can be accomplished either directly or through the state institutions. Thus the direct democracy should be one of the two main forms of democracy in Bulgaria and the constitutional people's initiative and the constitutional referendum should be permitted. On the other hand, Chapter IX devoted to the amendment of the Constitution does not provide for any form of direct democracy. It concentrates the constituent power in the two representative institutions – the National Assembly and the Grand National Assembly – which are eventually the only devices for constitutional reform.

*87.* The Direct Participation of the Citizens in the State Power and Local Self-Government Act (adopted in 2009) permits constitutional people's initiative and the constitutional referendum only if they concern issues outside the scope of Article 158. Consequently, these instruments of direct democracy are provided as an alternative only to the National Assembly but not to the Grand National Assembly. If the first logic is valid, namely that all forms of direct democracy should be considered as constitutionally permitted due to the principle of popular sovereignty, then the prohibition of constitutional referenda and constitutional people's initiatives on the issues enlisted in Article 158 of the Constitution is unconstitutional. On the contrary, if the 1991 Constitution prohibits all constitutional people's initiatives and the constitutional referenda, then the legislative provision of such direct democratic devices is unconstitutional. Thus the Direct Participation of the Citizens in the State Power and Local Self-Government Act is unconstitutional either way. This is mainly due to the very scarce and insufficient constitutional institutionalization of the direct democracy by the 1991 Constitution.

## IV. Entrenched Clause

*88.* The 1991 Bulgarian Constitution does not provide for unamendable or 'eternity' clauses. The provision of unamendable clauses seemed to the MPs in the VII Grand National Assembly as unnecessary, non-democratic and in contrast with the Bulgarian constitutional tradition. On the contrary, they believed that some of the most important elements of the constitutional design have to be safeguarded against rash and ill-considered amendment especially during the turbulent and to a great extent controversial and painful process of democratization of Bulgaria during the last decades of the twentieth and the first decades of the twenty-first centuries.

*89.* That is why the 1991 Constitution is a semi-rigid Constitution. Its most important provisions enlisted in its Article 158 can be amended only by the Grand National Assembly whereas the rest of the constitutional texts can be amended by the National Assembly.

*90.* Article 158 provides for the entrenched clause of the 1991 Constitution. According to it, only the Grand National Assembly can adopt new Constitution or can amend the form of government, the form of territorial distribution of power, the direct effect of the constitutional provisions and the primacy of the international treaties over the sub-constitutional legislation, the irrevocability of human rights and the inviolability of certain human rights in case of war and state of emergency as well as the procedure for the amendment of the Constitution. In addition, only the Grand National Assembly can take decisions regarding the alteration of the Bulgarian state territory and can ratify international treaties related to that issue.

*91.* It is clear that the entrenched clause of the Bulgarian Constitution is internally inconsistent. It does not contain a coherent system of interrelated constitutional principles, values or institutions. Article 158 of the Constitution is constructed as a shield against rash constitutional amendments. It safeguards those elements of the constitutional design which are perceived by the constitutional legislator as important for the stability of the state in the period of transition to democracy and rule of law. The entrenched clause covers elements of the constitutional design on macro (form of government and form of territorial distribution of power), meso (principles of the normative hierarchy) or micro (issues pertaining to different human rights) level. It also establishes the Grand National Assembly's reserve for the adoption of a new constitution.

*92.* The general conferral of the adoption of new Constitution in the exclusive competence of the Grand National Assembly is not bound to the preservation of specific values and principles (e.g., human dignity, rule of law, democracy etc.) or of concrete elements or aspects of the institutional design (e.g., the parliamentary republic or the unitary state). Moreover, it is context and content independent. That is why it can be hardly legitimated via the substantial constitutional axiology that has to be protected or by referral to the historic experience and the constitutional tradition of Bulgaria.

*93.* Moreover, the amendment of the territory can be conceived with great difficulty as a legitimate entrenched clause. It is substantially different from the rest of the elements enlisted in Article 158 of the Constitution and deserves enhanced protection not due to its crucial importance for the constitutional system but to its quality as an element of the statehood according to the theory of G. Jellinek.[23]

*94.* To sum up, the VII Grand National Assembly has established the entrenched clause of Article 158 due to the pragmatic concerns in order to safeguard the institutions enlisted in it from irrational and swift amendment by temporary parliamentary majorities. However, the entrenched clause is internally inconsistent, vague and cannot be justified by a coherent set of values. The vagueness of the concepts textually enshrined in Article 158 of the Constitution paves the way for misunderstandings and allows the Constitutional Court to develop activist jurisprudence based on its 'open texture'.[24]

## V. The Constitutional Amendments Which Have Already Been Accomplished

*95.* The 1991 Constitution has been amended five times since its adoption – in 2003, 2005, 2006, 2007 and 2015. Thus it is the most amended among the four Bulgarian constitutions. There are three main determinants for that fact.

23. Georg Jellinek, *Allgemeine Staatslehre*, 1–835 (Nabu Press, 2010).
24. For the open texture of law, *see* Herbert L.A. Hart, *The Concept of Law*, 124–136 (Oxford University Press, 1997).

*96.* First, currently Bulgaria is experiencing one of the relatively rare democratic periods of its historical development. Indeed, there are a lot of deficiencies of the Bulgarian democracy, and yet there is some degree of power polycentrism and political pluralism that allows for launching of different views on the constitutional model of the state. That is why some of the constitutional amendments are a result of renegotiation of the framework of the public power by the leading stakeholders in the current Bulgarian society and political system.

*97.* Second, the EU integration of Bulgaria has triggered and necessitated many of the amendments introduced in the 1991 Constitution in the pre-accession period. Some of these amendments – e.g., the introduction of EU integration clause, the lifting of the ban on acquisition of land property by EU citizens in Bulgaria and the permission for extradition of Bulgarian citizens to other EU Member States – have been inevitable results of the EU accession and membership. Other constitutional amendments such as the constitutional provision of parliamentary control over the governmental activity in the EU decision-making process have been optional. Moreover, the preparation for EU integration has been a powerful precursor of constitutional reforms related to the judiciary.

*98.* Third, the 1991 Constitution is semi-rigid as already discussed. However, Decision No. 3 of 2004 and Decision No. 8 of 2005 of the Constitutional Court have de facto broadened the sphere of competence of the National Assembly thus making the Constitution much more flexible than initially intended by the constitutional legislator. That is why the 1991 Constitution can be amended much more easily than the other democratic Bulgarian Constitution – the 1879 Tarnovo Constitution, which also explains the relatively high number of constitutional amendments.

*99.* Substantially the constitutional amendments concern three main groups of issues. These are: first, amendments that are related to the EU membership, second, amendments related to the judiciary and third, amendments related to other issues.[25] The 2003 amendment of the Constitution is related to the status of the magistrates. The 2005 amendment concerns the EU-related amendments such as the EU integration clause, the right of EU citizens to acquire land property, the extradition of Bulgarian citizens to other EU Member States, the elections for European Parliament, the procedure for transfer of constitutional competences to the EU and the information and control rights of the National Assembly with regard to the participation of the Council of Ministers and the Ministers in the EU decision-making processes.

*100.* The 2006 amendment appertains to the immunity of the MPs, the parliamentary hearings of the annual reports of the Supreme Court of Cassation, the Supreme Administrative Court and the State Prosecutor General, the status of the ombudsman, the adjustment of the functions of the state's prosecutors office, the establishment of constitutional preconditions for the creation of investigative police

25. *See* Evgeni Tanchev and Martin Belov, *supra* n. 13, 10.

officers, the status of the magistrates and the administrative directors of the institutions belonging to the judicial power and the constitutional proclamation of some of the competences of the Minister of Justice.

*101.* The 2007 amendment is related to the status of the military forces, the provision of a separate budget for the National Assembly as well as for quorum for its sessions, the partial tax decentralization increasing the tax revenue determination independence of the municipalities, the parliamentary hearing of reports of the institutions elected by the National Assembly, some reforms of the Supreme Judicial Council as well as of the status of the Minister of Justice and the magistrates and the constitutional provision of Inspectorate to the Supreme Judicial Council.

*102.* The 2015 amendment concerns the annual reports of the Supreme Court of Cassation, the Supreme Administrative Court and the State Prosecutor General to the Parliament, the division of the Supreme Judicial Council in two colleges – one for the judges and one for the state prosecutors and the competence of the Supreme Attorney's Council to approach the Constitutional Court with demand for declaration of unconstitutionality of acts of Parliament which infringe constitutional rights.

## §3. HIERARCHY

*103.* The 1991 Constitution is the supreme source of law in the Bulgarian legal order apart from the relative primacy of the EU law over the domestic law. The formal supremacy of the 1991 Constitution is safeguarded by both the difficult procedures for its amendment and the institutions and the forms of control for constitutionality of the sub-constitutional sources of law. The supremacy of the constitution is proclaimed in its Article 5, paragraph 1 according to which the constitution shall be the supreme law and no other law may be in conflict therewith. Moreover, Article 5, paragraph 2 proclaims the direct effect of the constitutional provisions.

*104.* The isolated reading of these two constitutional provisions may lead to the conclusion that all courts or administrative bodies are not only allowed but also obliged to apply directly the provisions of the constitution instead of contravening provisions contained in the sub-constitutional sources of law such as international treaties, acts of Parliament and normative acts of the government. Especially the courts are supposed to be the dispersed agents of the direct effect and the supremacy of the constitution as the fundamental law of the land.

*105.* However, Chapter VIII of the Constitution provides for centralized control for constitutionality of both the international treaties and the acts of the Parliament. The only court which is competent to declare the unconstitutionality of the provisions of international treaties and the acts of the Parliament is the Constitutional Court. Moreover, the Constitutional Court is formally not part of the judicial power in general and of the court's system in particular. In addition § 3, paragraph 1 of the Transitory and Concluding Provisions of the Constitution allows the ordinary courts to disregard and to not apply only the 'pre-existing laws' on grounds of unconstitutionality. These are acts of Parliament which have entered into force before the entering into force of the 1991 Constitution. Another question is what 'pre-existing laws' means since the acts of the Parliament may have been adopted before 13 July 1991 – the moment of entering into force of the 1991 Constitution but may have been consequently amended many times after that date.

*106.* The systematic reading of these provisions may lead to two contradictory conclusions. The first is that the principles of constitutional supremacy and the direct effect of the Constitution proclaimed by Article 5, paragraphs 1 and 2 enjoy primacy over the provisions of Chapter VIII that should serve as their safeguard and as their logical continuation and supplement. Following that logic, all courts and other state institutions which perform the function of law application must apply the constitutional provisions instead of contravening provisions of sub-constitutional legislation. Otherwise, the constitutional supremacy and direct effect would be only prerequisites for the provision of centralized constitutional control accomplished by the Constitutional Court while being of declarative nature with regard to the courts. This will limit the protective force of the constitutional supremacy for the constitutionally provided human rights, diminish the regulative force of the Constitution as directly applicable legal standard and thus undermine its nature as supreme legal act. The Constitution will have only indirect supremacy for the courts and for the parties to lawsuits mediated by the jurisprudence of the Constitutional Court. Having in mind the extremely austere case law of the Constitutional Court since 1991 related to constitutionally enshrined human rights one can conclude that the Constitution has, in practice, limited supremacy, direct effect and applicability with regard to human rights' protection in cases pending in front of the Bulgarian courts. This situation impedes the development of human rights' dimension of the Constitution.

*107.* The problem of this first explanatory logic of the supremacy and the direct effect of the Bulgarian Constitution concern the lack of constitutional ground for the accomplishment of diffuse control for constitutionality in combination with the lack of activist attitude as well as sufficient education of the Bulgarian magistrates with regard to their function as safeguards of the constitutionally provided human rights. The aggregate of these normative and sociolegal factors impedes the development of diffuse control for constitutionality of the acts of the Parliament and the international treaties based on the supremacy and the direct effect of the Constitution which are otherwise proclaimed by its Article 5, paragraphs 1 and 2.

*108.* Hence the second conclusion, based on another possible logic, which seems to be the predominating one not only in the Bulgarian constitutional theory but also in the practice of the courts, leads in quite the opposite direction. Indeed Article 5, paragraphs 1 and 2 proclaim the supremacy and the direct effect of the 1991 Constitution. However, the authority of the acts of the Parliament and the established centralized control for constitutionality by the Constitutional Court will be undermined if all courts and even all law-applying state institutions are allowed to disregard parliamentary legislation and to directly apply the Constitution instead of it.

*109.* That is why neither Chapter VIII of the Constitution devoted to the Constitutional Court nor the other parts of the Constitution explicitly provide for any form of diffuse control for constitutionality of the post-constitutional legislation. The competence of the ordinary courts to apply directly the Constitution instead of acts of Parliament can be legitimated only by referral to the principle of constitutional supremacy itself. Last but not least, the ordinary courts should not be allowed to disregard provisions of the international treaties due to their presumed unconstitutionality because this may lead to 'creeping', uncontrollable and diffuse violation of one of the main principles of the international law – *pacta sunt servanda.*

*110.* Moreover, no Bulgarian court can adopt precedent decisions. The lack of precedent decisions issued by Bulgarian courts reduces their ability to swiftly harmonize the practice of the courts regarding the direct application of the constitutional supremacy. There is a huge risk of incorrect and contradictory legal practice due to non-application of acts of Parliament and international treaties because of their presumed unconstitutionality. Such a risk results not so much from incompetence or corruption of the courts; it stems much more out of the vagueness and the openness of the constitutional provisions and the continental law training of the magistrates in Bulgaria as Montesquieuian 'mouths of the law'.

*111.* The conclusion is that the VII Grand National Assembly has established almost exclusively centralized control for the constitutionality of the acts of the Parliament. The Constitutional Court monopolizes the competence to declare acts of Parliament and international treaties unconstitutional. The ordinary courts are allowed to disregard pre-constitutional legislation, which has entered into force before 13 July 1991 (the date of the entering into force of the Constitution). When it comes to post-constitutional legislation which has been adopted after that date, they have theoretically three options.

*112.* The first option is to disregard the sub-constitutional legal provision and to apply the constitutional provision instead. Such diffuse control for constitutionality can be based on Article 5, paragraphs 1 and 2. However, it is very problematic due to the already-analysed concerns.

*113.* The second option is to try to interpret the legislative provision in conformity with the Constitution. However, not all legislative provisions can be interpreted so as to comply with the Constitution. Moreover, such interpretative activity of the ordinary courts may lead to creeping ascription of divergent content in the legislative provisions by the courts. Thus it may endanger the legal certainty and the predictability of the jurisprudence.

*114.* The third option is actually the option which is closest to the intent of the constitutional legislator. It consists in the competence of the ordinary courts to temporarily suspend the decision of the case and to approach the Supreme Court of Cassation (when it comes to civil or criminal courts) or the Supreme Administrative

Court (in case of administrative courts) with the demand to approach the Constitutional Court which then may declare the pretended unconstitutionality of the legislative provision in question.

*115.* Hence this so-called concrete control for constitutionality is the main instrument available to the Bulgarian courts to indirectly protect the supremacy of the constitution. However, this is rather lengthy procedure which is de facto dysfunctional and has almost never been applied. In practice, the courts try to avoid using this procedure by either neglecting the eventual unconstitutionality of legislation applicable to the case which is pending in front of them or interpreting the legislative provision in conformity with the constitution, if this is possible. There are several determinants of the self-restraint of the courts to initiate concrete control for constitutionality. One of them is the lack of confidence of the magistrates regarding the appropriateness of this procedure. This attitude is based on the perception of the Constitution as a predominantly political act without sufficient impact on the 'real law' consisting of normative acts of the Parliament and the government. Other determinants are the lack of training for detecting and defining the unconstitutionality of the sub-constitutional legislation and the fear of delaying the judicial process.

*116.* The direct effect of the Constitution is to some extent limited also by the openness and vagueness of the textuality of the constitutional provisions. The Constitution contains several types of normative regulators – legal norms, as well as principles, values and aims. The constitutional values and aims and to lesser extent the constitutional principles frequently do not provide for immediately applicable solutions for pending lawsuits and other legal disputes. They need interpretation, balance and adaptation.[26] Thus the direct effect of the constitutional values, aims and principles is mediated by the interpretative activity of the courts and other law-applying state institutions. Moreover, the so-called non-self-executable norms, e.g., the social and cultural rights, need additional concretization either by sub-constitutional legislation or by decisions of the Constitutional Court in order to acquire direct effect.[27]

*117.* The Republic of Bulgaria is a member of the EU since 2007. Hence the Bulgarian constitutional order is integrated with the supranational constitutionalism of the EU. Common issue for all constitutional systems of the EU Member States is the relationship between the national constitution and the EU law. The principle of constitutional supremacy, which is the formal aspect of the principle of state sovereignty, is modified, tempered and limited by the principle of the primacy of the EU law.

---

26. *See* Ronald Dworkin, *Taking Rights Seriously*, 22–28 (Harvard University Press, 2001).
27. Rosen Tashev, *General Theory of Law*, 144–145 (Sibi, 2004) (in Bulgarian).

*118.* The Bulgarian Constitution does not take a clear stance on the issue of its relation with the EU law. It does not contain any provision on the hierarchical status of the EU law in the Bulgarian legal order. The integration clause Article 4, paragraph 3 of the 1991 Constitution just declares that the Republic of Bulgaria shall participate in the construction and the development of the European Union (EU).

*119.* According to the Decision No. 7 of 2018 of the Constitutional Court, Article 4, paragraph 3 of the Constitution (the Bulgarian Constitution EU integration clause) has rich and complex normative content although it is austere and in laconic wording. Pertaining to the Constitutional Court the constitutional legislator differentiates between the Bulgarian participation in the construction and the Bulgarian participation in the development of the EU thus reflecting the dynamic and permanent character of the integration process.

*120.* Hence there are two possible solutions regarding the issue of the relationship between the 1991 Constitution and the EU law. The Treaty on the EU and the case law of the ECJ suggest the relative primacy of the EU law over all national laws the Constitution has included apart from the provisions forming the national constitutional identity. The Bulgarian Constitutional Court implicitly presumes the absolute supremacy of the Bulgarian Constitution by stipulating that the EU law equals international treaties.

# Chapter 2. Treaties

## §1. The Treaty-Making Power: Types of International Treaties According to the Bulgarian Constitutional Law

*121.* The 1991 Constitution distinguishes between two types of treaties. Article 85 of the Constitution enlists the international treaties which are of special importance and must be ratified or denounced by an act of Parliament. All other international treaties which do not fall into the scope of Article 85 can be approved or denounced by the Council of Ministers via governmental decree. According to Article 85 of the Constitution, the National Assembly ratifies and denounces the international treaties which: have political or military character, are related to the participation of the Republic of Bulgaria in international organizations, provide for correction of the state boundaries of the Republic of Bulgaria, contain financial obligations for the state, provide for participation of the state in arbitration or judicial resolution of international disputes, are related to human rights, concern the implementation of the acts of the Parliament or require the adoption of acts of Parliament, explicitly provide for parliamentary ratification, grant to the EU competences which stem out of the Bulgarian Constitution.

*122.* The acts of the Parliament for ratification of international treaties which provide for granting of constitutional competences to the EU have to be adopted via qualified two-thirds majority of all MPs. This qualified majority should serve as safeguard for reaching wide-ranging political consensus and thus for reasonable transfer of constitutional sovereignty.

*123.* However, this special procedure adopted in the course of the 2005 constitutional amendment allows the National Assembly to accomplish constituent power by transferring constitutional competences to the EU. This simplified procedure is not provided for in Chapter IX of the Constitution which is related to the procedures for constitutional amendment. According to Article 158 of the Constitution, constitutional amendments related to the procedure for amendment of the Constitution must be introduced by the Grand National Assembly. However, the procedure for transfer of constitutional competences to the EU has been introduced by the National Assembly.

*124.* The fact that the Constitution is not directly amended by the ratification of such international treaty may serve as an excuse. However, the transfer of constitutional competences to the EU by necessity presumes the accomplishment also of a constitutional amendment. This is because according to Article 85, paragraph 4 of the Constitution, the conclusion of international treaties which require amendments in the 1991 Constitution must be preceded by their adoption.

*125.* According to the International Treaties Act, the drafts for international treaties are prepared by the Ministers or other administrative directors of state institutions. These drafts should be prepared after careful consideration of their impact on the Bulgarian Constitution, legislation and the other international obligations of the

Republic of Bulgaria. In their proposal to the Council of Ministers, the above-mentioned institutions must include a report on these issues as well as on the impact of the international treaty on the EU membership of Bulgaria and on its financial consequences. All constitutional and legislative amendments required by the international treaty should be made in advance before its introduction in the Bulgarian legal system.

*126.* The conclusion of international treaty must be approved by the Council of Ministers which acts on the proposal of Ministers or other heads of state institutions. The National Assembly or the Grand National Assembly must have given their consent for the conclusion of the international treaties in the cases when such consent is required by the 1991 Constitution. The Council of Ministers approves via decision the conclusion of the international treaty and denominates the head of the delegation for negotiation and signing of the treaty.

*127.* Powers of attorney for negotiation and signing of international treaties are issued by the Minister of Foreign Affairs based on the decision of the Council of Ministers. The President of the Republic, the Prime Minister and the Minister of Foreign Affairs sign international treaties without the need for such explicit and formal powers of attorney.

*128.* The international treaties may be concluded by the President of the Republic, by the Council of Ministers or by the Ministers. The President concludes the international treaties in concordance with the government when the subject matter or the importance of the treaty so requires or in accordance with the agreement between the high contracting parties regarding the state institutions which have to conclude the treaty. Otherwise, the international treaties are concluded by the Council of Ministers. The Ministers conclude international treaties when they fall into their exclusive sphere of competence after the decision of the Council of Ministers.

## §2. Hierarchy

*129.* According to Article 5, paragraph 4 of the 1991 Constitution, the international treaties which are ratified, published and entered into force for the Republic of Bulgaria have primacy over all domestic legislation except for the Constitution. Hence such primacy is granted only to the most important international treaties enlisted in Article 85, paragraph 1 of the Constitution. According to Decision No. 3 of 2012 of the Constitutional Court, such primacy is unconditional.

*130.* From a formal point of view, these international treaties should have been allocated on the same level of the normative hierarchy as the acts of the Parliament. This is because they are ratified by act of the Parliament. However, there are two reasons for assigning primacy of these international treaties to the acts of the Parliament.

*131.* First, Bulgaria has adopted the monist system for implementation of international treaties. According to Decision No. 7 of 2018 in conjunction with Decision No. 7 of 1992 of the Bulgarian Constitutional Court, the constitutional legislator has adopted moderate monist approach. It does not require implementation of international treaties in the domestic legal order via special act. The formal ratification and entry into force should suffice for their introduction in the domestic law and for their primacy over contravening domestic legislation. Thus the international treaties are ratified through formal act of Parliament that serves as a tool for recognition of the treaty as part of the domestic system of sources of law without reproducing its normative content. Hence the international treaties are just formally introduced in the Bulgarian legal system through act of Parliament while at the same time they have direct effect.

*132.* The second and much more important reason is the political choice made by the VII Grand National Assembly to give primacy to the most important international treaties over the sub-constitutional legislation. This is an important safeguard for the international obligations of Bulgaria especially in the sphere of human rights from eventual violation by the parliamentary majority which simultaneously preserves the state sovereignty by non-infringing the supremacy of the 1991 Constitution over the international treaties.

*133.* Both reasons are related to the decision of the Bulgarian constitutional legislator to balance the principle of open statehood allowing for integration in the supranational constitutionalism with the principle of sovereignty safeguarded by the supremacy of the national constitution.

*134.* Supremacy over the sub-constitutional domestic legislation possesses only international treaties which are ratified by the National Assembly via act of Parliament adopted on two readings. In exceptional circumstances, the two readings may be accomplished in one parliamentary sitting. Moreover, the act of Parliament for ratification of the international treaty must be published in State Gazette (SG). Last but not least, they also have to enter into force. Usually the entering into force occurs on the third day of the publication of the acts of the Parliament in SG. However, the Parliament may explicitly deviate from this rule and provide a shorter or longer – *vacatio legis* – term for entering of the act of Parliament into force.

*135.* The international treaties which are not provided for by Article 85, paragraph 1 of the Constitution are introduced in the Bulgarian legal order via decrees of the Council of Ministers. They have the same hierarchical position as the governmental decree itself. This means that they are allocated under the EU law, the Constitution, the international treaties ratified by the National Assembly and the parliamentary legislation. Hence in case of conflict of norms contained in the international treaties which deserve parliamentary ratification and international treaties which are introduced by governmental decree, the former should automatically prevail over the latter.

*136.* The unclear stance of the Bulgarian Constitution on the issue of the hierarchical status of the EU law in the Bulgarian legal system may lead to very problematic situations in case of contradiction between the EU law and the international treaties ratified, published and entered into force. This problem has already been analysed in the paragraph concerning the hierarchical place of the Constitution.

## §3. System for Implementation of the International Treaties

*137.* The Bulgarian constitutional legislator has chosen the system of semi-perfect monism. It consists in the fact that the international treaties, once implemented, have direct effect in Bulgaria. The rights and the duties of the citizens and legal entities as well as the rights and the obligations of the Bulgarian institutions stem directly out of the text of the international treaty. This is because the international treaties are ratified by formal acts of Parliament or are adopted by formal governmental decrees. The formality of these domestic sources of law consists in the fact that they contain only one legal provision which proclaims the international treaty to be part of the Bulgarian legal order. Hence the international treaty itself regulates the social relations in Bulgaria, and the domestic legal act serves only as an instrument for their introduction as valid part of the Bulgarian legal order.

*138.* The Bulgarian variant of monism is semi-perfect because the international treaties need the formal mediation of domestic legal act – act of Parliament or decree of the government. Thus they do not become automatically part of the Bulgarian system of sources of law as of the date of their signing. The international treaties become part of the Bulgarian legal order from the moment of their introduction via act of Parliament or via decree of the Council of Ministers.

## §4. Mixed Agreements Concluded Jointly by the EU and Its Member States and Third Parties

*139.* The status, primacy and system for implementation of the mixed agreements which are concluded by the EU and its Member States and third parties are not explicitly provided by the Bulgarian Constitution. That is why the Constitutional Court has been approached in 2017 by the President of the Republic with the demand for an interpretative decision on this issue. Hence in 2018 the Constitutional Court had adopted one of its most important decisions related to the Bulgarian EU membership and addressing issues of the relationship between the domestic and the EU law. This is Decision No. 7 of 2018 on constitutional case No. 7 of 2017.

*140.* Although this is a decision for abstract interpretation of the Constitution, the concrete reason for approaching the Constitutional Court is the conclusion of the EU-Canada Comprehensive Economic and Trade Agreement (CETA) by the EU and its Member States. That is why this decision will be referred to as the CETA decision of the Constitutional Court.

*141.* The Constitutional Court has been approached by the President of the Republic with the demand to give binding interpretation of Article 4, paragraph 3, Article 5, paragraph 4, Article 85, paragraph 1, point 9, Article 19, paragraph 2 and Article 20 of the Bulgarian Constitution. The demand for abstract interpretation of these constitutional provisions is related to the following questions posed by the Bulgarian President to the Constitutional Court:

(1) Under which conditions do the mixed agreements concluded jointly by the EU and the Member States with a third party become part of the internal legal order of the Republic of Bulgaria and acquire primacy over contravening domestic legislation?
(2) Is the temporary application of mixed agreements, which is sometimes provided by them, dependent on the fulfilment of the conditions of Article 5, paragraph 4 of the Bulgarian Constitution?
(3) Is Article 85, paragraph 1, point 9 of the Constitution, regulating the procedure for ratification of international treaties for transfer of constitutional competences to the EU, applicable to the mixed agreements jointly concluded by the EU and the Member States with a third party?
(4) How should the expression 'competences stemming out of this Constitution' used in Article 85, paragraph 1, point 9 of the Constitution be interpreted? Is it limited to the transfer of competences provided only by the Constitution or is it applicable also for competences provided by the acts of Parliament which are sources of the Bulgarian constitutional law?
(5) Is Article 85, paragraph 1, point 9 of the Constitution applicable for mixed agreements providing for the establishment of institutions in which only the EU is represented but not the Member States under the condition that the competence of these institutions includes competences stemming out of the Bulgarian Constitution?
(6) How should the provisions of Article 19, paragraph 2, Article 20 and Article 5, paragraph 4 of the Constitution be interpreted with view to the following questions: the protection of which constitutional values justifies deviations from Article 19, paragraph 2 of the Constitution and are there legitimate exceptions from the principle of equality of the subjects of the economic life in the course of accomplishment of economic activity for the purpose of balanced development of the territory of the Republic of Bulgaria?
(7) What are the legitimate deviations from the principle provided by Article 19, paragraph 2 of the Constitution in the application of the primacy of the international treaties according to Article 5, paragraph 4 of the Constitution?
(8) In its reasons, the Constitutional Court provides for detailed analysis of the 'new generation' of international trade agreements concluded after the entering into force of the Lisbon Treaty, the nature of the 'mixed agreements' and their temporary application and the competence of the EU to conclude mixed agreements.

*142.* Initially, the Constitutional Court clarifies what is meant under the concept of 'new generation of trade agreements' and why does CETA belong to them. The Constitutional Court profoundly analyses the role of the common trade policy of the

EU for the establishment of the crucial role of the EU as global political and economic player and for the provision of its economic goals and political values and principles. The Constitutional Court clarifies the link between the common trade policy, the exclusive competence of the EU, the goals and values of the European integration and the role played by the 'new generation of trade agreements' for their achievement.

*143.* Furthermore, the Constitutional Court clarifies the reason for concluding of mixed agreements by the EU. It defines the mixed agreements and classifies them into two groups – compulsory and facultative. In that regard, the Constitutional Court provides an analysis of the different competences of the EU. The Constitutional Court links the need for conclusion of mixed agreements with the competences of the states in the international relations which are forming part of the 'hard core' of sovereignty. The Constitutional Court provides that the facultative mixed agreements are result of the desire of the EU to take the external sovereignty of the states into account. Thus, the Constitutional Court implicitly suggests that sovereignty is not anymore holistic concept but is composed of 'hard core' and, presumably, 'soft periphery'.[28]

*144.* Moreover, the Constitutional Court analyses the nature and effects of the temporary preliminary application of the mixed agreements. The Constitutional Court reaffirms that not only the parts of the mixed agreement which concern exclusive EU competences may be subject to temporary application before their ratification but also their parts which are related to shared competences in so far it is in compliance with the distribution of the competences between the EU and the Member States. The Constitutional Court reaffirms the position of the ECJ that the international agreements to which EU is a part (the mixed agreements included) are part of the EU law and their hierarchical status is under the primary but above the secondary EU law.

*145.* The Constitutional Court provides for textbook-like systematization of the competences of the EU, the distribution of the competences between the EU and the Member States and the principles regulating this distribution. It puts special emphasis on the principles of conferral and sincere cooperation.

*146.* The Constitutional Court underlines that both the integration clause provided by Article 4, paragraph 3 serving as basis for the primacy of the EU law and the rule of recognition of the primacy of the international treaties provided by Article 5, paragraph 4 of the Constitution are mutually harmonized. However, the primacy of the EU law 'stems from and is manifestation of the specific nature of the EU legal order and does not require any constitutional provision for its recognition'.

---

28. For the concept of fragmentation of sovereignty and the existence of sector-specific sovereignties, *see* Martin Belov, *Rule of Law in Space of Flows*, in Martin Belov (ed.) *Rule of Law at the Beginning of the Twenty-First Century* (Eleven Publishing, 2018), p. 129 and Martin Belov Финансов конституционализъм [*Financial Constitutionalism*] (Sibi, 2015), pp. 15–109.

*147.* Moreover, according to the Constitutional Court, the provisions of the mixed agreements related to the competences of the EU are valid in the domestic legal order of the Republic of Bulgaria with their entering into force. They enjoy primacy over contravening Bulgarian legal provisions not on the basis of Article 5, paragraph 4 but due to the principle of primacy of the EU law. The domestic constitutional and legislative procedures for implementation of treaties and for acquisition of primacy over domestic law are applicable only to their provisions which are falling into the scope of the competence reserved for the Member States. Consequently, these parts of such mixed international agreements will have primacy over contravening domestic provisions only after the fulfilment of the constitutional requirements of Article 5, paragraph 4 of the Constitution.

*148.* This line of argumentation leads to the conclusion that the Constitutional Court recognizes the case law of the ECJ on the primacy of the EU law. Moreover, the Constitutional Court ascribes to Article 4, paragraph 3 of the Bulgarian Constitution the function of rule of recognition for the validity of the EU law but derives its primacy from the jurisprudence of the ECJ. The joint reading and systematic effect of these lines of argumentation may let us to conclude that this is an implicit recognition of the primacy of the EU law over the domestic constitution. However, the Constitutional Court just implicitly hints at such possible interpretation without making the final and decisive step to confirm this conclusion by either taking an explicit stance on it or making it clear via engagement with judicial dialogue with the ECJ.

*149.* The Constitutional Court comes also to other important conclusions. According to it, the provisions of the mixed agreements concluded jointly by the EU and the Member States with a third county – such as Canada in the case of CETA – which are related to the competences of the EU are part of the EU law from the moment of their entry into force. This is the reason why they have primacy over contravening domestic law. The provisions of such agreements which are part of the competence of the Republic of Bulgaria acquire primacy over contravening provisions of domestic law under the conditions of Article 5, paragraph 4 of the Constitution.

*150.* The Constitutional Court stipulates that the temporary application of provisions of the mixed agreements which fall into the sphere of competence of the EU does not depend on the fulfilment of the conditions provided by Article 5, paragraph 4 of the Bulgarian Constitution. Furthermore, according to the Constitutional Court the provision of Article 85, paragraph 1, point 9 of the Constitution is not applicable to the mixed-trade agreements. This is because Article 85, paragraph 1, point 9 of the Constitution provides for the procedure for transfer of sovereign competences to the EU, whereas the exclusive or concurrent competences in the sphere of the international trade have already been transferred to the EU by the TEU and the TFEU.

*151.* According to the Constitutional Court, the mixed agreements do not grant new competences to the EU. On the contrary, they are concluded on the basis of already-transferred competences which are shared with the Member States. The Member States have already granted their consent for such competence conferral ratifying the treaties forming the primary law of the EU. Hence such mixed agreements should be ratified on the basis of the regular (simplified) and not via the qualified ratification procedure necessary for transfer of constitutional competences.

*152.* Finally, the Constitutional Court rejects the demand to answer the questions of the President listed above under points (f) and (g). The Constitutional Court believes that answering these questions will result in illegitimate virtual amendment of the Constitution by the Court. This is in fact a rare case of explicit judicial self-restraint by the Constitutional Court.

## Chapter 3. Legislation

### §1. Types of Legislation

### I. Acts of Parliament

*153.* Formally, there is only one type of acts of Parliament in Bulgaria. These are the acts of the Parliament adopted by the National Assembly. They may serve for amendment of the Constitution, for ratification of international treaties, for transfer of constitutional competences to the EU, for adoption of the state budget or for adoption of legal provisions in any field of the social relations. In other words, from a formal point of view and with regard to the used term for their denomination, there are only 'acts of Parliament' and no constitutional laws or organic laws.

*154.* However, from a substantial point of view as well as with regard to the procedure for their adoption, one can differentiate between constitutional laws, acts of Parliament for ratification of international treaties, act of Parliament for the adoption of the state budget and (ordinary) acts of Parliament. The term used for all of them is '*zakon*' (закон) which means act of Parliament. However, their subject matter, their scope and the specialized procedures used for their adoption qualifies them as distinct types of legislation.

*155.* The constitutional acts of Parliament are adopted by the Grand National Assembly or by the National Assembly when it acts as an institution of the constituent power. They differ from the ordinary acts of Parliament with regard to their subject matter (introduction of a constitutional amendment) and the more complicated procedure for their adoption (additional reading, qualified majorities and publication by the Chairman of the National Assembly or the Chairman of the Grand National Assembly). In fact, the constitutional acts of Parliament do not have independent existence. Once adopted, they become an integral part of the Constitution.

*156.* There are no organic laws in Bulgaria. Indeed there are many acts of Parliament which contain provisions related to the state institutions, human rights or the institutions of the public sphere thus regulating constitutional issues. These are, e.g., the Constitutional Court Act, the Judicial Power Act, the Local Self-Government and Local Self-Administration Act, the Direct Participation of the Citizens in the State Power and the Local Self-Government Act, the Political Parties Act, the Assemblies, Rallies and Manifestations Act, the Bulgarian Citizenship Act etc. However, these acts of Parliament do not possess the two distinct features typical for the organic laws. First, they are not especially denominated as 'organic laws'. Second, there is neither specific procedure for their adoption nor procedure for compulsory control for their constitutionality. Hence these are acts of Parliament which regulate constitutional subject matter but do not differ from the ordinary law with a view to their name, hierarchical status, procedure for adoption or procedure for control for constitutionality.

*157.* The act for adoption of the state budget is a formal act of the Parliament.[29] Its normative content consists of provisions regarding the financial revenues and the expenditures of the state and its institutions. The state budget is adopted in the form of act of Parliament as a safeguard for the public and parliamentary control over the state finances and for the primacy of the state budget over the normative acts of the government and other budgetary institutions with norm-setting competence. However, the state budget is much more an annual financial plan than a real and substantial act of Parliament.

*158.* The procedure for the adoption of the annual State Budget Act of Parliament is the same as the procedure for the adoption of the other acts of Parliament. The only difference consists in the fact that the Council of Ministers has monopoly over the legislative initiative for the draft state budget as a whole. In contrast to the other acts of Parliament, the MPs are not allowed to propose the whole act for the annual state budget but only amendments to it.

*159.* The acts for ratification of international treaties are formal in the sense that they just introduce the international treaties to the domestic legal order thus making them a valid source of law in Bulgaria. These acts of Parliament have no content which is independent from the content of the international treaty they implement. The acts for ratification of international treaties differ from the ordinary acts of Parliament not only with a view to their formality but also partially with regard to the procedure for their adoption. Both types of acts of Parliament have to be adopted on two readings with absolute majority. However, the two readings in the case of adoption of acts of Parliament for ratification of international treaties can be held in a single parliamentary sitting. This is because the Bulgarian Parliament cannot amend the content of the international treaty; it can be either ratified or rejected.

*160.* The acts of the Parliament for transfer of constitutional competences to the EU are provided by Article 85, paragraph 1, point 9 and Article 85, paragraph 2 of the Constitution. They have already been discussed above.

## II. Special Majority Acts

*161.* There are two types of acts of Parliament which are adopted by special majority. The first is the acts for amendment of the Constitution. The constitutional amendments which do not fall into the sphere of competence of the Grand National Assembly can be accomplished by the National Assembly on three readings with majority of three-fourths of all MPs or under the circumstances described in Article 155, paragraph 2 of the Constitution with a reduced majority of two-thirds of all MPs.

---

29. For the formal laws in the Bulgarian legal systems (the laws for adoption of the annual state budget and for ratification and denouncement of international treaties), *see* Rosen Tashev, *supra* n. 27, 59–60.

*162.* The second type of special majority acts is the above-mentioned acts of Parliament for transfer of constitutional competences to the EU provided by Article 85, paragraph 1, point 9 and Article 85, paragraph 2 of the Constitution. They require two-thirds majority of all MPs in two distinct readings.

*163.* In fact, both types of special majority acts introduce measures which reshape the constitutional model either via formal constitutional amendment or through transfer of constitutional competences to supranational constitutional system. In many instances the limiting of the sphere of constitutional autonomy of the EU Member States in general and of Bulgaria in particular may have much deeper consequences than the introduction of constitutional amendments related to provisions of secondary importance. However, the Bulgarian constitutional legislator has decided that the transfer of constitutional competences and thus of state sovereignty to the EU can be accomplished through much more simplified procedure than the formal reform of the Constitution consisting of introduction of amendments of secondary importance by the National Assembly.

*164.* According to Decision No. 7 of 2018 of the Constitutional Court, the provision of Article 85, paragraph 1, point 9 should be read in conjunction with the EU integration clause of Article 4, paragraph 3 of the Constitution. This is because both constitutional provisions form 'normative complex' and are joint structural pillar of the Bulgarian EU membership. According to the Constitutional Court, 'the integration and inclusion of the primary EU law in the national legal system is grounded on article 4, paragraph 3 of the Constitution whereas the ratification of international treaties for transfer of constitutional competences provided by article 85, paragraph 1, point 9 and preconditioned upon article 4, paragraph 3 of the Constitution makes possible the effective realization of its primacy, direct effect and universal application'.

*165.* Furthermore, in its Decision No. 7 of 2018, the Constitutional Court believes that the formulation of Article 85, paragraph 1, point 9 of the Constitution removes any doubts that it concerns international treaties by virtue of which partial transfer of national competence to the EU is accomplished. Hence these are specific international treaties for granting competences to the EU which previously belonged to the Bulgarian state. According to the Constitutional Court, an evidence of this is the required two-thirds qualified majority coinciding with the minimal majority for the amendment of the Bulgarian Constitution by the National Assembly

## III. Reasons for the Lack of Delegated Legislation

*166.* The 1991 Constitution does not allow for the adoption of either extraordinary or delegated legislation. Moreover, Article 2 of the Normative Acts Act prohibits the transfer of legislative or any other norm-setting competences by the Parliament.

*167.* The extraordinary legislation consists in the competence of institutions different from the national Parliament, e.g., the head of state or the government, to adopt normative acts with the rank and the force of acts of Parliament in case of state of siege, state of emergency or some other extraordinary situation. The delegated legislation consists in the competence of institutions different from the national Parliament, e.g., the head of state, the government or a parliamentary committee, to adopt acts with the rank and the force of acts of Parliament on the basis of authorization by the Parliament. Both types of legislation concern issuing of bills by institutions different from the Parliament. The extraordinary legislation may be adopted directly on the basis of the Constitution whereas the delegated legislation stems out of parliamentary empowerment.

*168.* In fact, there was no Bulgarian Constitution which provided for delegated legislation. The 1879 Tarnovo Constitution, however, provided for the competence of the monarch to adopt extraordinary legislation in the form of decree laws in case of external or internal threat to the state. The Bulgarian monarchs have misused this competence in order to establish their personal authoritarian regimes. They usually simulated the existence of an extraordinary situation imposing threats to state and society thus enabling them to adopt decree laws. This misuse of constitutional competence was especially evident in the context of the personal regime of Tzar Boris III in the period from 1934 to 1943 when the Parliament had been dissolved for some time, the political parties were prohibited and the monarch turned himself into a legislator adopting decree laws.

*169.* During the communist regime, the National Assembly was supposed to be the focal point and climax of all state power. In the political practice however, it turned into a nominal institution. Its presence in the system and political influence was of secondary importance. Some of the factors contributing to that situation were the concentration of power in the leader of the communist party and in the party oligarchy and the extremely short parliamentary sessions. That is why the Presidium of the National Assembly (under the 1947 Constitution) and then the State Council (under the 1971 Constitution) became the real legislative bodies adopting legislation in the form of decrees (‘*uka*z’ or *‘указ’* in Bulgarian). These decrees were consequently rubber-stamped by the National Assembly.

*170.* In fact the decrees adopted by the Presidium and the State Council were neither extraordinary nor delegated legislation. They resembled the extraordinary legislation because of their immediate constitutional ground and the lack of parliamentary delegation. However, they differed from it because they were adopted not in the context of an extraordinary situation.

*171.* The misuse with the above-mentioned forms of non-parliamentary legislation during both periods of the constitutional monarchy and the communist regime is the reason for the unwillingness of the VII Grand National Assembly to allow either delegated or extraordinary legislation in Bulgaria. Another reason is the belief of some of the MPs in the VII Grand National Assembly that the delegated legislation violates the separation of powers and limits the legislative function of the Parliament.[30] This belief has been grounded on arguments stemming out of the presumed although politically inexistent centrality of the Parliament under the communist regime.

## IV. Reasons for the Lack of Subnational Legislation

*172.* Bulgaria is a unitary state with a local self-government. That is why the institutions for local self-government – the municipal councils – are allowed to adopt normative acts with territorially limited scope of application which, however, do not have the quality of acts of Parliament. This is because they do not regulate substantial issues but rather provide for solutions of local issues which fall into the scope of competence of the municipal council. Thus the municipal councils possess norm-setting function but do not have legislative function in the proper sense of the meaning. They neither adopt subnational acts of Parliament in the formal sense nor may provide for initial normative solutions of fundamental social issues without being based on pre-existing national legislation. The fundamental reasons for the lack of subnational legislation coincide with and stem out of the reasons for the adoption of the unitary form of territorial distribution of power in Bulgaria.

### §2. Hierarchy

*173.* The acts of the Parliament are allocated below the Constitution, the decisions of the Constitutional Court, the EU law and the international treaties. They have primacy over the normative acts adopted by the Council of Ministers, the Ministers and the administrative agencies.

*174.* The only exception is the acts of the Parliament for ratification of international treaties. They are formal acts of Parliament which are nominally allocated on the level of the international treaties which are introduced by them in the Bulgarian legal order. However, they do not possess any substantial normative content different from the provision for introduction of the international treaty. Thus their substance is the introduced international treaty.

*175.* It should be underlined that the constitutional laws, which are the acts of the National Assembly for adoption of constitutional amendment, do not have independent existence. Once adopted, they become automatically part of the 1991 Constitution itself. Thus they have constitutional rank due to their integration in the text of the Constitution. The acts of the Parliament which concern constitutional subject matters, such as the status of state institutions, human rights, direct democracy, and

30. That argument is launched in the Bulgarian constitutional theory by Prof. St. Stoychev. *See* Stefan Stoychev, *Constitutional Law*, 526 (Ciela, 2002) (in Bulgarian).

political parties, have the same hierarchical place as the ordinary parliamentary legislation. The same is true for the act of Parliament for the adoption of the annual state budget.

## Chapter 4. Case Law

*176.* Traditionally Bulgaria belongs to the continental legal system since the establishment of the modern Bulgarian statehood in 1878–1879. Consequently, the judge is supposed only to apply the law but not to adopt sources of law in the form of judicial precedents. The judicial precedent has been rejected as valid source of the Bulgarian legal system during the epoch of the constitutional monarchy (1879–1947) for two main reasons. The first reason was the strong influence of the French legal ideas and especially the theory of Montesquieu of the judge as the 'mouth of the law'. The second reason was the lack of sufficient number of qualified magistrates who can be relied upon to adopt precedent judicial decisions. During the communist period (1947–1989), the courts were supposed to implement the will of the working class formed by the National Assembly as focal point of the state power. Hence the Bulgarian tradition established during the past almost century and a half clearly denies any norm-setting function of the courts and rejects the judicial precedent as a valid source of the Bulgarian law.

*177.* However, two phenomena contravene this seemingly durable tradition. The first consists in the fact that the supreme courts in Bulgaria have always possessed the competence to adopt interpretative decisions by virtue of which to define the appropriate way for application of unclear legislative provisions thus reaffirming the legal clarity and legal certainty. The supreme courts are supposed to function as instruments for re-establishment of the jurisprudential homogeneity by setting universal interpretative standards to the lower courts and thus indirectly to all parties that participate in a judicial process, e.g., the state prosecutors, the attorneys etc.

*178.* According to Article 124 of the Judicial Power Act, the civil, the commercial or the criminal departments of the Supreme Court of Cassation and the departments of the Supreme Administrative Court can adopt interpretative decisions in case of incorrect or controversial practice of the civil and the criminal courts as well as of the administrative courts. If there is such incorrect or controversial practice between the civil or criminal courts and the administrative courts, then the Supreme Court of Cassation and the Supreme Administrative Court can adopt interpretative decrees aiming at harmonization of the case law of these courts.

*179.* The incorrect practice is a result of improper application of legal provisions. The controversial practice may consist of proper and correct application of legal provisions which, however, are applied in quite a diverse way due to their vagueness and openness for different interpretations thus leading to inconsistency or unpredictability of the jurisprudence.

*180.* The interpretative decisions and the interpretative decrees of the supreme courts do not possess the characteristics of a judicial precedent. They do not concern any concrete lawsuit pending in front of a court and are not a form of law application. The interpretative decisions and the interpretative decrees are adopted by the supreme courts in the framework of distinct and specific procedure which are different from the procedures applicable by these courts in the civil, commercial, criminal or administrative law cases pending for decision in front of them.

*181.* Although the interpretative decisions and the interpretative decrees of the supreme courts are not judicial precedents, they are sources of law which are adopted by courts and not by the Parliament or the government. Hence they are a form of judicial norm-setting and thus they frame and form the judicial policy in the most important and controversial cases. That is why they serve as a very important exception from the traditional perception of the Bulgarian magistrate as 'law applying machine'.

*182.* It must be noted that not only the interpretative decisions and the interpretative decrees of the supreme courts but also the practice of all courts is increasingly perceived in the past decades as an important source of information for the appropriate solving of cases pending to the courts. The magistrates are getting used to search for, to study and in many instances to follow the case law of their colleagues not because it is a direct source of law and they are obliged to do so, but due to the need to adopt reasonable and well-grounded decisions.

*183.* To sum up, both the interpretative decisions and the interpretative decrees of the supreme courts as direct sources of law and the case law of the courts as an indirect source of law and as a source of legal argumentation and inspiration have increasing importance in the Bulgarian legal system.

*184.* The second phenomenon that changes the long-lasting perception of the Bulgarian legal system as entirely 'continental' in the sense that it rejects both the norm-setting function of the courts and the judicial precedent as valid source of law is a result of the integration of Bulgaria in forms of supranational constitutionalism. The most important example of such integration is the Bulgarian membership in the CE and in the EU.

*185.* The European Court of Human Rights (ECtHR) and the ECJ adopt precedential judicial decisions. The case law of these supranational courts is a valid source of law in the Member States of the CE and in the EU thus being also a valid source of law in Bulgaria. Hence the Bulgarian courts are not allowed to adopt precedential judicial decisions. However, the judicial precedent is a valid source of law in Bulgaria since 1992 with regard to the case law of the ECtHR and the number of judicial precedents has dramatically increased since 2007 – the date of the Bulgarian accession to the EU with a view to the case law of the ECJ.

*186.* Finally, the decisions of the Constitutional Court have to be analysed in the context of the debate on the norm-setting role of the courts in the Bulgarian constitutional and legal system. Indeed the Constitutional Court adopts three types of decisions: first, interpretative decisions, second, decisions for hierarchical norm control (unconstitutionality of international treaties and acts of Parliament as well as for contravention of acts of Parliament to international treaties and generally recognized principles of international law) and third, decisions for concrete matters falling into the sphere of competence of the Constitutional Court (e.g., constitutionality of political parties, impeachment of the President, resolution of conflicts of competences concerning the horizontal and the vertical separation of powers etc.).

*187.* The first two groups of Constitutional Court's decisions are sources of the Bulgarian constitutional law. However, the Constitutional Court's decisions are not judicial precedents due to two reasons. First, the Bulgarian Constitutional Court does not belong to the judiciary. Second, most of these decisions are not adopted with a view to concrete control for constitutionality related to the decision of a pending lawsuit. Even in the cases of concrete control for constitutionality, the Constitutional Court does not adopt judicial precedents because the lawsuit is pending in front of the ordinary court and not in front of the Constitutional Court itself.

*188.* According to Article 149, paragraph 1, point 1 of the Constitution, the Constitutional Court can issue interpretative decisions. By virtue of these decisions, it gives authoritative and binding interpretation of constitutional provisions. The theory of the self-restrained constitutional jurisdiction proclaims that the Constitutional Court just clarifies the intent of the constitutional legislator by virtue of historical, systematic and grammatical interpretation. That intent is already enshrined in the constitutional texts although in an unclear manner.

*189.* However, the Bulgarian Constitutional Court frequently uses teleological interpretation, analogy and in many instances broadens the scope of its interpretative activity to such a scale that it in fact ascribes meaning to the constitutional texts. The Bulgarian Constitutional Court on many occasions further develops the constitutional concepts thus functioning as a quasi-constitutional legislator.

*190.* This practice is legitimated in the Bulgarian constitutional discourse with arguments that an activist constitutional jurisdiction is needed in the context of transition to democracy in order to smoothly adapt the written to the ideal and factual constitution and to allow for the well-functioning of the constitutional model.[31] However, it is very doubtful with a view to the democratic legitimacy of the Constitutional Court and the principles of popular sovereignty, democracy and separation between the constituent and the constituted powers. The activist jurisprudence of the Constitutional Court is especially problematic if it is also controversial and inconsistent.

*191.* Anyway, the interpretative decisions of the Constitutional Court are a very important source of the Bulgarian constitutional law. There is no clear constitutional or legislative provision on their hierarchal rank. However, implicitly one can suggest that they have constitutional rank since they interpret constitutional provisions which must then be applied not with their 'plain' meaning stemming out only from the constitutional text but with the meaning which has been extracted, defined,

31. *See*, for example, Emilia Drumeva, *Constitutional Law*, 696 (Ciela, 2008) (in Bulgarian).

implied or ascribed by the Constitutional Court. The quantity, the scope, the substantial importance and the hierarchical standing of the interpretative decisions of the Constitutional Court inevitably produce their high practical and theoretical significance.

*192.* Another group of Constitutional Court's decisions, which are a source of law, comprises the decisions for the declaration of non-compliance of inferior to superior legal norm. There are two main types of such decisions. The first consists of decisions for declaration of unconstitutionality of international treaties before their ratification and decisions for the declaration of unconstitutionality of acts of Parliament and decrees of the President of the Republic. The second comprises the decisions for declaration of contravention of the acts of the Parliament and the decrees of the President with the international treaties and the generally recognized principles of international law. Both groups of decisions can be issued in the context of abstract as well as concrete norm control.

*193.* Similar to the interpretative decisions, there are no provisions regarding the hierarchical status of these decisions for norm control. One can presume that the decisions for unconstitutionality or for contravention to international treaties are allocated at least on the level of the sources of law which are declared to be void due to contravention with hierarchically superior provisions.

# Chapter 5. Unwritten Law

## §1. Conventions

*194.* The predominant viewpoint in the Bulgarian constitutional theory is that the conventions and the constitutional customs are not a source of the Bulgarian constitutional law. This conception is based on the understanding that the Bulgarian constitutional history is marked by discontinuity[32] and has been formed not on the basis of steady evolution but of persistent, continuous and frequent contradictory reforms usually based on reception and transplantation of foreign ideas and institutions.

*195.* This belief is generally true. Indeed there are just three practices which may eventually achieve the status of convention. The first is usually referred to as 'the first 100 days of the government'. It consists in the consensus among the political players – the party leaders and politicians, the MPs, the media, the civic activists etc. – that every new government should be granted an initial period of tranquillity amounting to a hundred days. During that period, the government should not be exposed to parliamentary control or harsh and intense public criticism. The idea is that the new government should have some time to establish its internal structure and to get oriented in the sociopolitical situation. Although not constitutionally or legally provided, this practice has been followed almost strictly since 1991. The only case in which this emerging constitutional convention was disregarded appeared in 2013 when the government under Prime Minister Plamen Oresharski was hit by a massive protest wave less than a month after its establishment. The public criticism was triggered by the appointment of a very unpopular businessman and politician – Mr Delyan Peevski – as Chairman of the State Agency for National Security.

*196.* The second practice gradually achieving the status of constitutional convention is the representation of the Republic of Bulgaria in the European Council by the President of the Republic and not by the Prime Minister in case of a 'caretaker government'. There have been already three cases for such representation of the parliamentary Republic of Bulgaria in the European Council by the President and not by the caretaker Prime Minister. In 2013 and in 2014, it was President Rosen Plevneliev and not the caretaker Prime Ministers Marin Raykov and Georgi Bliznashki who accomplished such representation. Similarly in 2017, President Rumen Radev represented Bulgaria in the European Council instead of the caretaker Prime Minister Ognyan Gerdjikov. These cases are temporary departure from the rules of parliamentary republic in which the state – in this case Bulgaria – should be represented in the European Council by the Prime Minister and not by the President. Indeed even in the case of parliamentary crisis when the state is governed by a caretaker Prime Minister, the form of governance remains parliamentary republic. However, there is tacit consensus that in such case the state should be represented

32. Georgi Bliznashki, *supra* n. 4, 21, Plamen Kirov, *supra* n. 4, 113.

by the President because he is the only 'regular' institution in the system (the Parliament is dissolved and there is no regular government) whereas the caretaker Prime Minister is appointed by him and serves for a very short period of time usually limited to three to four months

*197.* The third constitutional convention concerns the representative function performed by the Vice President. It is discussed in the paragraphs 334–335 of this book related to the competences of the Vice President.

## §2. General Principles of Law

*198.* The universally recognized general principles of international law are part of the domestic Bulgarian legal order. They have the same hierarchical standing as the international treaties. Consequently, they are allocated under the 1991 Constitution but above all sub-constitutional sources of law, including the acts of the Parliament, the normative acts of the government, the Ministers and the different administrative agencies, the normative acts of the municipal councils, the organizational regulations of the state institutions and the interpretative decrees and the interpretative decisions of the supreme courts.

*199.* This superior legal standing of the general principles of international law is safeguarded by the Constitutional Court. According to Article 149, paragraph 1, point 4 of the Constitution, the general principles of international law are also a criterion for compliance for the acts of the Parliament. Thus acts of Parliament may be declared void by the Constitutional Court if they contravene the general principles of international law.

# Chapter 6. Administrative Regulations and Orders

## §1. Classification

*200.* There are three main categories of administrative acts according to the Bulgarian law. These are the normative acts, the general administrative acts and the individual administrative acts. The normative acts contain legal provisions which concern non-specified number of cases and people. They differ from the acts of the Parliament either because they regulate less-important social relations or because they aim at further concretization of the legal provisions contained in the parliamentary legislation or in the international treaties. The general administrative acts contain provisions addressing undetermined but determinable number of cases or addressees. They possess some kind of normativity because they have regulative influence on a range of cases. However, their scope of application is much more limited than the normative acts. The individual administrative acts aim at the application of the law in concrete cases with a view to concrete addressees and concrete problems.

*201.* All normative acts of the central executive power institutions have the status of by-laws since there is no delegated legislation in Bulgaria. Moreover, only the central executive power institutions may issue normative acts. The regional governors and the mayors of municipalities, rayons and mayorships issue only orders which are individual administrative acts which in some cases can have the character of general administrative acts. However, they cannot adopt normative acts.

*202.* The Council of Ministers can adopt several administrative acts: decrees, ordinances, regulations, orders and decisions. The government adopts ordinances and regulations which are normative acts via decrees. The orders and decisions are individual administrative acts. The Council of Ministers adopts ordinances for the implementation of an act of the Parliament in its entirety whereas the regulations are by-laws which are adopted for the implementation of separate structural parts of the acts of the Parliament such as chapters or sections. Hence both the ordinances and the regulations are normative acts of the government which further develop the acts of the Parliament. The difference between them concerns the scope of the legal provisions which they contain.

*203.* The Ministers adopt ordinances, regulations, instructions and orders. The ordinances, regulations and instructions are normative acts whereas the orders are individual administrative acts.

*204.* Administrative acts – normative, general or individual – can be adopted also by the state agencies and the state committees. They have the same hierarchical standing as the acts of the other executive power institutions such as the government and the Ministers. The state agencies and the state committees adopt administrative acts in the field of their competence.

§2. HIERARCHY

*205.* The normative acts adopted by the Council of Ministers and the Ministers are allocated under the acts of the Parliament in the Bulgarian hierarchy of sources of law. Hence they must be in compliance with the 1991 Constitution, the EU law, the international treaties to which Bulgaria is a part, the general principles of international law and the acts of the Parliament. Otherwise, they will not be valid because they will be automatically derogated by the above-mentioned superior sources of law. Article 15, paragraph 3 of the Normative Acts Act allows the courts to disregard and to not apply provisions of decrees, ordinances, regulations and instructions if they contravene to the superior legal act. This diffuse control for legality is the most important safeguard for the supremacy of the acts of the Parliament, the international treaties, the EU law and the Constitution over the normative acts of the executive power institutions.

*206.* There are no explicit rules providing for some kind of hierarchy between the normative acts adopted by the Council of Ministers, the Ministers and the different administrative agencies. However, according to Article 107 of the Constitution, the Council of Ministers may abolish any legal act of the Ministers due to either its illegality or its contravention with the general policy implemented by the government. Hence the competence of the Council of Ministers to abolish all kinds of legal acts of the Ministers is not only a safeguard for their compliance with superior legal standards but it also serves as an assurance for their compatibility with the governmental programme and with the strategic and tactical decisions made by the Prime Ministers and the collegium of the Ministers.

*207.* Moreover, the Council of Ministers is on top of the executive power and the Ministers are the chiefs of different sector-specific hierarchies in the general framework of the executive power. In other words, the collegial principle of the organization of the executive power dominates over the ministerial principle, and the political branch of the executive power prevails over the administrative branch. That is why the normative acts of the Council of Ministers are superior to the normative acts adopted by the different Ministers. Moreover, the normative acts both of the Council of Ministers and of the Ministers prevail over the normative acts adopted by the administrative agencies and committees.

*208.* The derivative and supplementary character of the normative acts of the executive power institutions is clear also with regard to Article 13 of the Normative Acts Act. According to this act, the full or partial abolition of acts of Parliament automatically leads to the abolition of the decree, ordinance, regulation or instruction which is adopted on its basis and serves for its concretization and further development.

# Chapter 7. Codification, Interpretation and Publication

## §1. Codification

*209.* Bulgaria has codified constitution. It has already been mentioned that the codified nature of the Constitution is a constant characteristic of the Bulgarian constitutional tradition. The existence of different sources of constitutional law, such as the international treaties, the acts of the Parliament, the normative acts of the executive power institutions, the decisions of the Constitutional Court and the interpretative decisions and decrees of the supreme courts, naturally produces a degree of dispersion of the constitutional provisions. However, the existence of different sources of constitutional law is a natural feature of all constitutional systems. It cannot be defined as any form of deviation from the codified nature of the 1991 Constitution.

*210.* The increased importance of the jurisprudence of the Constitutional Court as well as the inclusion of a great number of precedent case laws of the ECtHR and the ECJ as valid sources of law of the Bulgarian legal order, especially in the field of human rights, contribute to the increasing 'de-codification' of the Bulgarian constitutional law. In fact, the jurisprudence of these two supranational courts both de-codifies the Bulgarian constitutional order and connects it with the supranational constitutionalism. The penetration of supranational constitutional standards, especially in the form of precedent judicial decisions, makes impossible the proper understanding of human rights' provisions enshrined in the texts of the 1991 Constitution without taking them into account. Thus the case law of the ECtHR and the ECJ produces further development of the open textuality[33] of the domestic constitution and leads to 'virtual de-codification'.

*211.* Moreover, the acts of Parliament, the Regulation for the Organization and Activity of the National Assembly, other regulations for the internal organization and functioning of state institutions (e.g., of the Constitutional Court and the Council of Ministers) and the international treaties especially in the field of human rights are also important sources of Bulgarian constitutional law. That is why they lead to proliferation of the constitutional law provisions and to de-codification of the constitutional law without de-codifying the 1991 Constitution itself.

## §2. Interpretation

*212.* All subjects of constitutional law interpret the Constitution in the course of its application. However, the Constitutional Court is the only institution which is competent to interpret the Constitution with binding force for all subjects of constitutional law.

---

33. *See* Herbert L.A. Hart, *supra* n. 24, 124–136.

*213.* The Bulgarian Constitutional Court has the competence for abstract interpretation of the Constitution which is relatively rare in a comparative perspective. It can adopt interpretative decisions on the initiative of one-fifth of the MPs, the President of the Republic, the Council of Ministers, the Supreme Court of Cassation, the Supreme Administrative Court and the State Prosecutor General. The Constitutional Court by virtue of these interpretative decisions actually accomplishes virtual amendment of the constitution based in its open texture. It accomplishes teleological interpretation, ascribes new meanings to constitutional concepts, broadens or limits the scope of application of different constitutional provisions. The Bulgarian Constitutional Court is rather activist and makes an extensive use of its interpretative power.

*214.* The Constitutional Court interprets the 1991 Constitution also in the course of accomplishment of its other competences. This is especially true with regard to the competence to declare the unconstitutionality of international treaties before their ratification, and to accomplish *ex post* control for constitutionality of the acts of the Parliament and the decisions of the Parliament. This is a concrete interpretation which serves as part of the argumentation of the Constitutional Court regarding the constitutionality or the unconstitutionality of the act under scrutiny. However, it is binding to all constitutional subjects – state institutions, organizations and citizens.

*215.* The Supreme Administrative Court and the Supreme Court of Cassation may issue interpretative decisions or interpretative decrees in case of incorrect or inconsistent and controversial practice of the courts. By virtue of these decisions and decrees, they give advice for the correct interpretation of the Bulgarian legislation in general and the acts of the Parliament and the Council of Ministers in particular.

*216.* It is not absolutely clear whether the Supreme Administrative Court and the Supreme Court of Cassation may also give interpretations of the Constitution. On the one hand, the ordinary courts may also interpret the Constitution incorrectly or inconsistently. Thus the harmonization of the jurisprudence is also needed with regard to the meaning and the correct interpretation of the constitutional provisions. On the other hand, the constitutional legislator has tried to concentrate the control for constitutionality and the constitutional interpretation in the Constitutional Court in order to prevent chaotic and controversial constitutional interpretation. More precisely, the emergence of eventual 'interpretative battles' between the Constitutional Court and the two supreme courts, especially if they are hidden and diffuse and not explicit, could be very problematic.

### §3. Publication

*217.* Most of the sources of the Bulgarian constitutional law are published in the official journal of the state – the SG, by the institution which adopts them. If the institution is collective, then the act is published by its Chairman. However, the acts of the Parliament in Bulgaria are published by the President of the Republic. This is because the President of the Republic has the competence to impose a moderately strong suspensive veto on the acts of the Parliament before their promulgation and publication. The President of the Republic has a fourteen days promulgation term in which he or she may either impose the veto thus returning the act of Parliament to the National Assembly for reconsideration or publish the act of Parliament in SG.

*218.* The only acts of Parliament which are not published by the President of the Republic but by the Chairman of the National Assembly are the constitutional laws which are the acts for amendment of the Constitution. This is due to the fact that in the course of the adoption of constitutional amendment the National Assembly acts as an institution of the constituent power whereas the President of the Republic is an institution of the constituted power. Consequently, the head of state cannot impose any veto on the acts for the amendment of the Constitution. Thus they are published by the Chairman of the National Assembly or by the Chairman of the Grand National Assembly within a short term amounting not to fourteen but to seven days as of the adoption of the act for the amendment of the Constitution.

# Part II. Form of Government

## Chapter 1. General Characteristics of the Bulgarian Form of Government

### §1. Introduction

*219.* The 1991 Constitution provides for republican and parliamentary form of government. This is the third republican constitution in Bulgarian history. The republic is a durable feature of the Bulgarian constitutionalism. Since 1946 it has permanently replaced the monarchy although there is no unamendable republican clause in the 1947, 1971 or the 1991 constitutions. Hence the republican form of government became a central element of the Bulgarian constitutional identity. A peculiar and a specific example which demonstrates the consensus regarding the republic is the fact that the last Bulgarian monarch – Tzar Simeon II – was elected as the Prime Minister in 2001, and he had sworn allegiance to the republican 1991 Constitution.

*220.* The parliamentary form of government, in contrast to the republic, is rather a novelty in the Bulgarian constitutional tradition. It should be perceived as rejection of both the constitutional monarchy provided by the 1879 Tarnovo Constitution and the Soviet type of people's democracy provided by the 1947 and the 1971 constitutions.

*221.* The VII Grand National Assembly, which has adopted the 1991 Constitution, opted for hybrid parliamentarism. The main reasons for choosing the parliamentary form of government have been its higher degree of social integration and political inclusiveness, its legal mechanisms for the solving of sociopolitical conflicts as well as the fear that a presidential republic may foster authoritarian tendencies whereas the semi-presidential republic may enhance the potential for clashes for power between the President and the Prime Minister.

*222.* It is again the fear of authoritarian rule – this time concentrated in the figure of the Prime Minister – which made the founding fathers and mothers of the 1991 Constitution to provide for some deviations from the pure parliamentary form of government. Thus the moderately weak President who enjoys direct democratic legitimacy due to his or her direct election, the lack of delegated legislation, the lack of right to discretionary dissolution of the Parliament by the President or the Prime

Minister and the incompatibility between the ministerial and MPs' positions are supposed to serve as a reinforced system for checks and balances remedying the concentration of power in the Prime Minister of a Parliamentary Republic. The role of safeguards against concentration of power in the political unit composed of the government and the parliamentary majority under the leadership of the Prime Minister is ascribed also to the strong Constitutional Court and to the judiciary which enjoys enhanced autonomy.

*223.* The main institutional novelties introduced in the Bulgarian constitutionalism by the 1991 Constitution are the President as a single and directly elected by the people republican head of state, the Constitutional Court, the Supreme Judicial Council and the ombudsman. The welfare state principle is also proclaimed for the first time by the 1991 Constitution.

*224.* The 1991 Constitution provides for predominantly representative republic. The institutes of direct democracy apart from the elections are not explicitly provided by the Constitution itself. Indeed the 1991 Constitution proclaims the principle of popular sovereignty and is not prohibitive of direct democracy. However, the lack of clarity regarding the permissibility of the different types of referenda and people's initiative and more precisely the doubtful constitutionality of the constitutional referendum expose the direct democratic developments in the political practice as well as their legislative foundations to a permanent threat of being declared unconstitutional.

*225.* Bulgaria is a party democracy. The political parties play an important role for the functioning of the system especially with a view to the fact that Bulgaria is parliamentary and not presidential republic. However, several factors render the party democracy in Bulgaria rather dysfunctional. The most important of them are the lack of real ideology-based parties (with some exceptions), the predominant character of the Bulgarian parties as leadership parties, the uncertainty of the ideological demarcation lines between the parties which are overshadowed by lobbyist and other hidden influences, the crisis of representation and the crisis of trust in the political parties and the party system by the Bulgarian citizens.

## §2. Intermediate Institutions of the Public Sphere

### I. Political Parties

*226.* The legal status of the political parties in Bulgaria is provided by the 1991 Constitution and the Political Parties Act. Other important sources of law which contain provisions regarding the political parties are the Election Code, the Direct Participation of the Citizen in the State Power and Local Self-Government Act and some decisions of the Constitutional Court.

*227.* The 1991 Constitution defines the constitutional status of the political parties in Bulgaria as an element and a logical consequence of the provision of the principle of political pluralism. Article 11, paragraph 1 of the Constitution declares that the political life in Bulgaria is grounded on the principle of political pluralism. Furthermore, Article 11, paragraph 2 prohibits the declaration of any political party or political ideology to be official party or ideology of the state. These two paragraphs are clear examples of the reflexivity and the reactivity of the 1991 Constitution to the 1971 Constitution, which proclaimed in its Article 1 the leading and dominant role of the Bulgarian Communist Party. The proclaiming of the political pluralism instead of the political monism should be read in conjunction with the proclamation of the separation of powers in Article 8 of the 1991 Constitution as a reflexive and a reactive replacement of the principle of unity of state power as a pillar of the Soviet-type constitutionalism which existed in Bulgaria from 1947 to 1991.

*228.* Article 11, paragraphs 3 and 4 are devoted to the constitutional status of the political parties. Paragraph 3 is a declaratory provision in which a role is to broadly outline the constitutional role of the political parties and to serve as a device for legislative delegation for further development of their status by the Parliament. It provides that the political parties contribute to the formation and the expression of the political will of the citizen. Moreover, the procedure for establishment and dissolution of political parties as well as the conditions for their activity should be provided by an act of Parliament.

*229.* Finally, Article 11, paragraph 4 provides for the grounds for unconstitutionality of the political parties which serve as quality limitations of the political pluralism. Two types of political parties are prohibited by the 1991 Constitution. First, political parties that are established on ethnic, race or religious basis are prohibited. Second, political parties that strive at the seizure of state power through violent means are also prohibited.

*230.* There are several principles of the status of the political parties provided by the Political Parties Act. The political parties are voluntary associations of citizens with electoral rights according to the Bulgarian legislation. Hence not only Bulgarian citizens but also EU citizens may form and participate in Bulgarian political parties. The political parties should contribute towards the formation and the expression of the political will of the people only through democratic means. The establishment and activity of the political parties are public. The political parties possess monopoly for the participation in elections. Organizations which are not political parties cannot participate in elections. The political parties must respect the Constitution and other sources of law in Bulgaria, and their activity must be performed only in Bulgarian language, which is the official language of the state. The political parties must be distinct and differentiated from the state, the institutions of public power and the religious institutions. Magistrates, some categories of civil servants, diplomats and members of the armed forces are not allowed to be members of any political party. Logical consequence of this principle is the prohibition of political parties to use in their symbols either the official symbols of the Republic of Bulgaria, or the symbols of any other state, or any religious symbols.

*231.* The procedure for the establishment of political parties encompasses several consecutive steps which are logically and legally intertwined. Initially, an initiative committee must be established. It must comprise at least fifty citizens possessing electoral rights according to the Bulgarian legislation. The initiative committee adopts a constituent declaration in written form and publishes it in at least one national daily journal or newspaper. In addition, the initiative committee gathers the necessary minimal number of signatures for the establishment of a political party which amounts to five hundred signatures.

*232.* The next step is the summoning of a Constituent Assembly by the initiative committee. The Constituent Assembly must adopt the statute of the political party and must elect its governing and controlling bodies in accordance with this statute. The Constituent Assembly is valid if at least five hundred establishing members of the political party are present on it.

*233.* The last step is the registration of the political party in the public register of the political parties at the Sofia City Court. The Sofia City Court will register the political party if all necessary documentation is provided, if there are at least 2500 members of the party and if its statute complies with the Bulgarian legislation. The decision of the Sofia City Court may be appealed in front of the Supreme Court of Cassation. If it is not appealed or if the appeal has been rejected by the Supreme Court of Cassation, then the decision of the Sofia City Court is published in SG.

*234.* The political parties are allowed to establish their local substructures on territorial principle. They may also establish women and youth sections and structures. However, the political parties are prohibited from establishing structures in workplaces, in public administrations as well as religious, military and children's structures (allowing for the membership of citizens with less than 18 years of age).

*235.* The activity of the political parties is financed by their own revenues as well as by state subsidy. The political parties cannot accomplish any economic or trade activity. The state subsidy is granted to political parties which are represented in the National Assembly as well as to political parties which have at least 1% of the votes in the previous parliamentary elections. The management of the party finances is controlled on an annual basis by the Court of Audits.

*236.* There are several grounds for the termination of the political parties. Some of them do not have the character of a sanction, but they are based on the will of the governing bodies of the political party. These grounds comprise merger with the other political party, the secession from the political party or the division of the political party into several parties as well as the voluntary termination of the existence of the political party.

*237.* Two other grounds for termination of political parties have the character of a sanction. They are a result of the will of state institution (the Constitutional Court or the Sofia District Court) and not of the will of the political party. These two grounds are the declaration of the unconstitutionality of the political party by the Constitutional Court and its termination by decision of the Sofia District Court.

*238.* The grounds for unconstitutionality of the political parties have already been presented above. The Sofia District Court may terminate the existence of a political party in the following cases: first, if the political party systematically infringes the requirements of the Political Parties Act; second, if its activity contravenes the 1991 Constitution; third, if the political party has not participated in parliamentary, presidential or local self-government elections during the last five years since its last registration; fourth, if the political party did not file its annual financial reports to the Court of Audits for two consecutive years; fifth, if the political party has not accomplished the sessions of its supreme body which are provided by its statute for more than two consecutive terms or at least once during the last five years and has not presented to the Sofia District Court the list of members of its newly elected governing body. The decision of the Sofia District Court for dissolution of the political party may be appealed in front of the Supreme Court of Cassation, whose decision is final.

## II. Non-governmental Organizations

*239.* The 1991 Constitution provides for the freedom of association as a human right and in parallel safeguards the (non-governmental) associations and organizations as objective constitutional institutions of the public sphere. The Constitution does not contain detailed provisions on the different aspects of the freedom of association such as the right to form association, the right to join association, the right to leave the association and the right to influence the organizational life and the activity of the association. Moreover, there are constitutional provisions only on the positive right to association – the right to form association, but no explicit constitutional provisions on the negative right to association consisting in the right not to join or not to participate in the formation of any association.

*240.* However, all these aspects of the broad freedom of association are actually presumed by the 1991 Constitution. They are not explicitly proclaimed by it due to the lack of a developed doctrine of human rights in general and of specific human rights, e.g., the freedom of association, in particular in Bulgaria during the late 1980s and the early 1990s that was able to expose the necessity of such detailed constitutional arrangement of the freedom of association.

*241.* The 1991 Constitution provides for several main issues related to the freedom of association. It proclaims the freedom of association as a subjective right and defines the main aims for which associations may be established. It determines some restrictions of the freedom of association and declares some limits to the activity of the associations. They serve as constitutional margins of the freedom of association and thus as qualitative limitations to the principle of political pluralism similar to the grounds for unconstitutionality of the political parties. The 1991 Constitution proclaims also several specific forms of associations which deserve special attention in the view of the constitutional legislator.

*242.* Article 44, paragraph 1 of the Constitution provides for the freedom of association as a subjective right. Although the wording of the text grants this freedom to 'the citizens', it must be interpreted widely since this is a universal human right and not a right reserved only for the Bulgarian citizens. Article 12 proclaims the objective constitutional institution of the association. According to this article, the associations of the citizens serve for satisfaction and protection of their interests. Again this text must be interpreted extensively so as to include also the associations of non-citizens.

*243.* Article 12, paragraph 2 of the Constitution prohibits the accomplishment of political activity by the associations in Bulgaria. According to the Constitution, such activity may be performed only by the political parties. Indeed there is some logic in restricting one of the forms of the freedom of association – the trade unions – to participate in the political life since their aim is to protect the social and labour and not the political rights of the people.

*244.* The limitation of the political life to party politics is rather inaccurate and a reductionist understanding of the institutional infrastructure of the civil society and the public sphere in the context of a modern democracy. It can be understood with regard to the rather early phase of the transition to democracy during which the 1991 Constitution was adopted. Thus it can be explained with the lack of sufficient experience of the constitutional legislator with full scale and fully fledged democracy for which the political engagement of the NGOs is of central importance. As a matter of fact, the political life in Bulgaria is not structured exclusively around political parties although they have a central place in it. The NGOs and other forms of associations also intensely participate and play a crucial role in the Bulgarian civil society and public sphere.

*245.* Article 44, paragraph 2 of the Constitution imposes restrictions on the freedom of association. It prohibits the establishment of organizations whose activity is directed against the sovereignty, the territorial integrity, the unity of the nation, which are inciting racial, national, ethnic or religious hatred or infringing human rights. Organizations which create secret or paramilitary structures or aim at violent achievement of their goals are also constitutionally prohibited.

*246.* According to Article 44, paragraph 3 of the Constitution, the acts of the Parliament determine the types of organizations and associations which should be registered, the procedure for their registration and their interrelations with the state. The Constitutional Court has pronounced via Decision No. 10 of 1994 that in principle the organizations and the associations can be established directly on the basis of the Constitution without the necessity for legislative permission and without registration, except if such procedures or registrations are required explicitly by an act of the Parliament in accordance with the Constitution. Hence if the association is constitutionally permitted, there is no need for a special legislative provision of its status. The acts of the Parliament may provide for restrictions of the associations if they comply with the Constitution and if they concern legitimate state or social interest. Last but not least, according to the Constitutional Court's decision, an act of Parliament may authorize associations and organizations to perform state functions. In that case, the associations and organizations must agree to accomplish the assigned tasks voluntarily.

*247.* The 1991 Constitution provides also for some special forms of associations. Article 49, paragraph 1 of the Constitution provides for the freedom of association of the workers and the civil servants in trade unions. The trade unions should serve for the protection of their labour and social security interests. Article 49, paragraph 2 of the Constitution safeguards the reciprocal right of the employers to form and join employer's organizations. Article 19, paragraph 4 of the Constitution provides for the freedom to establish specific associations with a commercial purpose. According to this article, the acts of the Parliament should establish the necessary conditions for the association of the citizens in cooperatives and in other associations for the achievement of economic or social prosperity.

*248.* Last but not least, Article 137 of the Constitution provides for the freedom of association not of the citizens but of the municipalities. According to this article, the self-governing territorial communities may establish or join associations for the solving of their common issues. The Local Self-Government and Local Administration Act establishes the concrete conditions for these specific types of associations allowing for both national and regional associations of the municipalities.

## III. Media

*249.* The 1991 Constitution does not contain provisions related to the different types of media – classical, electronic or Internet based. The only constitutional provision in that regard is paragraph 6 of the Transitory Provisions of the Constitution related to the temporary competences of the National Assembly in relation to the Bulgarian National Television and Bulgarian National Radio accomplished in the period until the adoption of the new democratic act of Parliament on electronic media. Hence this provision has lost its importance almost immediately after the adoption of the 1991 Constitution.

*250.* The 1991 Constitution does not provide for the media as objective constitutional institutions but grants information and communication rights to the people based on which they can establish and develop media as instruments for their accomplishment. These information and communication rights will be discussed in the chapter devoted to the fundamental rights and liberties. Consequently, the approach of the constitutional legislator on the constitutional foundations of the media differs from its approach to the political parties and the associations which are proclaimed as objective constitutional institutions and as players of the public sphere in parallel with the assignment of the subjective constitutional rights such as the freedom of association in general and the freedom to establish and join political parties in particular.

*251.* The legal status of electronic media is regulated by the Radio and Television Act. The Electronic Communications Act also has some relevance since it provides for the conditions for granting of licenses to radio and TV operators. The Radio and Television Act defines the types of media services delivered by different media. It determines the status of media service providers, establishes safeguards for the political and economic independence of media service providers, for media pluralism, for the freedom of information and for the respect for human rights. The Radio and Television Act enlists the main principles and guidelines serving as pillars for the organization and the functioning of electronic media in Bulgaria. Some key issues such as the freedom of information, the protection of sources of information, the rights of media providers and the journalists to access public information and the safeguards for the critical function of media on public figures are also provided by the Radio and Television Act.

*252.* Furthermore, the Radio and Television Act provides for the status of the Electronic Media Council which is the state institution accomplishing supervision and control over electronic media in Bulgaria. The Electronic Media Council is an independent body comprising five members. Three of the members of the Electronic Media Council are elected by the National Assembly and two are appointed by the President of the Republic.

*253.* The Radio and Television Act determines also the status of the Bulgarian National Radio and the Bulgarian National Television. It provides for the compulsory requirements regarding their programmes, management and financing. The Radio and Television Act contains numerous provisions on the advertisement, financing, licensing and registration of electronic media apart from the just mentioned two state-owned media institutions.

## IV. Lobbies

*254.* The lobbies and lobbyism are not legally institutionalized in the Bulgarian legal system. There are only provisions for the prevention of the conflict of interests as well as provisions related to the protection against dependencies of the state office holders and the civil servants from improper influence by private companies, associations and citizens which serve as an indirect limitation of the lobbyist activity. The most important sources of law which contain such provisions are Chapter XII, Section II of the Regulation for the Organization and the Activity of the National Assembly devoted to the ethical norms of the behaviour of the MPs and the Prevention and Detection of Conflict of Interest Act. They will not be analysed here due to the fact that these acts do not regulate directly the lobbies or lobbyism.

# Chapter 2. The President

## §1. Constitutional Status in the System of Separation of Powers

*255.* There is widespread thesis in the Bulgarian constitutional theory that the President of the Republic is neutral power. According to that theory, the President is not a part of the 'classical' state powers – the legislative, the executive and the judicial power – but has competences in all of them serving as a safeguard of the Constitution and the national interests and as an arbiter between the state institutions.[34]

*256.* In fact, this theory is an attempt to apply the nineteenth-century theory of Benjamin Constant regarding the '*pouvoire moderateur neutre*' (the neutral moderating power) of the king of the constitutional–parliamentary monarchy[35] in the republican context of a post-communist society at the end of the twentieth and the beginning of the twenty-first centuries. The aim of this attempt at transplanting normative ideologies developed in different constitutional systems and political context is to allow the President to function as a factor of political neutrality that can pacify and moderate the political process and can mediate between the state institutions.

*257.* The theory of the neutral moderating power of the head of state has been initially launched in the Bulgarian constitutional discourse by some intellectual circles, gathered around the Radical Democratic Party and the *Democraticheski pregled* magazine at the end of the nineteenth and the beginning of the twentieth centuries during the reign of Tzar Ferdinand I. The idea of the modern authors relaunching the notion of neutral power of the head of state[36] is to build upon the democratic traditions of the pre-communist period thus demonstrating a kind of continuity between the Tarnovo Constitution and the 1991 Constitution and to establish the President as a moderator in times of severe political battles for power.

*258.* However, there are several arguments against the theory that the President of the Republic can perform the role of neutral power. The President, in contrast to the monarch, is directly elected by the people on the basis of party political nomination and competition. Hence all Bulgarian Presidents are party politicians or at least have been supported by political parties. Indeed some of them have been formally nominated by initiative committees and not directly by a political party. Moreover, some of the Bulgarian Presidents have been experts who have lately started a political career. Anyway, no Bulgarian President has been elected without the massive support of a political party or party coalition. Last but not least, the 1991 Constitution does not prohibit the party membership of the President and the Vice President.

---

34. *See supra* n. 4 Georgi Bliznashki, *supra* n. 4, 12–14 and 59–80 ('St. Kliment Ohridski' University Press, 2009) (in Bulgarian), Plamen Kirov, *supra* n. 4, 137–140.
35. Benjamin Constant, *Cours de politique constitutionnelle*, 13 et seq. (Paris, 1814).
36. *See* Georgi Bliznashki, *supra* n. 10, 64.

*259.* Another argument against the theory of the President as neutral power centre is the fact that he or she has a fixed term of office. Thus the Bulgarian President not only has a political past but may have and in practice frequently has a party political future. Hence, it is naïve to expect that the President, who has been a party politician before his or her election as head of state and will probably continue to have a political career after the lapse of his or her mandate to behave during his or hers mandate in compliance with the principle of party political neutrality.

*260.* Actually, there is an internal controversy enshrined in the 1991 Constitution with regard to the role and the functions of the President of the Republic. Pertaining to Article 92, paragraph 1 of the Constitution, the President symbolizes the unity of the nation. This provision suggests that the President should be a non-party political figure who is equally remoted from all political parties, lobbies and fractions in the Bulgarian political life and society and who can serve as a symbol for self-identification of all Bulgarian citizens. However, according to Article 95, paragraph 2 of the Constitution, the President can be a member of a political party. Moreover, the direct elections for President, the electoral campaign which is led on party political lines and the natural involvement of the President in party politics before, during and frequently even after his or her term of office are clear evidence of the impossibility of the political neutrality of the President. It is unclear how a party politician or an expert who is supported by a political party or a coalition of parties can become a neutral moderator equally remoted from all political factors thus symbolizing the unity of the nation as of the day of the elections.

*261.* At first glance it might seem that the 1991 Bulgarian Constitution allows the President to perform a relatively wide range of political roles. The President can try to behave as a neutral power, a reactive veto player and a proactive veto player.[37]

*262.* There are several preconditions which must be fulfilled in order for the President to pretend to be a neutral power. The candidate for the presidential office must not have engaged in party politics in the past, nor during the electoral campaign and the elections. He or she must have never been a member of a political party. In other words, the President should be absolutely politically impartial. He or she has to refrain from both imposing veto on the acts of the Parliament and approaching the Constitutional Court with any demands for unconstitutionality. Otherwise, the President will be involved in the legislative process and the legislative politics which are naturally political phenomena. Last but not least, the President will have to avoid intervening in any controversial political discussions. Thus the President should in fact avoid acting because any action and any accomplishment of competence is *per se* divisive and usually has a party political connotation.

37. For the concept of veto players in general and of proactive veto player in particular, *see* George Tsebelis, *Veto Players. How Political Institutions Work*, 1–344 (Russell Sage Foundation/Princeton University Press, 2002).

*263.* The question is whether such intentional neutrality of the President does not transform the institution into a nominal head of state which is neither necessary, nor possible in the Bulgarian context. Moreover, it is questionable whether a systematic de-politicization of the head of state, which makes redundant the presidential competences, is in compliance with the Constitution and with the intention of the constitutional legislator.

*264.* The Bulgarian President has no constitutional competences to initiate the decision-making processes. The President cannot initiate either legislation, or governmental policies or governmental legal acts. He or she cannot impose his or her own strategy for internal or external policy of the state. If the President is a respected politician who has instruments for personal and political influence due to his charisma, contacts or experience, he or she can be an important factor in the discussion and the determination of the Bulgarian political process. However, the President has only political but no legal means to initiate formal decision-making processes. Consequently, the Bulgarian President does not possess the competences to perform the role of proactive veto player and to serve as a policy initiator.

*265.* The President has only two competences by virtue of which he or she can act as a proactive policy initiator. These are the right to propose national referenda to the Parliament and the right to propose amendments to the Constitution. The President cannot impose his or her will on the Parliament. The National Assembly is the institution which is competent to approve or reject the presidential proposal for the accomplishment of national referendum or for constitutional amendment.

*266.* Consequently, the Bulgarian President can be politically active. He or she may try to function as a policy initiator and thus as a proactive veto player. However, the number and the character of the competences granted to the President by the 1991 Constitution do not allow him or her to become a permanent policy initiator. The President cannot compete for the role of an active leader of the state which is vested in the institution of the Prime Minister by the current Bulgarian Constitution. The President can never become a strategic power centre generating and implementing policies alternative or contrary to the policies launched by the government and its parliamentary majority.

*267.* Actually, the typical role of the Bulgarian President shaped by the 1991 Constitution is the reactive veto player. The President is an important part of the system of checks and balances established by the 1991 Constitution. The main task of the President is to compensate the concentration of power in the Prime Minister heading the power unit composed by the government and the parliamentary majority.[38] Such concentration of power is typical for all parliamentary systems.

*268.* The Bulgarian constitutional legislator tries to remedy this natural tendency of the parliamentary form of government especially by virtue of the combined influence of the President and the Constitutional Court on the balance of

38. Vasil Kirov, *supra* n. 4, 208.

power. The President can veto legislation which is typically initiated by the government and approved by its parliamentary majority. He or she can initiate the Constitutional Court's proceedings by virtue of which a control for the conformity of the acts of the Parliament with the Constitution and the international treaties can be accomplished. The President can reject the proposal of the Supreme Judicial Council for the appointment of the Chairman of the Supreme Court of Cassation, the Chairman of the Supreme Administrative Court and the State Prosecutor General thus blocking these very important nominations for the top positions in the judicial power.

*269.* Last but not least, the President serves as a check on other state institutions through his or her competence to appoint the office holders of some of the most important state bodies. The competence of the President to appoint one-third of the Constitutional Court's judges, members of the Governing Board of the Bulgarian Bank, members of the Electronic Media Council and members of important state agencies actually serve as instruments for counterbalance of the influence of other state institutions with regard to not only the personal but also the substantial policy of the state.

*270.* Hence the President is a reactive veto player who has also some symbolic functions resembling the neutral moderating power of the constitutional–parliamentary monarch and some limited competences for policy initiation. The President is an institution which possesses competences belonging to different branches of the state power. The competences of the President concern predominantly the external power, the executive power, the patronage power and the communication power although he or she has also competences in the legislative and the financial power.[39] The influence of the President is most limited with regard to the judicial power where he or she has only the right to pardon for criminal offences.

## §2. Election

*271.* The President and the Vice President are elected as a team directly by the people. They are the only institutions at the national level which possess 'input' direct democratic legitimacy[40] apart from the National Assembly. The direct election of the President is one of the differences of the Bulgarian constitutional model from the pure parliamentary republic.

---

39. For more about these branches of state power, *see* Martin Belov, *Separation of Powers Reconsidered: A Proposal for a New Theoretical Model at the Beginning of the 21st Century*, in *Law, Politics and the Constitution. New Perspectives from Legal and Political Theory*, 47–63 (Antonia Geisler, Michael Hein and Siri Hummel eds., Peter Lang, 2014).
40. For the 'input' democratic legitimacy, *see* Paul Craig and Grainne de Burca, *EU Law. Text, Cases and Materials*, 65 (Oxford University Press, 2008); Philip Kiiver, *The National Parliaments in the European Union: A Critical View on EU Constitution-Building*, 95 (Kluwer Law International, 2006).

*272.* Two main ideas lay behind the direct election of the President in the contemporary Bulgarian constitutional model. The first is that the people should be allowed to have direct influence on the recruitment of the most important state institutions. The logic of this concept is that the more institutions the people elect the more involved in the decision-making process they will feel and the more integrated and active the civil society will be. This is especially important in the context of post-totalitarian society in transition to democracy in which the democratic habits and attitudes for self-responsibility, democratic control over the state power and active involvement in the political process have to be (re)created and fostered. Hence the direct election of the President seemed an important tool for civic engagement and additional democratic influence on the state power. The direct presidential elections are supposed to serve as a channel for linking the civil society and the state power.

*273.* The second idea which is implied in the direct elections of the President is related to the search of additional checks and balances which can remedy the natural concentration of power in the Prime Minister of a Parliamentary Republic. Hence the directly elected President, who enjoys immediate popular support and direct democratic legitimacy, should function as a counterbalance and a corrective factor to the power unit composed of the government and the parliamentary majority and topped by the Prime Minister.[41] The direct elections for President allow for eventually divergent party political affiliation of the head of state and the above-mentioned power unit. Indeed in the political practice the President becomes more active and makes use of his or her role as a reactive veto player exactly in the cases when he or she belongs to a political force different from the government and the majority in the National Assembly.

*274.* The President and the Vice President are elected via absolute majority electoral system in two rounds. They can be elected also in the first round if two requirements related to achieved majority and threshold are simultaneously met. Thus the election of the President and the Vice President in the first round is possible if they receive the absolute majority of votes cast where an absolute majority of the people with the right to vote have participated in the elections. If one of these two conditions is not fulfilled, then one week later a second round of voting is accomplished. In the second round, the electoral activity and the threshold are not relevant and the candidate pair that has received most of the votes is elected as President and Vice President.

*275.* Compulsory voting for all types of elections as well as for referenda held in Bulgaria was introduced in 2016 via a reform of the Electoral Code. However, in 2017 the Constitutional Court by virtue of its Decision No. 3 of 2017 declared the sanction provided by the Electoral Code to be unconstitutional. The sanction for refraining to cast a vote has been anyway rather weak and meagre. The citizens who have not participated in the last elections of a specific type, e.g., presidential elections, are not included in the list of the electorate for that type of elections the next

41. For this single power unit *see* Vasil Kirov, *supra* n. 4, 208.

time they are held. However, the citizen can vote in the elections for other state institutions or in referenda. If the citizen explicitly declares his or her desire to participate in the next elections for which he or she has lost his or her right to vote, the citizen gets immediately inscribed in the electoral register and regains his or her active electoral rights.

*276.* Thus even before the abolition of the sanction by the Constitutional Court, compulsory voting in Bulgaria was not supported by real sanction and actually resembled an indirect, hidden, partial, diffuse and ad hoc active registration. It is indirect because there is no requirement that the people should register for voting if they regularly go to vote. It is hidden because it is masqueraded as sanction. It is partial because it concerns only distinct types of elections and referenda and does not count for the active right to vote for all elections. It is ad hoc and diffuse because it concerns only specific citizens who did not go to the polling station in the last elections for one or another state institution.

*277.* Hence currently the Electoral Code provides for compulsory voting with no sanction,which as a result is not compulsory at all. This absurd situation is even more problematic because of the fact that despite the compulsory voting only 57.47 % of Bulgarian citizens had participated in the first round and 51.62 % in the second round of the 2016 presidential elections.

*278.* All Bulgarian Presidents and Vice Presidents have been elected in the second round. This can be explained by the procedural hurdles and by the fact that there are many 'dead souls' in the electoral register. This definition is applicable to citizens who are still part of the list of citizens with the right to vote although they should be at an age at which they should be presumably deceased thus factually increasing the quorum with several per cents. Moreover, there is no Bulgarian political party or political leader who was able to accumulate sufficient popular support as to be elected as President in the first round.

*279.* The candidates for President and Vice President can be proposed and supported by political parties, coalitions of political parties, initiative committees or initiative committees with the support of political parties. The right of initiative committees to nominate candidates for President and Vice President is a result of the legislator's desire to allow for extensive political pluralism and to enable also actors without explicit party political affiliation to participate in the electoral process and eventually in the political life. However, in practice, the nomination by initiative committees has been typically used by the political parties and coalitions in order to generate wider support for their candidate by pretending that he or she is 'neutral' or to conceal the party support for different reasons.

*280.* The President and the Vice President have five years term of office. They may be elected only for two terms of office irrespective of whether they are consecutive or are interrupted by a certain period of time. Until now, only one President – Georgi Parvanov – has been re-elected and has served two terms of office as a head of state.

*281.* There are several requirements for the eligibility of the candidates for President and Vice President. The candidate must be at least 40 years old, should possess only Bulgarian citizenship by birth, has to live at least for the last five years in Bulgaria, must not have been put under custody, must not have served a term of imprisonment.

*282.* According to Decision No. 12 of 1996 of the Constitutional Court, the requirement that the candidate for President or Vice President has Bulgarian citizenship by birth is fulfilled if he or she has acquired the citizenship not via naturalization but through the principles *ius sanguinis* or *ius soli* according to the law which was valid at the moment of the birth of the candidate.

*283.* Moreover, according to Decision No. 3 of 2001 of the Constitutional Court, the requirement that the candidate should have lived in Bulgaria during the last five years before the elections is satisfied if he or she had lived actually and physically in the Bulgarian territory during periods amounting to at least more than the half of each of these five years. The idea is that the candidate must be sufficiently acquainted with the sociopolitical context in Bulgaria and that is why he or she must be durably linked to the society whereas the territorial presence is an indication of such a durable bond.

## §3. Immunity and Removal from Power

*284.* The President and the Vice President enjoy absolute immunity. They can be removed from power only in case of state treason or violation of the Constitution. Otherwise, they cannot be held liable for any action or inaction and they enjoy full freedom of expression. In contrast to the immunity of the MPs, the immunity of the President or the Vice President cannot be removed. If the President or the Vice President is removed from power, they lose also their immunity due to the fact that they are not office holders any more, but ordinary citizens. However, if the President or the Vice President is still in office even in case of pending impeachment procedure, they enjoy full immunity.

*285.* There are four grounds for preterm termination of the term of office of the President and the Vice President: death, durable inability to accomplish the functions due to serious illness, resignation or impeachment. The first two of them are objective factors which do not depend on the will either of the office holder or of any state institution. The resignation is a ground for preterm termination of the office which is triggered by the will of the resigning President or Vice President.

*286.* The removal of the President or the Vice President from office through impeachment procedure is the only ground which has the character of a sanction and is a direct result of their political responsibility. The ground for impeachment as well as the main aspects of the impeachment procedure are provided by Article 103 of the Constitution and are further developed in the Constitutional Court Act.

*287.* The President or the Vice President may be removed from office on two alternative grounds. These are state treason and violation of the Constitution. There is ambiguity whether the state treason as grounds for removal of the head of state according to Article 103 of the Constitution coincides with the state treason as a criminal offence according to the Criminal Code. It seems that the most logical and reasonable solution is to assume that these two concepts coincide in the sense that the parameters and the elements of state treason as a ground for preterm termination of the term of office of the head of state have to be found in the criminal law concept of state treason. Based on the use of some objective legal standards, this option safeguards a degree of clarity and legal certainty.[42]

*288.* Article 103 of the Constitution does not clarify whether the state treason should be accomplished intentionally and guilty by the President or the Vice President and whether there is some specific type of the guilt that has to be at hand as a precondition for the impeachment. If the analogous and complementary application of the Criminal Code continues, then all modalities regarding the intention and the guilt provided by it should be applied also in the case of impeachment.

*289.* It has to be underlined that if the Constitutional Court adopts a decision for impeachment of the President or the Vice President due to state treason or violation of the Constitution, the sanction is just political and consists in preterm termination of their term of office. The Constitutional Court is not a criminal court, and it cannot apply any form of criminal liability. The impeached President or the Vice President is not considered convicted of a criminal offence. That is why they should be put on trial in front of a criminal court after the impeachment if there is sufficient evidence that they have accomplished a criminal offence. This will most probably be the case with state treason. It is also important to note that the state prosecutors' office and the criminal court are independent from the Constitutional Court. They are not bound by the conclusions or the procedural activities of the Constitutional Court although they can make use of them.

*290.* The constitutional text is also vague with regard the kind of violation that the Constitution can constitute a ground for impeachment. More precisely, it is unclear whether all types of constitutional violations, even the formal and minor violations, can provoke the impeachment of the President or the Vice President. The comparative and historic analysis of the impeachment provisions contained in the constitutions of other states may lead to the conclusion that only violations which are serious and intentional and which are anti-systemic and directed against the established constitutional model can be sufficient to engage the political responsibility of the President or the Vice President resulting in their impeachment.[43] However, such conclusion cannot pretend for immediate validity in the Bulgarian context until there is either explicit constitutional provision clarifying the issue, or interpretative decision of the Constitutional Court or practice of the impeachment procedure.

42. For the contrary opinion, *see* Emilia Drumeva, *supra* n. 31, 435.
43. For these considerations, *see* Emilia Drumeva, *supra* n. 31, 435.

*291.* The impeachment procedure has two phases – parliamentary phase and Constitutional Court's phase. The parliamentary phase is compulsory and whether there will be any Constitutional Court's phase depends on its result. If the National Assembly rejects the motion for impeachment, then the procedure does not continue in front of the Constitutional Court. Hence the Constitutional Court's phase is facultative.

*292.* The parliamentary phase commences on the initiative of one-fourth of the MPs who can introduce a motion for impeachment of the President or the Vice President. The motion has to be motivated and supplied with evidence. If more than two-thirds of all MPs after the parliamentary deliberations support the motion and vote in favour of a parliamentary decision that the President or the Vice President have accomplished state treason or violation of the Constitution, then the parliamentary phase ends and the Constitutional Court is approached by the National Assembly with a suggestion for impeachment.

*293.* Thus the Constitutional Court's phase begins. There are several peculiarities of the impeachment procedure which are deviations from the regular parameters of the Constitutional Court's procedure. The Constitutional Court's decision is prepared not by one but by three judges–rapporteurs. There is a fixed term of the duration of the impeachment procedure – the decision must be adopted in a one-month term after the initiation of the procedure. This is an extremely short term in comparison to the usual duration of the Constitutional Court's proceedings which may last between several months and a year. In fact, there is no legally provided deadline for deciding the Constitutional Court's cases apart from the procedure for impeachment.

*294.* Moreover, the proceedings in front of the Constitutional Court are closed, and there are no oral hearings and usually only written evidence is accepted. The impeachment procedure is open and is based on oral hearings and exchange of arguments between the MP who presents and defends the parliamentary motion for impeachment and the President or Vice President who also has the right to counsel. All types of evidences are applicable. The parties to the case can present not only written but also oral and material evidence.

*295.* If the Constitutional Court adopts a decision that the President or the Vice President has accomplished state treason or violation of the Constitution, then they are removed from office. If the President is impeached, then the Vice President becomes the President. If there is no Vice President, then the Chairman of the National Assembly accomplishes the competences of the President until preterm presidential elections are held. If the Vice President is impeached, then the President continues his or her mandate without a Vice President. In case there is evidence of a criminal offence having been committed, the Constitutional Court submits it to the state prosecutors' office.

§4. Functions and Competences

*296.* The Bulgarian President has several functions. He or she possesses the four classical functions that belong to all heads of state but are especially evident in the case of the Presidents and the monarchs of the parliamentary republics and monarchies. These are the symbolic, integrative, representative and communication functions.[44] Moreover, the Bulgarian President has a function which is specific for the hybrid parliamentary systems and especially for the current Bulgarian constitutional model.[45] This is the function of the President as a safeguard[46] for the Constitution and the international treaties resulting from his status as a reactive veto player. The Bulgarian President has rather limited functions of policy initiation and determination and execution of the external policy of the state. According to some authors, the Bulgarian President has also arbitrating and moderating function.[47]

*297.* According to Article 92, paragraph 1, the President symbolizes the state, the statehood and the unity of the nation. Moreover, he or she serves as an integrative factor for the society. The President is presumed to be a key pillar of political integration.[48] Due to his or her direct democratic legitimacy which is equal to the legitimacy of the Parliament, the President represents the statehood in the shared beliefs of the nation, serves as a tool for reunification of the pluralistic society and has the integrative force of other elements of the symbolic pantheon of the state and the nation such as the hymn, the flag, the national symbols.

*298.* Such direct transposition of these essentially monarchic functions – the symbolic and integrative functions – to the institution of the President as a republican head of state is dysfunctional and artificial. It is not clear why a party politician or even an expert figure supported by political parties such as the President should symbolize the unity of the nation and the holistic nature of the statehood. Moreover, it is difficult for a single, non-composite institution, such as the President, to serve integrative function. This is because all elections are divisive. The elections for non-collective institutions such as the President are even more divisive. This is because in such elections there are clear winners and losers. Hence it is questionable why the citizens that have supported the alternative candidates should feel represented and integrated by the person against whom they have actually voted. That is why the symbolic and integrative functions of the Bulgarian President are rather dysfunctional and fictitious although they are launched in theory and despite the fact that they are even proclaimed by the 1991 Constitution.

---

44. For the functions and competences of the Bulgarian President, *see* Georgi Bliznashki, *supra* n. 10, 59–81, Plamen Kirov, *supra* n. 4, 148–149 and Emilia Drumeva, *supra* n. 31, 437–448.
45. Georgi Bliznashki defines three categories of functions of the Bulgarian President. These are the traditional functions, the arbitration functions and the safeguarding functions. *See* Georgi Bliznashki, *Parliamentary Law*, 122 ('St. Kliment Ohridski' University Press, 2015).
46. *See* Plamen Kirov, *supra* n. 4, 140.
47. *See* Emilia Drumeva, *supra* n. 31, 437 and Plamen Kirov, *supra* n. 4, 141.
48. *See* Georgi Bliznashki, *The Parliamentary Government in Bulgaria*, 60 ('St. Kliment Ohridski' University Press, 2009) (in Bulgarian).

*299.* The communication function of the President consists in his or her institutional capability to influence the public opinion and public debate in Bulgaria through his or her political acts as instruments for political communication. The President as a directly elected institution has enhanced legitimacy to engage in strategic political communication with other central state institutions regarding issues concerning the constitutional politics and the external and military policy of the state. This is because the President has important competences in these spheres of social governance.

*300.* The strength of the Bulgarian President is hidden in his or her direct democratic legitimacy combined with his or her relative remoteness from the effective daily policymaking. In other words, the President may engage in political communication regarding the priorities of the nation from the position of the directly elected alternative to the main power centres of the state – the government and the Parliament. Thus the President can serve as an alternative source for political ideas, as a mediator and as a channel for expression of public concerns.

*301.* The President has instruments for engagement in both horizontal (inter-institutional) and vertical (society related) political communication. He can take part in political discourses with the other state institutions through his or her addresses being instruments for horizontal (inter-institutional) political communication. Moreover, the President can form public opinion via his or her messages whose addressee is the civil society, the institutions of the public sphere and the citizens.

*302.* The last function belonging to the 'traditional functional core' of the institution of the head of state is the representative function of the President. According to Article 92, paragraph 1 of the Constitution, the President represents the state in the international relations. Indeed the President has several important competences in the external power – the power related to the participation of the state in international and supranational relations. The President can represent the state in different international forums, conferences and organizations. He can visit other states and can deliver speeches in front of international organizations. The President is also authorized by the Constitution and the International Treaties Act to conclude international treaties exactly because of his or her representative function and the fact that the President can express the will of the state in international relations.

*303.* It is the Prime Minister and not the President who represents Bulgaria in the European Council. However, in the event of a caretaker government the role shifts and the President represents the state in the European Council instead of the caretaker Prime Minister. This is not an explicit constitutional or legislative provision but a matter of legal practice based on the implied logic of the Constitution. Thus Presidents Rosen Plevneliev and Rumen Radev represented Bulgaria in the European Council instead of the caretaker Prime Ministers Marin Raykov, Georgi Bliznashki and Ognyan Gerdjikov.

*304.* The President has also a safeguard function. Being a reactive veto player, he or she serves as a safeguard for the Constitution and the international treaties.

The President has two main competences by virtue of which he or she can serve as a safeguard for the above-mentioned acts and thus of the normative hierarchy and the consistency of the legal order as well as of the rule of law. The first is the presidential veto and the second is the right of the President to approach the Constitutional Court with demands for control of constitutionality of international treaties and acts of Parliament as well as for control of the compliance of the acts of the Parliament with international treaties.

*305.* The President possesses moderately strong suspensive legislative veto. The veto is suspensive because it can be outvoted by the National Assembly. Thus the head of state just returns the act for reconsideration and for new debate and voting in the Parliament without the possibility to permanently prevent its entering into force. The Presidential veto is moderately strong because it can be overcome with absolute majority of all MPs.

*306.* The President is allowed to impose veto on the acts of the Parliament not only with regard to their eventual non-compliance with hierarchically superior legal standards such as the Constitution, the EU law, the international treaties and the generally recognized principles of the international law but also with a view to their substantial qualities. In other words, the President may impose veto on the act of Parliament not only because it is illegal in the broader sense but also because he or she deems that it will be ineffective, unjust, or just because the head of state considers it as inappropriate.

*307.* Hence the presidential veto in Bulgaria is not only an instrument for safeguarding the normative hierarchy in general and the supremacy of the Constitution and the primacy of the EU and the international law in particular. It is also a device for the realization of some influence of the President on the legislative politics of the state. Thus the President is also a participant in the legislative power. He or she cannot introduce legislation but can temporarily prevent its entering into force through the imposition of veto. In fact, the President is a reactive veto player on the output side of the legislative process.

*308.* The Bulgarian Presidents make practical use of their legislative veto. The use of the veto intensifies especially in times when the President belongs to a political party or political power centres which are different from or in opposition to the governing majority in the National Assembly and in the Council of Ministers. This fact is evidence of the existence of semi-presidential dynamics in the political process in general and in the legislative process in particular although Bulgaria is not semi-presidential but hybrid parliamentary republic.

*309.* The second instrument by virtue of which the President serves as a safeguard for the Constitution and the international treaties is the competence to approach the Constitutional Court with demands for control of the constitutionality of international treaties and acts of Parliament as well as for control of the compliance of the acts of the Parliament with the international treaties. In contrast to the presidential veto, the approaching of the Constitutional Court can be accomplished only with arguments concerning the contravention to superior source of law and not with arguments related to the substantial qualities of the act such as its efficiency, compatibility with the Bulgarian legal order, or justice.

*310.* Similar to the presidential veto the instances in which the President makes practical use of his or her competence to approach the Constitutional Court with demands for declaration of unconstitutionality of the acts of the Parliament or the international treaties or for contravention of the acts of the Parliament with the international treaties and the generally recognized principles of international law increase in case of 'cohabitation'[49] with government and parliamentary majorities dominated by parties hostile to the President.

*311.* The President may ask the Constitutional Court to declare the contravention of the act of the Parliament to both the Constitution and the international treaties. Although the 1991 Constitution does not explicitly grant the President the right to demand the control for compliance with the EU law, the head of state implicitly subsumes the EU law under a broader concept of international law. This practice has the advantage that it allows for the protection of the EU law from violations by the Bulgarian Parliament. However, it is doubtful with regard to the fact that the President is not explicitly constitutionally allowed to provoke such control. Moreover, the subsuming of the EU law under the category of international treaties may put the relative primacy of the EU law over the Constitution in question which contravenes the established case law of the ECJ.

*312.* The President has limited competences in the constituent power. He or she can propose amendments to the Constitution which then have to be adopted by the National Assembly. Thus the President may serve as one of the policy initiators for constitutional reform. This is one of the rare competences of the President as a proactive veto player.

*313.* Another competence of the President by virtue of which he or she functions as an agenda setter and a proactive veto player[50] is his or her right to propose the accomplishment of constitutional referendum on issues which fall within the competence of the National Assembly. This competence of the President, however, is questionable with regard to its constitutionality. In fact, there are solid arguments that the constitutional referendum introduced by the Direct Participation of the Citizens in State Power and the Local Self-Government Act infringes the constitutional model for the accomplishment of the constituent power provided by Chapter IX of the 1991 Constitution and thus may turn to be unconstitutional.

*314.* The President has only one competence that concerns the judicial power. This is the right to pardon. This competence may be assigned to the Vice President. In fact, the right to pardon is not a form of accomplishment of any jurisprudential

49. For the concept of 'cohabitation', *see* Maurice Duverger, *The Semi-Presidential Regime. Check to the King* ('St. Kliment Ohridski' University Press, 1998) (in Bulgarian).
50. For the concepts of agenda setter and proactive veto player, *see* George Tsebelis, *supra* n. 37.

activity. It is supposed to be an instrument for the delivering of humanism based on extralegal criteria such as justice which does not abolish or reassess the court's verdict. The President or the Vice President issues the decree for pardoning the sentenced person after considering the non-binding opinion of the Pardons Council which is a consultative body belonging to the presidential administration.

*315.* The President has also the competence to release uncollectable public revenues. This competence of the head of state in the sphere of public finance is comparable to the right to pardon because it is based on the general concept of justice. Both competences of the President are a result of the desire to satisfy metalegal criteria of justice by overcoming the rigidity of the valid law. They both are remnants from the monarchical prerogative which have been inherited by the republican form of government.

*316.* The President has important patronage power. This power concerns the personal politics of the state and results in competences for appointment and dismissal of the office holders of different state institutions. The President can appoint one-third of the Constitutional Court's judges, members of the Electronic Media Council, members of the Governing Council of the Bulgarian National Bank and members of different state agencies and committees. Moreover, the President appoints the members of the presidential administration. The appointments to the just enlisted positions are made on the discretionary judgment of the President. In other words, the President does not act on proposal or with the consent of any state institution for the appointment of the above-mentioned office holders.

*317.* There is also a second group of competences related to patronage power which are accomplished on the proposal of other state institutions. The President appoints and dismisses the diplomats, the high-ranking officials in the army and the police as well as some of the office holders in the state administration on a proposal of the Council of Ministers. The Council of Ministers acts on a proposal of the responsible Minister. Thus the appointment or dismissal of the generals is made by the President on a proposal of the government which acts on a proposal of the Minister of Defence or the Minister of Interior. The appointment or dismissal of the diplomats is accomplished by the President on a proposal of the government acting on a proposal of the Minister of Foreign Affairs. The proposal of the Minister is not binding whereas the proposal of the government is binding for the President. Hence these appointments and dismissals are not made on the discretionary will of the President. Here the President is just a formal last procedure in the process for appointment and dismissal. The appointment by the President has rather symbolic meaning although it might be questionable whether the President may have also some signalling and controlling function for appointments and dismissals which are gravely inappropriate.

*318.* There is also one case of presidential patronage power in which the head of state has limited discretion. The Chairman of the Supreme Court of Cassation, the Chairman of the Supreme Administrative Court and the State Prosecutor General are appointed and dismissed by the President on a proposal of the Supreme Judicial

Council. The Supreme Judicial Council acts on a proposal of either one-fifth of its members or of the Minister of Justice. The President is allowed to reject once the proposal for appointment or dismissal of these office holders. In case of a second proposal, however, he or she is obliged to follow the Supreme Judicial Council's proposal to appoint or dismiss them.

*319.* The President possesses also important competences in the external relations and the military. It has already been mentioned that the President is one of the institutions which can represent the state in international relations. Moreover, according to Article 100 of the Constitution, the President is the supreme commander of the armed forces in times of peace or during war. It fact, he or she is just a symbolic commander-in-chief whereas the strategic and tactical government of the armed forces is accomplished by the Ministers of Defence and Interior as well as the professional leaders such as the Chief of Defence and the high-ranking military officials.

*320.* In his quality as supreme commander of the armed forces, the President presides and may summon the Consultative Council for National Defence. On a proposal from the government, he or she appoints and dismisses the high-ranking officials in the armed forces, assigns high military ranks and decorations and proposes general or partial mobilization of the armed forces. Moreover, the President can propose the declaration of war, state of siege or state of emergency to the Parliament. The President declares war in the event of an armed attack against Bulgaria or in response to the need of urgent honouring of international commitments of Bulgaria or proclaims state of siege or state of emergency whenever the National Assembly is not in session. In such cases, the National Assembly has to be convened forthwith to pronounce the decision.

*321.* The President has several competences concerning the symbolic policy. The President represents the state in official festivities and parades where he or she may pronounce speeches. The President distributes state awards, decorations and medals, gives names to objects of national importance, cities, towns and villages, confirms the borders and the centres of the administrative–territorial units in Bulgaria, grants or deprives Bulgarian citizenship and grants asylum. The granting of asylum is based on a non-binding recommendation of Asylum Council which is a part of the presidential administration. The granting or depriving of citizenship is accomplished on non-binding recommendation of the Minister of Justice based on the expert opinion of the Citizenship Council attached to the Ministry of Justice.

*322.* In conclusion, the President of Bulgaria has various competences which are spread in different branches of the state power. Most of them concern the external, the executive and the patronage power. However, there is no predominating power centre of the presidential competences which can justify the allocation of the presidential institution in a single branch of the state power. The typical role and function of the Bulgarian President is the reactive veto player acting as a safeguard for the Constitution, the EU law and the international treaties and serving as a key element in the system of checks and balances. The additional competences, which the

Bulgarian President has in contrast to the nominal heads of state of the pure parliamentary systems, are the extensive patronage power, the suspensive legislative veto and the right to approach the Constitutional Court.

## §5. Legal and Political Acts

*323.* The President issues decrees, addresses and messages. The decrees are legal acts whereas the addresses and messages are political acts. The decrees are individual administrative acts. In some very rare occasions, they may possess also some degree of normativity due to the fact that they may concern a broad number of addressees and widely defined scope of issues. The decrees for proclamation of general or partial mobilization and for exceptional proclamation of war, state of siege or state of emergency are examples of such decrees with broader regulative scope and quasi-normative character.[51]

*324.* Most of the presidential decrees have to be countersigned. The countersignature is an instrument by virtue of which the government through the Prime Minister or the Ministers takes the responsibility for the acts of the President. The countersignature makes possible the existence of a non-responsible head of state in the context of responsible government.[52] The decrees which have strategic and general importance are countersigned by the Prime Minister whereas the decrees with secondary importance directed towards specific sector policy are countersigned by the respective Minister.

*325.* It is doubtful whether the instrument of countersignature is really up to date and in line with the functional logic of the modern republics. It is questionable whether the President has to be non-responsible and whether the responsibility for his or her acts has to be borne by the government which might be composed of parties which are in opposition to the President. Anyway, the 1991 Constitution follows the classical logic of the parliamentary form of government that the head of state should be non-responsible and thus his or her acts need also to be countersigned.

*326.* However, some of the decrees of the President are excluded from the list of decrees that need compulsory countersignature for their validity. According to Article 102, paragraph 2 of the 1991 Constitution, the following decrees of the President do not need to be countersigned: decrees for appointment of caretaker government, decrees for assigning mandate for forming government, decrees for dissolution of the National Assembly, decrees for imposing a veto, decrees for determining the structure and for appointment of the members of the presidential administration, decrees for scheduling elections and referenda and decrees for publishing of acts of Parliament in the SG.

---

51. *See* Plamen Kirov, *supra* n. 4, 216.
52. *See* Georgi Bliznashki, *supra* n. 10, 74, Plamen Kirov, *supra* n. 4, 203–204.

*327.* The addresses and messages are the political acts of the President. They are instruments for political communication of the President with other state institutions as well as with the citizens and the civic society. The addresses and messages do not require countersignature.

## §6. THE VICE PRESIDENT

*328.* The existence of a Vice President in the context of parliamentary republic, even if it possesses some features of semi-presidentialism, is a rarity in comparative perspective. Indeed none of the classical reasons for the provision of the institution of the Vice President can be found in the Bulgarian context. The reserve function played by the Vice President of some presidential republic can easily be performed also by other institutions, e.g., the Chairman of the National Assembly. Bulgaria is a nation state with a liberal–republican model for the structuring of the statehood. Hence the Vice President is no balancing institution allowing for entrenched representation of any kind of ethnic, religious, national or other types of minorities.

*329.* That is why the figure of the Vice President seems to be rather senseless. It may be explained to a certain extent with the fact that in the time of the functioning of the VII Grand National Assembly there has been a political compromise between the former communist party and the opposition that the President will be Jelju Jelev from the latter whereas the Vice President will be Atanas Semerjiev from the former political force. Both the President and the Vice President have been provisionally elected by the Grand National Assembly until the adoption and entering into force of the 1991 Constitution allowed for the first direct elections of the head of state.

*330.* However, this historical precedent does not really predetermine the institutional design of the President and the Vice President under the 1991 Constitution. This is because they are directly elected by the people as a team which automatically excludes any continuation of such compromise between the leading parties. Naturally, the office of the Vice President may be given to a politician from a party which is a coalition partner to the political party that nominated the President, but this is politics as usual and represents no form of consensus democracy.

*331.* Some authors have launched the thesis that the Vice President is the 'guardian of the mandate' given to him or her together with the President by the direct vote of the people.[53] This thesis is in conflict with another very popular normative ideology namely that the President, even if he or she is nominated by a political party or coalition and is constitutionally permitted to retain his or her party membership, becomes a 'neutral power' and an integrative symbol of the state after the presidential elections.[54] Thus the question is can a supposedly neutral Vice President be a guarantor of a party political mandate?

---

53. Plamen Kirov defines the Vice President as 'the guardian of the mandate' due to his or her reserve function. *See* Plamen Kirov, *supra* n. 4, 268–284.
54. *See* Georgi Bliznashki, *supra* n. 258.

*332.* The 1991 Constitution grants no competences to the Vice President himself or herself. The Vice President has no competences of his or her own apart from the reserve function consisting in his or her role to become a President in case of preterm termination of the presidential office.

*333.* The President is constitutionally permitted to transfer to the Vice President four of his or her competences. These are the right to pardon for criminal offences, the right to grant asylum, the right to grant or deprive Bulgarian citizenship and the right to appoint or dismiss civil servants from office specified by act of Parliament. The President may grant to the Vice President all or some of these competences, or even none of them. There has been already a situation in which President Jelev had not transferred any competence to Vice President Blaga Dimitrova. It must be noted that the President and the Vice President are not allowed to accomplish simultaneously the above-mentioned competences. Hence if the President wants to make use of them he or she has to withdraw the empowerment of the Vice President to accomplish the competence in question.[55]

*334.* Finally, in the political practice, the Vice President also accomplishes a representative function. He or she participates in official ceremonies and national celebrations representing the President and serving as a symbol of the statehood. Moreover, the Vice President also visits abroad representing the Bulgarian state, e.g., in meeting with NGOs, with representatives of the Bulgarians living abroad etc.

*335.* This political practice, however, is questionable from the viewpoint of the written constitutional law. The Bulgarian Constitution assigns representative function and representative competences only to the President but not to the Vice President. The Constitution explicitly enlists the competences that the President can transfer to the Vice President and the representation of the state is not among them. That is why the representative competence of the Vice President is derived by his or her task to aid the activity of the President. In fact, this is a constitutional convention formed by virtue of extensive interpretation of the supportive function of the Vice President towards the President in the political practice. Hence the representative competence of the Vice President is not based so much on the text of the Constitution but stems out of the factual normativity of the political practice and is grounded on the permissive consensus in the theory and among the political players to allow the Vice President to accomplish representative missions on issues of secondary importance.

*336.* The President and the Vice President are elected as a team. However, they are not members of collective presidential body but are two distinct and separate state institutions. Despite the fact that they are nominated by one and the same initiative committee, political party or party coalition, there have been many instances in which the President and the Vice President have formed and demonstrated in the

55. *See* Plamen Kirov, *supra* n. 4, 283.

course of time different and even controversial visions for the strategical and tactical priorities of the state. A clear example is the resignation of Vice President Blaga Dimitrova due to controversies with President Jelju Jelev as well as the rather uneasy coexistence between President Rosen Plevneliev and Vice President Margarita Popova.

# Chapter 3. The Parliament

## §1. Constitutional Status and Structure

### I. Constitutional Status

*337.* The National Assembly has a central status in both the constitutional system provided by the written constitution and in the ideal constitution[56] comprising the supportive ideologies and the shared beliefs of the members of the political community. The National Assembly has been proclaimed as the supreme organ of the state and as an institutional focus of the unity of state power by the communist 1947 and the 1971 constitutions. The transition to democracy took the shape of replacement of the Soviet-type peoples' democracy with parliamentary republic. Thus parliamentarism has been associated especially in the initial years of the functioning of the new Constitution with supremacy of the Parliament and with its monopoly over the legislative function. The concept of the Parliament as the exclusive legislator is supported by some constitutional law scientists.[57] There are authors who even assert that the legislative process encompasses only the activity accomplished in the Parliament.[58] The concept of the Parliament as legitimate monopolist of the legislative power is prohibitive also for the introduction of the delegated legislation.

*338.* However, the 1991 Constitution establishes a hybrid parliamentary republic. According to that model, the Parliament is neither monopolist and the sole institution of the legislative power nor are its competences limited to that power. In other words, there are several institutions which influence the process of adoption of acts of Parliament, thus being important participants in the legislative power. Indeed the Parliament is an insurmountable factor in the legislative process. This is due to the centrality of the parliamentary phase of the legislative process and the lack of extraordinary and delegated legislation. However, the actual driving force of the legislative power is the single power unit composed by the government and its parliamentary majority.[59] The President via his or her veto and to a much lesser extent the people through the legislative people's initiative and the legislative referendum may also influence the legislative process.

*339.* Although the institutional focus of the National Assembly is the legislative power, the Bulgarian Parliament possesses competences in other state powers as well. This is especially true for the patronage, external and financial power. Hence the National Assembly is an institution with crucial importance for the Bulgarian constitutional model which is institutionally and to some extent functionally centred in the legislative power. However, the Parliament is also complexly engaged with the power polycentrism scheme provided by the 1991 Constitution. This

56. For the concept of ideal constitution, *see* Evgeni Tanchev, *supra* n. 20, 112.
57. *See* Emilia Drumeva, *supra* n. 31, 375 et seq. and Stefan Stoychev, *supra* n. 30, 387.
58. *See* Stefan Stoychev, *supra* n. 30, 413–414.
59. *See* Georgi Bliznashki, *supra* n. 4, 31 et seq., Vasil Kirov, *supra* n. 4, 208.

engagement is realized by both cooperating with other institutions in the legislative process and having key stance and important influence in other branches of the state power.

## II. Unicameral Parliamentary System

*340.* The unicameral structure of the Parliament is one of the most durable and resilient elements of the Bulgarian constitutional and legal tradition. All four Bulgarian constitutions provided for unicameral National Assembly. Indeed the initial project of the 1879 Tarnovo Constitution contained provisions for either State Council or Senate. However, both of them have been rejected by the members of the Constituent Assembly. The official reason has been that the founding fathers of the first Bulgarian Constitution aimed at the establishment of the egalitarian model of the statehood which necessitated the abolition of both the second chamber of the Parliament and the electoral census. The idea was that the Bulgarian society was rather egalitarian and homogeneous and the establishment of a second chamber would introduce artificial internal fragmentation of the society and will foster the emergence of political elite on the basis not so much on the merits but on the services to the monarch.

*341.* Indeed these arguments were correct. The Bulgarian society was egalitarian and the establishment of a second chamber could have been instrumental for disproportionate influence of its very small wealthy strata. The second chamber, especially if it was structured as State Council, would have served for the enhancement of the monarchical influence on the political process.

*342.* However, there have been also geopolitical arguments which contributed to the unicameral structure of the National Assembly. Russia was the main driving force behind the adoption of the Tarnovo Constitution. On the one hand, the imperial Russian government wanted to establish a moderately conservative design of the emergent Bulgarian statehood. Thus it launched the second chamber as a tool for the establishment of conservative monarchical constitutionalism. On the other hand, the Russian government believed in the pro-Russian sentiment in the Bulgarian people who were just liberated by the Russian army from Ottoman rule. Hence a strong, coherent and unicameral pro-Russian Parliament might have been an important counterbalance against pro-Western monarchs. Moreover, although the Bulgarian society was very egalitarian, there has been small economic and political elite which was established during the Tansimat epoch of reforms in the nineteenth-century Ottoman Empire. A second chamber would have allowed for the institutional reinforcement of this elite and for its co-opting in the new political reality of the liberated Bulgarian statehood.

*343.* The unicameral structure of the Parliament was preserved during the whole period of application of the Tarnovo Constitution (1879–1947) with the exception of the period from 1881 to 1883 when the Constitution had been suspended and knjaz Alexander I ruled as de facto absolute monarch with the help of a State Council. The reasons for the durability of the unicameral model in Bulgaria are at least twofold.

*344.* First, the Bulgarians were bound to their egalitarian traditions. The arguments against the second chamber proposed in the Constituent Assembly were appealing to the Bulgarian mentality. The authoritarian regime of knjaz Alexander I discredited the idea of State Council. The unicameral National Assembly gradually became a part of the Bulgarian constitutional culture and tradition.

*345.* Second, the Bulgarian monarchs actually did not need a second chamber in order to establish their personal regimes. The second Bulgarian monarch – Tzar Ferdinand I – took note of the failure of knjaz Alexander I and developed his personal regime predominantly through means which were already provided for by the Tarnovo Constitution. The same is true for his successor Tzar Boris III. Both of them did not make any attempts at introducing either Senate or State Council because they were rather successful in dominating the political system also in the context of unicameral Parliament.

*346.* The unicameral structure of the Parliament has been a natural element of the institutional design of the Soviet model which has been adopted in Bulgaria with the constitutions of 1947 and 1971. The unicameral structure of the National Assembly has been a logical continuation of the principles of supremacy of the Parliament and the unity of the state power. The National Assembly as a focal point of the unified state power has had to be necessarily unicameral.

*347.* The 1991 Constitution continued the tradition of the unicameral Parliament. This is because the Bulgarian constitutional legislator tried to both abolish these elements of the institutional design which were incompatible with the parliamentary democracy at the end of the twentieth century and borrow the cornerstones of the Bulgarian tradition such as the unicameralism. Moreover, many of the typical grounds for the establishment of bicameral Parliament such as the federalism or the representation of class or estate interest were not present in the Bulgarian context. Some of the deficiencies stemming out of the lack of second chamber, e.g., the inexistence of an additional check on the compliance of the legislation with the Constitution and the international law, have been remedied by the provision of the Constitutional Court.

## III. Horizontal and Vertical Structure of the Parliament

### A. *Horizontal Structure of the Parliament*

#### 1. Parliamentary Groups

*348.* The parliamentary groups are associations of MPs. Their status is regulated by the Constitution and the Regulation for the Organization and the Activity of the

National Assembly. The 1991 Constitution mentions the parliamentary groups only with regard to the procedure for election of a new government. More precisely, the 1991 Constitution provides for the compulsory consultations and interaction of the President with the parliamentary groups in the context of the assignment of a mandate for forming new Council of Ministers. Hence the Bulgarian Constitution does not provide either for definition of a parliamentary group or for the requirements of the forming of a parliamentary group or for any other aspects of their status, organization and functions. Thus the legal status of the parliamentary groups is provided exclusively by the Regulation for the Organization and the Activity of the National Assembly. This Regulation is adopted by each new Parliament and usually has similar content although there might also be some important differences.

*349.* There are two criteria for the establishment of a parliamentary group. These are the quantity criterion and the quality criterion.

*350.* The quantity criterion concerns the minimal number of MPs required for the formation of a parliamentary group. According to Regulation for the Organization and the Activity of the National Assembly, the minimal number of MPs required for the formation of a parliamentary group is ten MPs. If the number of MPs drops below that number, it ceases to exit.

*351.* The quantity criterion aims at safeguarding the functionality and efficiency of both the Parliament and the parliamentary groups. It assures the existence of parliamentary groups that are sufficiently feasible in size in order to contribute to the normal and efficient accomplishment of the parliamentary functions and especially of the legislative function of the Parliament. A reasonably high number of MPs required for the establishment of a parliamentary group safeguards that the Parliament would not be fragmented into unmanageable plurality of parliamentary groups. A reasonably low number of MPs required for the establishment of a parliamentary group is a safeguard for the principles of democracy and political pluralism guaranteeing the freedom of association of the MPs. In Bulgaria, the quantity criterion is set at 10 MPs in the context of National Assembly consisting of 240 MPs is reasonable and satisfies the above-mentioned requirements.

*352.* The quality criterion consists in the requirement that the MPs forming the parliamentary group must belong to the same political party or coalition of parties or at least must have common political views. This requirement has been provided for by the Regulation for the Organization and the Activity of some of the previous Bulgarian National Assemblies. However, it is not explicitly fixed by the Regulation for the Organization and the Activity of the previous forty-third and the current forty-fourth National Assembly. Anyway, it is an implicit requirement which is a logical precondition for the existence not only of the parliamentary groups but also of the representative party democracy itself. This is because the parliamentary groups are both substructures of the Parliament and institutions for the representation of the political parties in it.

*353.* Consequently, the quality criterion has also to be met by the parliamentary groups in the Bulgarian Parliament. An indirect indication of the quality criterion is the provision of Article 15, paragraph 6 of the Regulation for the Organization and the Activity of the forty-fourth National Assembly. According to this article, Bulgarian (Member of the European Parliament (MEP) from the same political family can participate in the work and deliberations of the respective parliamentary group of the Bulgarian Parliament without the right to vote.

*354.* A traditional problem of the Bulgarian parliamentarism has been the relatively frequent secession of MPs from their parliamentary groups, which in some cases led to their dissolution. These MPs either joined other already-existing parliamentary groups or established new ones. This phenomenon was figuratively defined in the media and in the constitutional and political theory as 'parliamentary nomadism'. It produced different negative outcomes, such as fragmentation of the Parliament, impediments and increased unpredictability of the parliamentary process, distorted representation of the initial vote of the electorate.

*355.* The 1991 Constitution proclaims the free mandate of the MPs. Thus the MPs are supposed to be not 'party soldiers' but free representatives of the Bulgarian people. On the contrary, the Bulgarian Constitution and legislation establish the preconditions for the development of party democracy. Moreover, the people vote not just for the personalities of the candidates for MPs but also with a view to their party political affiliation. This is especially true in the context of proportional representation electoral system. Hence if the MP who is elected from one political party or party coalition decides to leave its parliamentary group and to become an independent MP, or even more, to become a member of another parliamentary group, then this is a deviation from the will of the electorate, which clearly distorts the representative character of the Parliament.

*356.* That is why the Regulation for the Organization and the Activity of the National Assembly establishes several safeguards for the continuous representation of the will of the electorate and for the stability of the party political representation in the Parliament. The MPs are permitted to secede from their initial parliamentary groups. However, they may become only independent MPs but cannot form a new parliamentary group or join existing ones. Thus the independent MPs are not permitted to form or join parliamentary group. The MPs of a parliamentary group that has ceased to conform to the quantity criteria also become independent MPs, and they are not allowed to form or join another parliamentary group. Moreover, the MPs may be members of only one parliamentary group. Last but not least, existing parliamentary groups which have been established at the beginning of the legislature cannot merge with each other at a later stage.

*357.* If the MP secedes from the parliamentary group, he or she ceases to be its representative in the parliamentary committees. Moreover, the MP loses his or her position in the parliamentary delegations or the governing bodies of the Parliament.

These provisions apply not only when the MP has voluntarily quit his or her membership in the parliamentary committee but also if he or she is expelled from it by virtue of the decision of his or her colleagues in the group.

*358.* The parliamentary groups have organizational autonomy in the framework set by the Constitution and the Regulation for the Organization and the Activity of the National Assembly. They may determine the membership conditions and requirements as well as the rights and the obligations of their members.

*359.* There is a special register of the National Assembly containing information for the parliamentary groups. All changes in the leadership and in the list of members of the parliamentary groups should be reflected in that register.

*360.* The parliamentary groups have material safeguards for their proper functioning. They are allowed to hire paid experts and assistants. The parliamentary groups enjoy also the support of the experts of their political parties. They have also a number of premises in the buildings of the Parliament. Hence the independent MPs are in a worse position than the MPs belonging to a parliamentary group. They cannot rely on these material safeguards and preconditions for their proper activity.

### 2. Parliamentary Committees

*361.* The parliamentary committees are substructures of the National Assembly. They are composed of MPs belonging to different parliamentary groups as well as of independent MPs.

*362.* The political parties which have parliamentary representation are represented in the parliamentary committees proportionally to their representation in the plenum of the National Assembly. Similarly, they are proportionally represented in the governing bodies of the parliamentary committees. The exceptions from the principle of proportional representation are the parliamentary committee for combat against corruption, conflict of interests and parliamentary ethics, the parliamentary committee for EU issues and control over the EU funds and the parliamentary committee for control of the secret services and the special intelligence means. They are formed on the basis of parity principle. According to this principle, each parliamentary group elects two of its members as members of the just-mentioned parliamentary committees.

*363.* There are two main types of parliamentary committees. These are the standing committees and the temporary committees. The standing committees may form subcommittees whose activity should concern more concrete sectors of social relations or should address very specific issues. The most narrow and specialized substructures of the standing committees are the working groups. The subcommittees and the working groups are part of the standing committees and are composed of their members. The subcommittees and the working groups are aided by the experts of the respective standing committee.

*364.* The subcommittees and the working groups are established by virtue of the decision of the standing committees. The Regulation for the Organization and the Activity of the National Assembly provides for the compulsory establishment of three standing subcommittees. These are the subcommittee on accountability of the public sector as part of the budget and finance committee, the consumer protection and protection of the competition subcommittee as part of the economic policy and tourism committee and the subcommittee for control over the activity of the Energy and Water Regulation Commission as part of the energy committee.

*365.* The standing parliamentary committees may also decide to establish public councils. The public councils should include representatives of the NGOs and the civil society. They have only advisory functions because the opinions of the representatives of the civil society are not binding on the parliamentary committees. The idea of the public councils is to increase the transparency of the functioning of the standing committees and to foster the linkage and the cooperation between the Parliament and the civil society.

*366.* The governing body of the parliamentary committees consists of the Chairman and up to four Vice Chairmen. They are elected *en bloc* by the Parliament by virtue of an open vote on a proposal of the parliamentary groups or the MPs except in the case when objections for the proposal of some of the members of the governing body are made. In that case, the members of the governing body are elected one by one. The Regulation for the Organization and the Activity of the National Assembly specifies the competences of the governing body of the parliamentary committees as well as the grounds and the procedure for their removal from power.

*367.* The standing committees cover different governmental departments and spheres of social relations. The Bulgarian system of standing parliamentary committees is composed of numerous committees which cover a vast range of social spheres. It mirrors to some extent the system of governmental departments ("resorts") around which the separation of the ministries in the Council of Ministers is structured. Thus the Bulgarian Parliament at least formally has the institutional capacity to be coequal partner of the government in the decision-making processes.

*368.* According to Article 37 of the Regulation for the Organization and the Activity of the National Assembly, the temporary committees may be established for concrete occasion, for research and exploration of specific problems or for accomplishment of parliamentary enquiries. Thus the temporary parliamentary committees may be established either for additional research on specific, new, difficult or complex issues in the context of the legislative process or for clarification of problems related to parliamentary control. In the political practice, the temporary parliamentary committees are most frequently created exactly for the accomplishment of parliamentary enquiries as a form of parliamentary control.

*369.* The establishment of temporary parliamentary committees can be proposed either by the Chairman of the Parliament or by one-fifth of the MPs. They are established by virtue of a decision adopted by the National Assembly. The temporary parliamentary committees cease their existence either with the expiration of the term for which they are initially established or through a decision of the National Assembly. The provisions for the organization and the functioning of the standing committees are applied also to the temporary parliamentary committees.

*370.* The Regulation for the Organization and the Activity of the National Assembly provides that the MPs can be elected only in two standing parliamentary committees. Moreover, they can be elected as members of the governing boards of only one of them. The Chairman and the Vice Chairmen of the National Assembly cannot be elected as members of the governing board of the standing parliamentary committees in order to prevent the accumulation and the concentration of power and to safeguard some degree of independence and autonomy of the work of the standing parliamentary committees from the leaders of the Parliament.

*371.* All MPs are allowed to participate in the sessions of the standing parliamentary committees without having the right to vote. The Bulgarian MPs in the European Parliament can also participate in their work and in the discussion, but they cannot participate in the voting due to the fact that they can express only advisory opinions.

*372.* The Regulation for the Organization and the Activity of the National Assembly organizes the functioning of the parliamentary committees on the basis of the principle of publicity. It provides that the sessions of the parliamentary committees are in principle open to the public. Consequently, it permits the presence of citizens, NGO representatives and media during the sessions of the parliamentary committees. Moreover, the parliamentary committee may make a decision that its session will be transmitted online via the Internet site of the National Assembly.

*373.* The parliamentary committees may decide that some of their sessions will be non-public. In that case, the presence of all the above-mentioned persons is not permitted. The Regulation for the Organization and the Activity of the National Assembly provides that the sessions of the parliamentary committee for control over the security services, use of special intelligence means and access to the data required by the Electronic Communications' Act are not public in principle. This committee may make decisions for concrete sessions to be open to the public as a matter of exception.

*374.* The parliamentary committees' sessions are regular and extraordinary. The members of the parliamentary committees may be summoned in extraordinary session by their Chairmen on his or her initiative, on the initiative of the Chairman of the National Assembly or on a proposal of one-third of their members.

*375.* The standing parliamentary committees discuss and adopt reports, proposals and statements on draft acts of Parliament, opinions on the annual programme for the participation of the Republic of Bulgaria in the decision-making processes in the EU, drafts for parliamentary decisions, declarations and addresses and all other legislative or non-legislative matters which are distributed to them by the Chairman of the National Assembly. The standing parliamentary committees may also adopt reports for evaluation of the practical application of the acts of the Parliament. These reports present and assess the efficiency of the application of the acts of the Parliament in the social practice.

*376.* The parliamentary committees have also very important functions with a view to the parliamentary control. They can invite state officials or citizens to give information on issues of social and political importance. The Ministers are invited on a monthly basis to answer the questions of the members of the parliamentary committees. Moreover, the standing parliamentary committees with regard to their specialization accomplish control for the legality and the efficiency of the use of the resources stemming out of the EU funds and programmes.

### 3. Parliamentary Delegations

*377.* There are two types of parliamentary delegations – permanent and temporary. Only the permanent delegations have explicit legal standing provided by the Regulation for the Organization and the Activity of the National Assembly. The temporary delegations are elected by the National Assembly on an ad hoc basis by virtue of analogous application of the rules regarding the permanent delegations.

*378.* The members of the permanent as well as the temporary parliamentary delegations are elected by the Parliament among its own members by virtue of a parliamentary decision. The composition of the parliamentary delegations is proportional to the representation of the parliamentary groups in the plenum of the National Assembly.

*379.* In order to comply with this principle of proportional representation, the MPs who have lost their membership in the parliamentary group from which they are elected are deprived also of their membership in the parliamentary delegation. This rule is adopted in order to allow the parliamentary group to maintain its influence and representation on the participation of the Parliament in external policy and to replace the MP who is no more its member with the MP who belongs to the parliamentary group.

*380.* The Chairman of the Parliamentary Delegations usually belongs to the parliamentary majority, but there are no legal obstacles for the opposition MPs to chair them. The parliamentary delegations must give an account of their activity to the Chairman of the National Assembly.

### 4. The Independent MPs

*381.* The Bulgarian constitutional law permits the existence of independent MPs. The status of an independent MP may be acquired in two ways. The MP may be initially elected by the people in the parliamentary elections as an independent MP. This is rather a rare situation since the independent candidates for MPs cannot rely on the organization, information and financial support of a party and are usually not sufficiently well known to the wide public, which naturally diminishes their chances to be elected.

*382.* The typical way for emergence of independent MPs is their subsequent transformation from an MP who belongs to a political party and its parliamentary group into an independent MP after the parliamentary elections. Such independent MPs usually emerge as a result of either their own will due to resignation from the party and parliamentary group membership or their dismissal from the parliamentary group.

*383.* The independent MPs enjoy many of the rights of the party political MPs. They can participate in the plenary sessions of the National Assembly and there they can vote, take part in the discussions, raise questions and interpellations to the Ministers and the Prime Minister, participate in the budgetary process etc. Moreover, the independent MPs may be elected as members of the parliamentary committees and the parliamentary delegations.

*384.* However, the status of the independent MPs is limited to a certain degree in comparison to the MPs who belong to a political party. The independent MPs cannot be elected as members of the governing bodies of the Parliament and of the parliamentary committees and parliamentary delegations because such election will produce distortions in the principle of proportional representation of the parliamentary groups in the substructures of the National Assembly. The independent MPs may introduce draft acts of Parliament. However, in practice, such draft legislation usually has no real chance to be adopted. The independent MPs cannot introduce motions for vote of no confidence to the government and for adoption of decisions of the National Assembly for disapproval of the governmental policy since these rights belong to a quota of one-fifth of the MPs and it is very unlikely that so many independent MPs will be available in the Parliament. Thus the independent MPs have de facto limited ability to participate in the legislative, budgetary and controlling processes in the Parliament. Last but not least, the independent MPs have limited organizational support in comparison with the MPs belonging to political parties and their parliamentary groups.

## *B. Vertical Structure of the Parliament*

### 1. Parliamentary Plenum

*385.* The plenum of the National Assembly consists of all MPs. The 1991 Constitution prescribes its exact number, which amounts to 240 MPs. When the Constitution and the rest of the legislation ascribe some functions to the National

Assembly, they implicitly address the parliamentary plenum. The parliamentary plenum is the main arena for political deliberation and the main and ultimate decision-making body of the Parliament. The legislation and the state budget are adopted with the crucial involvement and the final sanction of the parliamentary plenum. It is the main forum for parliamentary control and it is the only decision-making factor for the adoption of vote of no confidence in the government or for rejection of a vote of confidence. The plenum of the National Assembly makes the most important decisions in the patronage power such as the election of the government, one-third of the judges of the Constitutional Court, the ombudsman, the Court of Auditors.

## 2. Governing Bodies of the National Assembly

### a. Chairman of the National Assembly

*386.* The Chairman of the National Assembly is elected on the first day of the first session of the newly elected Parliament. All MPs can propose candidates for Chairman of the National Assembly. He or she is elected by an open vote and through absolute majority of the MPs. Although each MP is legally permitted to stand for election in the political practice, the Chairman of the National Assembly has always been elected among the MPs belonging to the largest parliamentary group.

*387.* The Chairman of the National Assembly can be dismissed from office on the basis of one of several alternative grounds. These are: death, resignation, motion initiated by the parliamentary group which has proposed the Chairman, motion of one-third of the MPs due to objective inability to accomplish his or her duties, systematic misuse of the competences or systematic non-accomplishment of the competences of the Chairman. The Chairman of the National Assembly is dismissed if majority of the MPs who are present at the session have voted in its favour. Moreover, the Chairman and the Vice Chairmen of the National Assembly are dismissed if they leave or are dismissed by the parliamentary group which had proposed them, or if this group ceases to exist.

*388.* The competences of the Chairman of the National Assembly are provided by Article 77 of the Constitution as well as by Article 8 of the Regulation for the Organization and the Activity of the National Assembly. These are non-exhaustive lists because the Chairman of the National Assembly has also other competences, which are contained in other legal provisions.

*389.* The competences of the Chairman of the National Assembly can be divided into two main groups.[60] The first group encompasses competences related to the functioning of the Parliament. These are competences which concern the internal

60. Emilia Drumeva divides the competences of the Chairman of the National Assembly into four groups: first, competences related to the government of the state; second, competences related to the government of the National Assembly; third, competences related to the plenary sessions of the

organization of the parliamentary activity. The second group comprises competences by virtue of which the Chairman of the National Assembly participates in the inter-institutional dynamics of the constitutional model, engages in interactions with other state institutions and accomplishes influence reaching beyond parliamentary corporation.[61]

*390.* The Chairman of the National Assembly has two main functions in the broad constitutional model outside the framework of the parliamentary corporation. First, he or she has representative functions. The Chairman of the National Assembly represents the Parliament in front of other state institutions, the institutions of the EU and international organizations. Moreover, he or she represents the Republic of Bulgaria during his or her visits to international organizations and foreign states or in the course of the participation in different international forums.

*391.* The second function of the Chairman of the National Assembly outside of the parliamentary corporation is his or her reserve function. The Chairman of the National Assembly accomplishes the functions of the President of the Republic in case of preterm termination of the office of the head of state if there is no Vice President. The Chairman of the National Assembly accomplishes the presidential functions in parallel to his or her functions as leader of the Parliament. However, the Chairman of the National Assembly accomplishes the functions and the competences of the President until the preterm presidential elections which have to be held not later than three months from the date of the vacancy of the position in contrast to the Vice President who becomes President at the end of the mandate of the head of state.

*392.* The Chairman of the National Assembly has several functions in the framework of the parliamentary corporation. These are representative, organizational and disciplinary functions as well as the function for safeguarding the parliamentary integrity and autonomy. The Chairman of the National Assembly opens, directs and closes the parliamentary sittings, proposes draft parliamentary agenda, safeguards the observance of the order in the Parliament as well as the parliamentary procedure. More precisely, the Chairman of the National Assembly announces the draft legal and political acts that have to be discussed and voted by the Parliament, gives and takes away the word to the speakers, assigns the draft legal acts to the standing committees and determines the leading committee and applies the parliamentary procedure in all its aspects. The Chairman of the National Assembly certifies the authenticity of the parliamentary acts and publishes decisions, declarations and addresses adopted by the Parliament in the SG.

---

National Assembly; and fourth, competences related to the legislative activity of the National Assembly. *See* Emilia Drumeva, *supra* n. 31, 360–361.

61. Georgi Bliznashki classifies the functions of the Chairman of the National Assembly as follows: representative function, organizational function, guidance function, certification function, administrative function, budgetary function, police function and other functions. *See* Georgi Bliznashki, *Parliamentary Law*, 210–216 ('St. Kliment Ohridski' University Press, 2015).

*393.* The Chairman of the National Assembly imposes sanctions on the MPs in accordance with the Regulation for the Organization and Activity of the National Assembly. Thus he or she has disciplinary power over the MPs.

*394.* The Chairman of the National Assembly organizes the smooth functioning not only of the parliamentary plenum but also of the parliamentary corporation in cooperation with the Vice Chairmen, the Chairman's Council and the Chairmen of the Parliamentary Groups. The Chairman of the National Assembly assures the necessary conditions for the work of the MPs, the parliamentary committees and the parliamentary groups.

*395.* The Chairman of the National Assembly safeguards the integrity and the autonomy of the Parliament. He or she controls the guards of the Parliament, determines the rules for internal security, allows or prohibits the entering of people who are not MPs or civil servants of the National Assembly to its premises, implements the parliamentary budget and organizes the use of material resources of the Parliament. The Chairman of the National Assembly gives consent for the detaining of MPs who have been arrested during the accomplishment of *flagrante delicto* in the time periods when the Parliament is not in session.

b. Vice Chairmen and Chairman's Council

*396.* The Chairman of the National Assembly is aided in the accomplishment of his or her functions by Vice Chairmen as well as by Chairman's Council. The Vice Chairmen are elected by the plenary of the National Assembly by virtue of an open vote with absolute majority of the MPs. Similar to the Chairman, the Vice Chairmen are elected on the first day of the first session of the newly elected Parliament. They are proposed by the parliamentary groups and usually all parliamentary groups have one Vice Chairman of the National Assembly. If there are too many parliamentary groups and thus Vice Chairmen, they accomplish their activity on the basis of rotation. The grounds and the procedure for dismissal of the Vice Chairmen are the same as those which apply to the Chairman of the National Assembly. The Vice Chairmen accomplish the activities which are assigned to them by the Chairman of the National Assembly in the framework of the 1991 Constitution and the Regulation for the Organization and Activity of the National Assembly.

*397.* The Chairman's Council consists of the Vice Chairmen of the National Assembly and of the Chairmen of the Parliamentary Groups. The latter can appoint their substitutes who can represent them in the Chairman's Council. The Chairman's Council is summoned by the Chairman of the National Assembly on his or her initiative or on a proposal of one-third of its members.

*398.* The Chairman's Council is a consultative body attached to the Chairman of the National Assembly. It accomplishes consultations for the draft legislative programme and for the agenda of the National Assembly. Moreover, the Chairman's Council should be periodically, at least once a month, informed regarding the accomplishment of the legislative programme of the Parliament as well as of the work of the parliamentary committees on the draft acts of Parliament, decisions, declarations and addressees. Another important function of the Chairman's Council is that it contributes for the reaching of consensus in case of conflicts between the parliamentary groups as well as on procedural or organizational matters.

c. Secretaries and Questors

*399.* The secretaries and the questors support the Chairman and the Vice Chairmen of the National Assembly with regard to the maintenance of the order and the due functioning of the Parliament. The secretaries are MPs who have been elected to perform organizational functions in parallel to their functions as parliamentarians. The National Assembly elects eight secretaries by open voting and absolute majority. The questors are employees in the administration of the National Assembly. They are appointed and dismissed by the Chairman of the National Assembly.

## §2. Electoral System

*400.* The 1991 Constitution does not provide for the concrete type of the electoral system for the parliamentary elections. However, since the beginning of the post-communist period of the Bulgarian history developed under the 1991 Constitution, all elections for National Assembly have been accomplished on the basis of proportional representation system.

*401.* The preference of the political elite for the proportional representation system is based on its theoretical advantage to establish parliamentary representation which is both inclusive and well reflecting the political preferences of the different groups in the society. The proportional representation system is believed to foster both the political pluralism and the political integration of the Bulgarian society.

*402.* Two variants of the proportional representation system have been used so far. These are the pure proportional representation system and (the currently applicable) proportional representation system with preference voting.

*403.* Under the current version of the proportional representation system, the voters can cast their vote for a political party candidate or for an independent candidate for MP. If they choose to vote for a political party, then they have also the option to cast their preference for one of the candidates of this party included in the party list. Hence the system remains proportional but the lists are semi-flexible allowing for limited rearrangement of the consequence of the candidates for MPs.

*404.* On 6 November 2016, a referendum on the electoral system was held. The referendum was initiated by national people's initiative launched by an initiative committee supported by a TV show called *Slavi's Show*. Two of the questions of this referendum concerned the electoral system. The first question was 'Do you support the proposal that the MPs should be elected via majority voting system with absolute majority in two rounds?' 71.95 % of the voters voted in favour of the proposal to replace the proportion with majority voting system with absolute majority. The second question was 'Do you support the introduction of compulsory voting in the elections and in the referenda?' 61.89 % of the voters supported that proposal.

*405.* The decision of the referendum is not binding for the Parliament. This is because the degree of participation was lower than the required voter turnout necessary to oblige the National Assembly to amend the Electoral Code accordingly. Moreover, the compulsory voting is unconstitutional because the Bulgarian Constitution provides for election rights but not for election duties of the citizens. Anyway, the 2016 referendum started extensive debate on the electoral system. There are several legislative proposals for introduction of different variants of majority voting system or of mixed voting system which are currently introduced in the Parliament.

## §3. Legal Status of the Members of the Parliament

### I. Mandate of the Members of the Parliament

#### *A. Character of a Mandate*

*406.* Article 67 of the Constitution proclaims the free mandate of the MPs. According to this article, the MPs represent not just their own voters but the entire Bulgarian population. The imperative mandate is explicitly declared null and void. Moreover, the MPs are required to act only in accordance with the Bulgarian Constitution and legislation and with a view to their own conscious, convictions and beliefs.

*407.* Thus the Bulgarian Constitution proclaims the free mandate in its classical form as traditional element of the constitutional heritage of the West European constitutionalism of the twentieth century. It reinstates the free mandate in the Bulgarian constitutional law which has existed under the 1879 Tarnovo Constitution of Bulgaria but which has been abolished by the 1947 and the 1971 communist constitutions.

*408.* The 1991 Constitution represents a clear departure from the Soviet regime. It provides for political pluralism and democracy. Thus the re-establishment of the free mandate is a device for creating the necessary preconditions for representative democracy.

#### *B. Duration of a Mandate*

*409.* The MPs in the National Assembly have four-year term of office. There are two moments that may theoretically serve as the initial moment of the term of office of the MPs.[62] According to the so-called representative theory, the term of office commences as of the day of the elections due to the fact that this is the moment when the Bulgarian people as a sovereign express their will on the composition of the Parliament. The idea is that the MPs are representatives of the people, and they get this position by the will of the electorate as expressed at the moment of casting the ballot papers. Alternatively, according to the so-called organ theory the term of office may start from the first sitting of the newly elected National Assembly. This is because the main goal of the parliamentary elections is the establishment of the National Assembly as collegiate and collective institutions. Consequently, the term of office of the MPs ends either with the new parliamentary elections (according to the representative theory) or with the first sitting of the next Parliament (according to the organ theory).

*410.* The 1991 Constitution does not contain any explicit provision regarding the moment when the term of office of the MPs begins. This moment has been clarified by Decision No. 5 of 2001 of the Constitutional Court. The Constitutional Court opts for the representative theory and provides that mandate of the MPs is invested in them by the electorate in the moment of the elections. Consequently, their term of office begins and ends with the parliamentary elections. In fact, the concrete moment is not the date of the parliamentary elections but the date when the Central Electoral Commission adopts its final decision for the official announcement of the results of the parliamentary elections and for the distribution of the parliamentary seats.

### *C. Preterm Termination of the Mandate*

*411.* According to Article 72 of the Constitution, the mandate of the MPs may be terminated before the elapse of the regular four-year term of office in case of death, resignation, determination of incompatibility with the office of MP, existence of facts that prevent the election of the MP, lack of prerequisites for the election of the MP and sentencing of the MP. The Constitution does not contain any specific provisions on the official establishment of the death of the MP.

*412.* The resignation of MP has to be established by the Parliament via a decision which has to be voted in the plenary session. This is rather a strange provision since it leaves open the question what will happen if such a decision is not adopted at all due to intentional or non-intentional inaction of the Parliament. There is lack of clarity regarding the question of how long can the Parliament postpone the voting of the resignation of an MP.

*413.* Moreover, there is structural asymmetry in the legal background of the resignation of the MPs as such and their resignation from key positions within the Parliament, e.g., as the Chairman of the National Assembly or as Chairmen or Vice

62. *See* Emilia Drumeva, *supra* n. 31, 345.

Chairmen of the parliamentary committees and parliamentary delegations. The resignation of the MPs (including the resignation of the Chairman as MP) requires explicit decision of the National Assembly whereas the resignation from the abovementioned leading positions in the National Assembly is neither discussed nor voted. If the reason of the voting of the resignation is to verify the true will of the MP to resign, then such a check is necessary safeguard for the truthfulness and voluntariness of all types of resignations.

*414.* There has been a curious precedent in the contemporary Bulgarian parliamentary practice related to the rejection by the Parliament of an MP's resignation. In October 2017, Mr Delyan Dobrev filed his resignation as an MP. However, the National Assembly rejected his resignation with the argument that he is very valuable for the Parliament. The Constitutional Court was seized with a petition to declare unconstitutional the parliamentary decision of rejecting the resignation. The Constitutional Court in its Decision No. 2 of 2018 concluded that the National Assembly is not competent and is not allowed to reject the resignation of MPs. According to the Constitutional Court, the National Assembly has only to verify whether there is a resignation and whether it has been submitted voluntarily by the MP. In that regard Decision No. 2 of 2018 is a continuation of the practice of the Constitutional Court established with Decision No. 14 of 2013 according to which, in the case of a resignation, the National Assembly has only to establish whether the MP has voluntarily and clearly objectivized his or her decision to discontinue acting as an MP. According to both decisions of the Constitutional Court, the motives for resignation are absolutely irrelevant. In Decision No. 2 of 2018, the Constitutional Court provides also that the power claimed by the National Assembly to reject resignations of MPs stands in contradiction to the freedom of will and the freedom of choice of profession provided by the Bulgarian Constitution

*415.* The term of office of the MP is terminated also in case of entering into force of a court's verdict for imprisonment due to commitment of intentional crime if the execution of the sentence is not suspended. The MP can continue to accomplish his or her competences if he or she is sentenced to a punishment different from imprisonment, e.g., probation or fine, or if the implementation of imprisonment is postponed for a moment after the elapse of the mandate. There have been already concrete cases in which an MP has been sentenced to probation and has served his sentence during the accomplishment of his parliamentary mandate.

*416.* The establishment of incompatibility or the ascertaining of the existence or lack of prerequisites for the election as an MP is accomplished by the Constitutional Court by virtue of decision. The idea of the constitutional legislator is to ascribe this competence to an independent institution that is also competent to pronounce on the legality of the parliamentary elections.

*417.* There is also one more hypothesis for preterm termination of the office of the MPs which is not explicitly mentioned in Article 72 of the Constitution. The inability of the National Assembly to elect a Council of Ministers produces governmental and parliamentary crisis. It produces preterm termination of the office of the

MPs due to dissolution of the National Assembly by the President and the scheduling of preterm parliamentary elections. In that case, the preterm termination of the mandate is a result neither of resignation of the MPs nor of self-dissolution of the Parliament. The Bulgarian National Assembly does not possess the competence to self-dissolution due to reasons related to the stabilization of the parliamentary system. In that case, the preterm termination of the office of the MPs is a result of the dissolution of the National Assembly by the President via decree. In fact, this dissolution is not discretionary since the President is obliged to dissolve it after three unsuccessful attempts of the National Assembly to elect a new Council of Ministers.

## II. Incompatibilities, Immunities, Rights and Duties

### *A. Incompatibilities*

*418.* The incompatibilities with the position of MP are provided by Article 68 of the 1991 Constitution. According to that constitutional provision, the MPs cannot accomplish any other state service or take another state office. Thus the MP cannot be at the same time President or Vice President, magistrate, member of the state administration, member of any state agencies and committees, ombudsman, member of the Court of Auditors, member of the governing board of the Bulgarian National Bank etc. Moreover, the MP cannot be also a member of the government (Ministers, Deputy Prime Minister or Prime Minister).

*419.* The incompatibility between the ministerial office and the position as an MP is a peculiarity of the Bulgarian parliamentarism. In most of the parliamentary systems, the election as an MP is compatible with the ministerial position. In such a way, the constitutions try to assure the strong bond between the government and the parliamentary majority and the reinforced influence of the voters on the composition of the government ascribing direct input democratic legitimacy[63] to the Ministers.

*420.* The 1991 Bulgarian Constitution deviates from this traditional rule applicable to the 'classical' parliamentary systems. It tries to provide for an increased autonomy of the government from the Parliament. Thus the 1991 Constitution introduces an element of the rigid separation of powers which is typical for the dualist systems, e.g., the presidential republics, in the predominant parliamentary institutional outlook of the system.

*421.* In fact, the incompatibility between ministerial position and mandate as an MP leads to a different result. It allows for the partial emancipation of the parliamentary majority from the government. This incompatibility prevents the merger of the leadership positions in the Parliament (usually occupied by the parliamentary

63. For the 'input' democratic legitimacy, *see* Paul Craig and Grainne de Burca, *supra* n. 38, 65 and Philip Kiiver, *supra* n. 40, 95.

majority) and the ministerial offices. Thus the leaders of the parliamentary majority are by necessity different from the members of the Council of Ministers. In very limited but sometimes important occasions, this separation of key positions in the power unit composed of the government and its parliamentary majority may allow for an additional check on the Ministers and the government as a whole by its parliamentary group.

*422.* The MPs can be elected as Ministers. However, during the period when they are Ministers they are replaced in the National Assembly by the next person from the list of the political party or coalition from which they have been elected as MPs. This substitute becomes full and regular member of the Parliament. He or she loses his or her position only in case the substituted person ceases to be Minister and decides to return to the National Assembly. Hence the MPs who have been elected as Ministers retain the option to regain their parliamentary mandate under the condition that they cease to be members of the government.

*B. Immunities*

*423.* The MPs in the National Assembly enjoy both criminal immunity and criminal inviolability. The criminal immunity is provided in Article 69 of the Constitution and the criminal inviolability, in Article 70 of the Constitution.

*424.* The MP's criminal immunity consists in the freedom from criminal prosecution for speeches and votes in the Parliament. The explicit text of Article 69 of the Constitution provides for the freedom of opinion and expression of the MPs only in the National Assembly. The concept of 'Parliament' can be interpreted extensively in order to include all structures of the National Assembly – its plenum as well as its governing and supportive bodies such as the Chairman's Council, the parliamentary groups and the parliamentary committees.

*425.* The parliamentary delegations are in fact territorially remoted structures of the National Assembly. In spatial aspect, they do not work in the parliamentary premises. The same may be true also for the investigative parliamentary committees which may hold some of their sessions also outside the parliamentary buildings. However, the speeches and the votes of the MPs are protected also if they are delivered or cast in the parliamentary delegations or in the investigative parliamentary committees. This is because they are both structures of the Parliament which function on the basis of a functionally extended parliamentary spatiality.

*426.* Hence according to Article 69 of the Constitution the freedom of voting and expression of the MPs is a special privilege aiming at safeguarding the normal functioning of the National Assembly. The National Assembly is understood as a composite structure with some cases of extended territoriality.

*427.* Consequently, it seems that outside of the Parliament the freedom of the MPs to express their opinion in order to participate in the general political communication in the society and to form the public opinion is safeguarded not by the criminal immunity provided by Article 69 of the Constitution but by the information and communication rights provided in Articles 39, 40 and 41 of the Constitution. These rights are granted to all citizens and to all people.

*428.* In practice, such distinction between the criminal immunity of the MPs and the freedom of opinion, information and expression would not produce very different results. This is due to two reasons. First, the single MPs cannot initiate cases in front of the Constitutional Court for violation of their criminal immunity. Second, there is no direct constitutional complaint by virtue of which the MPs as citizens can approach the Constitutional Court.

*429.* However, the Constitutional Court by virtue of its Decision No. 10 of 1992 has extended the scope of criminal immunity of the MPs. According to the Constitutional Court, the MPs are not responsible for their statements if they are made not only in the Parliament and its substructures but also outside of the National Assembly. Thus the Constitutional Court has expanded the scope of the MP's criminal immunity by interpreting widely the initially clear provision of Article 69 of the Constitution. As a result of this extensive interpretation, the criminal immunity as a special enhanced protection of the freedom of speech of the MPs takes over the regulative and protective scope of the general freedom of speech.

*430.* The logic of this Constitutional Court's decision can be understood in the context of transition from authoritarianism to democracy. It is provoked by the desire of the Constitutional Court to provide for enhanced protection of the freedom of speech of the MPs understood as a safeguard for the emerging parliamentarism, political pluralism and representative democracy.

*431.* However, Decision No. 10 of 1992 of the Constitutional Court is problematic in two aspects. First, it is an example of overt judicial activism. Second, it may shape the criminal immunity in a way that would seem as an unjustified privilege going beyond the initial intent of the constitutional legislator.

*432.* Article 69 of the Constitution ensures protection against criminal liability of the MP for expressions and voting. However, the other forms of liability are not excluded. Thus the speeches of the MPs in the National Assembly can be an object of disciplinary liability effectuated by the Chairman of the National Assembly. The MP is also responsible for civil law delicts caused by their speeches resulting, e.g., in degrading the reputation of other people.

*433.* The criminal inviolability is provided in Article 70 of the Constitution. It has two main aspects consisting in the prohibition for detention and prohibition for criminal prosecution of the MPs. The MPs cannot be arrested or detained. This prohibition is directed towards all state institutions having functions related to criminal prosecution, delivering of criminal justice or combat against crime in Bulgaria. Hence the police officers cannot detain the MPs even with the permission of a judge, state prosecutor or state investigator.

*434.* The National Assembly is the only institution which may allow the arrest or detention of an MP. Such permission must be granted via a decision of the National Assembly adopted by a majority vote. If the National Assembly is not in session, the permission for the arrest and detention of an MP may be granted by the Chairman of the National Assembly. The permission of the National Assembly or of its Chairman for the arrest or detention of an MP can be withdrawn through the same procedure which was applied for its granting.

*435.* Permission by the National Assembly or by its Chairman is not required in case of *flagrante delicto*. In that case, if the MP has been caught in the course of accomplishment of grave criminal offence, he or she can be detained immediately by the competent state institutions which are usually the police officers. However, they have to immediately inform the National Assembly of the arrest and the detention. If the Parliament is not in session, then the Chairman of the National Assembly has to be immediately informed instead. According to the Bulgarian law, grave criminal offences are offences for which a penalty of at least five years' imprisonment is provided in the Criminal Code.

*436.* The second aspect of the criminal inviolability consists in the prohibition for initiation of criminal prosecution against MP without parliamentary consent given in advance. In the case of initiation of criminal prosecution, in contrast to the safeguards for due detention of the MP, the consent cannot be given by the Chairman of the National Assembly. If the Parliament is not in session, the initiation of criminal prosecution against its member has to be postponed until its next sitting when all MPs can discuss and vote in favour or against the decision for granting permission for a criminal trial.

*437.* Another difference between the two components of the criminal inviolability consists in the fact that the permission for detention can be waived at any time by discretionary decision of the Parliament whereas the permission for initiation of criminal proceedings cannot be waived once it has been granted by the National Assembly. Otherwise, the Parliament may intervene in the autonomy of the judiciary and can influence, frequently with political motives, the outcome of the criminal prosecution and the criminal trial.

*438.* The MPs can be prosecuted only for the so-called criminal offences of general character. According to the Bulgarian criminal law, these are the criminal offences which expose typically high degree of social danger. That is why they are prosecuted by the state on the initiative of the state prosecutors. The other type of criminal offences according to the Criminal Code – the 'criminal offences of private character' – is prosecuted on demand of the victim.

*C. Rights and Duties*

*439.* Most of the rights and the duties of the MPs stem out of their competences as members of the Parliament as collective representative institution. They can be classified into three main groups: first, rights and duties stemming out of the functions of the Parliament in the different state powers and in the various decision-making processes; second, rights and duties which are elements of the immunities of the MPs; third, personal rights and duties of the MPs safeguarding the necessary preconditions for the accomplishment of their functions.

*440.* The first group of rights and duties of the MPs comprise their competences for participation in the legislative, controlling, budgetary and other decision-making processes. It concerns also the influence of the MPs on the political functions of the Parliament, including the political representation and integration of the people and the recruitment of the political elite based on the patronage power of the Parliament. In other words, the MPs have rights concerning the competences of the National Assembly to influence and determine not only the substantial but also the symbolic and the personal policy of the state. This category of rights of the MPs will be discussed in the next paragraph in conjunction with the functions and the competences of the Parliament.

*441.* The second group of rights and duties has just been discussed in paragraph 423 and the following related to the immunities of the MPs. Thus only one further clarification is needed here. Until 2006, the immunity of the MPs comprised the system of elements described above which were simultaneously rights and duties. The reason was that the MPs were prohibited from giving up their immunity. More precisely, they were not allowed to renounce their criminal inviolability by granting consent for initiation of criminal proceedings against them.

*442.* However, in 2006, the Constitution was amended due to the critical public opinion on the immunity of the MPs. It was a widespread belief that the absolute character of the immunity of the MPs is not only unjustified but also leads to the prevention of criminal prosecution against MPs who were supposed to have committed serious criminal offences. Thus in 2006 a new paragraph 2 to Article 70 of the Constitution was added. According to this article, the MPs are allowed to renounce their criminal inviolability related to the initiation of criminal proceedings. The renouncement of that element of the MPs' immunity has to be done in written form and has to be addressed to the Chairman of the National Assembly.

*443.* The third group of rights of the MPs – the personal rights and duties of the MPs safeguarding the necessary preconditions for the accomplishment of their functions – can be divided into two subgroups. The first comprises the rights of the MPs to be elected in the governing bodies and positions of the Parliament as well as in the parliamentary committees and delegations. It includes also the rights of the MPs to participate, to vote and to express their opinions in the Parliament and its substructures. In fact, this subgroup of MPs' rights is directly related to the accomplishment of their competences with regard to the main functions of the National

Assembly. That is why they have to be analysed in conjunction with the first group of MPs rights because they are formal preconditions for their accomplishment.

*444.* The second subgroup comprises MPs rights which secure the social preconditions for the normal accomplishment of their functions. It includes the rights of the MPs to have logistical, technical and expert support by advisers and personnel, the rights of the MPs to receive a monthly wage, social and health insurance, and the rights of the MPs to have some additional social benefits related to their job. These rights are provided by the Regulation for the Organization and Activity of the National Assembly. They form a part of the autonomy of the Parliament and are supposed to safeguard not the high living standard of the MPs but the preconditions for the normal accomplishment of the functions of the National Assembly.

## §4. Functions and Competences

### I. Legislation

#### A. *Phases of the Legislative Process*

*445.* There are three phases of the legislative process in Bulgaria. These are the pre-parliamentary, the parliamentary and the post-parliamentary phases.[64] They are all compulsory and comprise the necessary stages and elements of the legislative process in Bulgaria. The compulsory character of all the three phases, which include the participation of different institutional actors, demonstrates that the legislative process is not limited to the activity of the Parliament and its substructures – the MPs, the parliamentary groups and the parliamentary committees and its governing bodies. According to the 1991 Constitution, important players in the legislative process are the Council of Ministers and to a limited extent, the President of the Republic. In addition, the Direct Participation of the Citizens in the State Power and Local Self-Government Act provides for the legislative peoples' initiative and the legislative referendum which make the people also potential players – both proactive and reactive – in the legislative process.

#### B. *Legislative Initiative*

*446.* The legislative initiative belongs to the single MPs and to the Council of Ministers. The 1991 Constitution gives a chance to each MP to have a proactive role in the legislative process. That is why it does not limit the right to legislative initiative to a qualified minimal number of MPs. The founding fathers and mothers of the current Bulgarian Constitution believed that this liberal approach is a natural consequence of the principles of democracy and political pluralism. Indeed the 1991 Constitution is the first Bulgarian Constitution which allows not only a group of

64. *See* Emilia Drumeva, *supra* n. 31, 379.

MPs but also single MPs to initiate legislation. In the political practice, however, the single MPs do not have any real chance to carry the bill through the parliamentary phase of the legislative process without the support of the majority of the MPs formed usually on party political and more rarely on lobbyist basis.

*447.* Thus the use of the right to legislative initiative by the single MPs typically serves two main goals. First, it is a 'political marketing devise' for launching and promoting the ideas of opposition or inner party opposition MPs who make visible their views by initiating legislative reforms. Second, it is an oblique way to initiate the adoption of acts of Parliament which are not deemed appropriate to be launched directly by the parliamentary majority or by the government. The reasons for such an approach may be the introduction of unpopular reforms or the desire not to expose contextual legislative coalitions with some of the opposition parties based on lobbyism or going against the main ideology and principles of the ruling party.

*448.* Most of the draft acts of Parliament are introduced in the National Assembly by the Council of Ministers. There are three main reasons for that phenomenon. First, according to the 1991 Constitution, Bulgaria is hybrid parliamentary republic. In most parliamentary systems, the key proactive veto player in the legislative process is the government. Second, Bulgaria is party democracy. Hence the party political affiliation of the government and the parliamentary majority and minority predetermine the dynamics and the trends in the decision-making processes in general and in the legislative process in particular.

*449.* The combination of these two reasons related to the form of government and the political regime produce important consequences also for the policy initiation framed as draft legislation. This is because the government and the parliamentary majority in Bulgaria being a parliamentary party democracy form a non-institutionalized but decisive political power centre. This power centre generates the strategical ideas for the public governance and thus is the main driving force behind the legislative process in general and the legislative initiative in particular.

*450.* The government dominates the proactive phase of the legislative process because it has information, organization and motivation advantages over its MPs and the Parliament as a whole with a view to the initiation of legislation. Hence there is unwritten but evident and durable internal separation of functions in the above-mentioned power unit in the context of the legislative power. It consists in the factual monopoly of the Council of Ministers over the initiation and the legal monopoly of the parliamentary majority over the adoption of the acts of the Parliament. That is why the legislative process in Bulgaria as well as in most parliamentary systems is concerted action comprising the activities of both the government and its parliamentary majority.

*451.* The third reason for the dominant position of the Council of Ministers in the initiation of legislation is the lack of delegated legislation. Thus the Council of Ministers has to rely only on the parliamentary legislation for getting the legislative basis for its policy. This fact fosters its appetite for initiating acts of Parliament.

*452.* The draft acts of Parliament which are introduced in the National Assembly have to be motivated and have to contain preliminary evaluation of their impact on the Bulgarian legal order and on the society. The motives and the preliminary evaluation are attached to the draft acts of Parliament. They should address the compliance of the draft acts of Parliament with the EU law, the international obligations of Bulgaria and the 1991 Constitution. The motives to the draft acts of Parliament which are related to the EU membership of Bulgaria must point out the concrete part of the EU legislation which necessitates their adoption. Moreover, they should assess the adequacy of the proposed act of Parliament to the Bulgarian legal tradition and its adjustment to the system of the valid law. Last but not least, they have to contain evaluation of their financial, budgetary and social impact. The motives and the preliminary evaluation of the impact serve as a basis for the debates on the merits of the draft act of Parliament during the parliamentary phase of the legislative process.

*453.* When the draft acts of Parliament are introduced by the Council of Ministers, they contain also several compulsory appendixes. The governmental draft acts of Parliament are supplemented by document reflecting the compulsory or facultative opinions that the Council of Ministers has assembled from other state institutions. If the draft act of Parliament is introduced with a view to harmonizing the Bulgarian law with the EU law, the government must present also reference for the compliance with the EU law. Last but not least, all draft acts of Parliament contain also evaluation for their compliance with the EConvHR and with the case law of the ECtHR.

*454.* It is clear that such complex preliminary evaluation can hamper the legislative initiative of the ordinary MPs who do not possess the institutional capacity and the experts of the government. The MPs must also provide such preliminary evaluation of the draft acts of Parliament introduced by them. However, they are prepared on the basis of a special methodical guidelines provided by the Parliament in order to facilitate the introduction of MPs' legislative initiative.

*455.* The draft acts of Parliament which do not contain motives, preliminary evaluation of the impact, or the compulsory appendixes in the case of the governmental draft bills are not processed and discussed by the Parliament until the initiator eliminates the irregularities. Hence these are compulsory properties of the draft acts of Parliament which help the MPs to get oriented to the goals, the effects and the merits of the proposed legislation and are supposed to rationalize the legislative process.

### *C. Parliamentary Legislative Process*

*456.* The draft acts of Parliament which are introduced in the National Assembly are registered in a public register. The Chairman of the National Assembly distributes the draft acts of Parliament among the standing parliamentary committees. In case of interdisciplinary draft acts of Parliament (acts of Parliament that concern more than one sphere of social relations and public government), the Chairman of the National Assembly may distribute them to more than one standing committee. In that case, he or she determines one of them as the leading committee. The leading standing committee is determined on the basis of the subject matter of the draft acts of Parliament. The leading standing committee has a key role to clarify the advantages and the disadvantages of the draft act of Parliament and an important coordination role especially in the case of draft acts of Parliament which are distributed to more than one standing committee.

*457.* The Chairman of the National Assembly regularly informs the MPs regarding the introduced draft acts of Parliament, their initiator and their distribution among the standing parliamentary committees. The standing parliamentary committees, which are interested in being involved in the legislative process regarding certain draft acts of Parliament, may raise objections against their distribution. The Chairman of the National Assembly has the final word on that matter.

*458.* The legislative procedure in Bulgaria is structured in two readings. They are organized around a scheme according to which the draft acts of Parliament are first discussed in the standing committees and then in the plenum of the National Assembly. This organization of the parliamentary procedure allows for relatively simple and fast adoption of the acts of the Parliament. At the same time, it makes possible the thorough deliberation of the draft acts of Parliament both from political and expert perspectives.

*459.* The draft acts of Parliament are discussed and voted on the first reading with regard to their general philosophy, principles and basic merits. During the first reading, the National Assembly has to evaluate the necessity of the act of the Parliament, its general appropriateness with regard to its compliance with the other sources of law and with a view to its efficiency and justice. In other words, the first reading is devoted to the assessment of the principle compliance of the draft acts of Parliament with the legal order and its general adequacy to provide sound, reasonable and durable solutions to important social problems.

*460.* The second reading is devoted to the improvement of the details of the draft acts of Parliament. During the second reading, the draft acts of Parliament are discussed and voted chapter by chapter, section by section or text by text. The aim of the second reading is to contribute for the adoption of coherent acts of Parliament which contain logical, well-formulated and efficient legal provisions.

*461.* Both the first and the second readings consist of standing committee phase and plenary phase. The standing committee phase precedes the plenary phase and has preparatory function. This consequence of the legislative process allows the MPs to have a thorough discussion on the substantial merits of the draft acts of Parliament in the standing committees before conducting a ‘political battle’ in the plenary session of the National Assembly.

*462.* The adoption of the draft acts of Parliament is accomplished in two different sittings of the National Assembly. Typically, they are divided by discussions both in the plenary and in the standing committees on the first and second readings. However, the National Assembly may decide to accomplish both votes in one sitting if during the discussion of the draft acts of Parliament no amendments have been proposed.

*463.* The first reading of the draft acts of Parliament in the committee phase is focused on their philosophy, macrostructure and the conceptual issues. The standing parliamentary committees decide upon the compliance of the draft acts of Parliament with the Bulgarian legal order, with the requirements of the supranational law which are valid for Bulgaria and with the standards set by the Normative Acts Act, the decree for its implementation and the Regulation for the Organization and Activity of the National Assembly.

*464.* In fact, such a check for compliance with the requirements of the just-mentioned acts is compulsorily accomplished only by the leading committee. The other committees which are involved in the adoption of the draft act of Parliament may also raise arguments on that issue and they frequently do so. The standing committees have to present reports for the first reading of the draft acts of Parliament to the Chairman of the National Assembly within two months. These reports are published on the Internet site of the Parliament.

*465.* The MPs discuss and vote on the draft acts of Parliament during the first plenary reading on the basis of several sources of information. Naturally, the most important one is the text of the proposed acts of Parliament. However, the MPs may rely also on information which is contained in the motives of the initiator attached to the draft act of Parliament, the report of the leading parliamentary committee for the first reading, the preliminary evaluation of the impact and the compulsory appendixes.

*466.* In case of draft acts of Parliament initiated by MPs, the Council of Ministers or the respective Minister have to present their opinion on the act of Parliament. If they do not present such opinions within two weeks, the Parliament may proceed also without it. The Regulation for the Organization and Activity of the National Assembly requires the presentation also of some additional opinions by different organizations, e.g., by the National Council for Tripartite Cooperation or by the National Council of the Disabled Persons, in case a sector-specific bill is discussed and voted. The Regulation for the Organization and Activity of the National Assembly allows also the citizens to present their written opinion on the draft acts of Parliament.

*467.* The report of the leading committee contains summary of all the above-mentioned documents. It provides also an assessment for the impact of the application of the draft act of Parliament on the legal order and on the social life.

*468.* If a draft act of Parliament has been rejected by the plenum of the National Assembly in the first reading, it may be reintroduced in the Parliament only after the lapse of the three months' period of time and only after serious and profound amendments in its concept and general logic. This general rule is not applicable in case of draft acts of Parliament which aim at harmonization of the Bulgarian law with the requirements of the EU law or at addressing and remedying the determinants for initiated procedure for sanctioning of Bulgaria for non-compliance with the EU law. In these two instances, the draft act of Parliament can be introduced without awaiting the lapse of the three months' period.

*469.* The initiator of the draft act of Parliament can withdraw it until the accomplishment of the voting on the first reading in the plenary of the Parliament. After the National Assembly has expressed its will in favour of the draft act of Parliament by adopting it on the first reading, the initiator may withdraw it only with the consent of the Parliament expressed via adoption of a parliamentary decision.

*470.* The Parliament takes into consideration and the MPs discuss and vote on the second reading only proposals for amendment of the draft act of Parliament which are made by the MPs in writing. Such proposals must be submitted by the MPs to the Chairman of the Leading Standing Committee via the Chairman of the National Assembly. The Council of Ministers may be asked to give an opinion on the suggested amendments.

*471.* There are cases in which more than one draft act of Parliament on the same topic have been introduced to the National Assembly. In such a situation, the standing committees and the plenary of the National Assembly discuss them in parallel on the first reading. However, the MPs vote separately for each one of them. The Parliament may adopt more than one of the introduced draft acts of Parliament on the first reading because more than one of them could be sufficiently well elaborated and provide for adequate and desirable solutions to the issues concerned. If this is the case, then the leading standing committee produces with the active involvement of the initiators a common draft act of Parliament which is then submitted to the second reading.

*472.* The National Assembly adopts the acts of the Parliament via absolute majority of the MPs. There is also a requirement for a necessary quorum consisting in the compulsory presence of 50% plus one of the MPs during the voting. The double requirement for quorum and majority is necessary for both the first and the second readings of the draft acts of Parliament.

### *D. Post-Parliamentary Legislative Process*

*473.* After the adoption of the act of Parliament, the National Assembly must send it to the President of the Republic for promulgation and publication in SG. The Chairman of the National Assembly certifies that the act of Parliament which is sent to the President is identical with the one which has been adopted by the Parliament.

The President has a promulgation term amounting to fifteen days after the adoption of the act of Parliament. During the promulgation term, he or she has to promulgate and publish the act of Parliament or impose a suspensive veto and return it to the National Assembly for reconsideration. If the National Assembly adopts anew the act of the Parliament thus rejecting the presidential veto, then the President must publish the act of Parliament in SG within seven days. These seven days are necessary for the technical activities related to sending and publishing of the act of Parliament.

*474.* Typically, the acts of the Parliament enter into force three days after their publication in SG. However, the National Assembly may provide for different *vacatio legis*. The Parliament is prohibited to provide for retroactive entering into force for criminal and tax acts of Parliament which establish criminal responsibility, raise the criminal sanctions or worsen the status of the tax-obliged persons. These requirements are safeguards for the principle of legal certainty and thus for the rule of law. The National Assembly may also provide that the acts of the Parliament enter into force as of the day of their publication. The Parliament provides for longer *vacatio legis* sometimes amounting to several weeks or months for codes or more complex acts of Parliament.

### E. *Implementation of Supranational Law*

*475.* Two types of supranational law need implementation via parliamentary legislation. These are the international treaties and the EU directives. Bulgaria has adopted the monistic system for implementation of international treaties. Thus the international treaty is implemented through a formal act of Parliament that does not have any normative content of its own apart from the provision recognizing the legal force of the international treaty in the Bulgarian legal system. That is why the ratified international treaties have direct effect in the Bulgarian legal order.

*476.* The international treaties provided in Article 85 of the Constitution must be ratified by act of Parliament. The ratification act of Parliament is adopted through the same procedure as the ordinary acts of Parliament. The only difference is that the two readings for the adoption of a ratification act of Parliament can be accomplished in one parliamentary sitting because of the formality of the act of the Parliament. This is because the National Assembly has to either adopt it or reject the ratification the act of Parliament but cannot introduce any amendments in the text of the international treaty which is subject to ratification.

*477.* The EU directives may be implemented by acts of Parliament or by normative acts of the Council of Ministers. However, in most of the cases they are implemented via acts of Parliament due to two main reasons. First, this is the way the National Assembly can preserve some discretion and control over the multilevel legislative process in the EU. Second, the Bulgarian political culture is rather reluctant towards the seizure of the legislative competences of the Parliament by the government. The implementation of the EU directives is tackled predominantly as an important legislative activity. That is why it is believed that the National Assembly should have the final influence over the implementation of the EU directives.

## II. Supervision of and Control over the Executive

### *A. General Classification of the Forms for Parliamentary Control*

*478.* The forms for parliamentary control may be classified with regard to four criteria: the subject who is accomplishing the control, the consequences of parliamentary control, the object of parliamentary control and the sphere of social governance towards which the parliamentary control is accomplished. In other words, both the general classification of parliamentary control and the distinct forms in which it is accomplished concern the system of questions: who controls whom with what instruments and in which policy domains. Thus the forms for parliamentary control may be systematized into four main groups.

*479.* The first group is structured around the subject that is competent to accomplish parliamentary control. According to the Bulgarian constitutional law, the parliamentary control can be accomplished by single MPs, by the parliamentary committees and by the plenum of the Parliament. All parliamentary committees have controlling functions. However, the temporary committees for enquiries are established with a special emphasis and with the exclusive task to accomplish parliamentary control.

*480.* It has to be taken into account that the parliamentary groups as such do not have special controlling competences. However, they are the driving force behind the controlling function of the Parliament in general and its specific and concrete forms in particular. The tension and the political dynamic between the pro-governmental majority in the Parliament and the parliamentary opposition is the main driving force behind the system for parliamentary control in Bulgaria as in all parliamentary republics.

*481.* The second group of forms for parliamentary control concerns the object of that activity. The control over the governmental activity in general and of the performance of the Prime Minister, the Deputy Prime Ministers and the Ministers in particular lay at the centre of the controlling function of the National Assembly.

*482.* The control over the government does not exhaust the objects of parliamentary control. Theoretically, the activity of all state institutions may be controlled by the National Assembly. However, this principle needs further clarifications.

*483.* The activity of the state administration, especially on medium or lower level, can hardly be systematically and directly controlled by the Parliament. Much more frequently, its activity is supervised and evaluated by virtue of control over the government and the Ministers.

*484.* The judiciary is partially excluded from the scope of parliamentary control because the National Assembly cannot control the concrete jurisprudential activity of the judges, state prosecutors and state investigators. This is a compromise made in favour of the principle of rule of law to the detriment of the principle of democracy. Actually, the activity of the judiciary is indirectly subjected to the parliamentary control with a view to the fact that the Chairmen of the Supreme Court of Cassation and the Supreme Administrative Court as well as the State Prosecutor General have to present annual reports to the National Assembly for the functioning of the judicial power.

*485.* Last but not least, the activity of non-state actors as well as some objective phenomena and processes may also be an object of parliamentary control. They may be at the centre of the parliamentary discussions raised through questions and interpellation. They may also trigger the procedure for vote of no confidence or be an object of investigation accomplished by a temporary committee of enquiry.

*486.* The third group of forms of parliamentary control concerns the sphere of social and political governance towards which they are directed. Abstractly it may seem reasonable to distinguish between parliamentary control concerning the different spheres of governmental activity, e.g., military and defence, public finance, culture, healthcare, education, economy etc. However, the constitutional law does not make any difference between the forms of parliamentary control that can be used for control of these policy fields. In other words, the constitutional law provides for universal set of parliamentary control instruments applicable in all policy sectors.

*487.* The only exception is the public finance. This is due to the emancipation of the public finance as a strategic field of governance that influences all sector-based policy domains. Hence the budgetary function of the Parliament not only concerns directly the adoption of the state budget but also implies the control for its implementation.

*488.* An important distinction can be made between the forms of parliamentary control concerning the domestic politics and the forms of parliamentary control on EU issues and on the participation of the Bulgarian institutions in the decision-making processes of the EU. Hence there is partial overlapping and important differences between the forms of parliamentary control of the domestic and of the supranational domains for policymaking. In contrast to the parliamentary control on domestic and on EU issues, there is no distinct, well-elaborated and institutionalized system for parliamentary control regarding the traditional, non EU-related international policy accomplished by the state institutions. Thus the control that the National Assembly accomplishes with regard to the international policy domain is performed on the basis of the general instruments for parliamentary control used also with a view to the domestic policymaking.

*489.* A fourth grouping or classification of the forms for parliamentary control can be made with regard to their consequences and legal effects. Most of the institutions for parliamentary control are directed towards the assembling of information for governmental or other state activity or for other objective processes with key sociopolitical impact. Thus they are not targeting directly the removal of the government from power. This first type of parliamentary control instruments aiming at forming public opinion and gathering of publicly important information comprise the questions, the interpellations, the enquiry committees and the parliamentary debates that follow a motion for interpellation.

*490.* The only form that is directly aiming at the removal of the government from power is the vote of no confidence. The vote of confidence can also lead to preterm termination of the office of the Council of Ministers, but due to the fact that it is triggered by the government itself it is rarely defined as a form of parliamentary control. Thus the vote of no confidence and indirectly the vote of confidence both result in procedures for parliamentary control that not only lead to information gathering and public opinion formation but also may remove the government from power.

*491.* In political practice however, the distinction between the forms for parliamentary control aiming at political communication and these forms, which may also lead to political responsibility of the Council of Ministers and to preterm termination of its mandate, is not as sharp as it may theoretically seem. On the one hand, most of the votes of no confidence in Bulgaria are initiated with the clear intention to provoke debate, to expose the weaknesses of governmental policy and to focus the public attention on them rather with the sincere hope to remove the Council of Ministers from power. On the other hand, the government may be politically forced to resign in the context of the accomplishment of other 'softer' versions of parliamentary control that cannot legally engage its responsibility ending with legally safeguarded preterm termination of the governmental term of office.

### *B. Forms of Parliamentary Control Aiming at Information Gathering*

*492.* The instruments for parliamentary control which aim at public opinion formation and information gathering comprise questions, interpellations, discussions following an interpellation and hearings in the standing committees. The enquiry committees also belong to this group of forms for parliamentary control with the specificity that they are both instrument and forum for the accomplishment of the controlling function of the Parliament.

*493.* According to the criterion who can initiate the form of parliamentary control? One can differentiate between forms belonging to single MPs (questions, interpellations and invitation for hearings in the plenum or in the standing committees) and forms belonging to a qualified number of MPs (initiation of discussion following an interpellation and initiation of inquiry committees). Another classification can be made with regard to the forum in which the control is accomplished. Here one can distinguish between forms of parliamentary control that can be accomplished in the plenum of the National Assembly (questions, interpellations, discussions following an interpellation and plenary hearings) and forms of parliamentary control that can be accomplished in the standing committees or in the enquiry committees of the National Assembly (committee hearings).

*494.* The questions and the interpellations are the most frequently used instruments for parliamentary control. The right to pose a question or interpellation belongs to every single MP. Addressees of the questions or interpellation can be the Prime Minister, the Deputy Prime Ministers or the Ministers, which means all members of the government. On the contrary, the MPs cannot pose questions or interpellations to persons and office holders who are not part of the Council of Ministers such as the Vice Ministers, the members of the different state agencies and state committees or the civil servants in the state or local administration.

*495.* If the MPs would like to be informed about the activity of the members of the administration, they will have to try to acquire this information from the members of the government. This is the reason why the members of the government and especially the Ministers are supposed to bear the consequences of the activity of the sector administration which they govern and thus to be held also liable for its failures. In fact, such responsibility is objective because the Minister is held accountable and liable for deeds which he or she had not accomplished or about which he or she does not even know. Anyway, holding the members of the government accountable and liable for the activity of the whole administration is the most important tool for securing an indirect parliamentary and thus democratic control over the executive power and for safeguarding that its performance complies with the standards of the rule of law and the good administration.

*496.* The questions have to address current and topical issues which concern public interest that fall into the sphere of competence of the Minister or his or her subordinate administration. The interpellations have to address fundamental issues of the activity of the Ministers. In other words, the interpellations are a qualified type of questions which are related to the key aspects of the activity of the members of the Council of Ministers. The questions and the interpellations to the Prime Minister must concern the general activity of the government.

*497.* Both the questions and the interpellations can be oral or written. The choice whether the information gathering and the public opinion formation will be accomplished via question or interpellation and whether they should be written or oral is made by the MPs. The answer to the question or interpellation is written if the MP has preferred to get a written answer. Moreover, the answer to a question is written if it concerns personal rights or interests or in case concrete arithmetical data have to be provided. The questions and interpellations are addressed to the Prime Minister, the Deputy Prime Ministers or the Ministers via the Chairman of the National Assembly. The written answers are received by the MPs the same way – through the formal mediation of the Chairman of the National Assembly.

*498.* There are some procedural differences between the questions and interpellations which stem out of their substantial differences. The time for delivering of the answer is longer in the case of interpellation than in the case of question. The time for posing an oral question by the MP as well as for its answer by the Prime Minister, the Deputy Prime Minister or the Minister is shorter than the time for posing and answering of interpellation. Moreover, the interpellation procedure allows for an extended exchange of opinions between both parties structured as discussions. Last but not least, one-fifth of the MPs can propose to have a general discussion on the interpellation which is not limited to exchange of opinions between the initiator and the member of the government and in which also other MPs may participate. Such discussion ends with a decision of the National Assembly by virtue of which it gives an evaluation on the issue that is concerned.

*499.* The main purpose of the procedure for general discussion on the interpellation is to allow a more thorough examination of the issue at stake and to focus the public opinion on it. It allows the opposition to have a chance for a more exhaustive debate on the conceptual problems of the governmental activity. It must be underlined that the National Assembly cannot force the Council of Ministers or some of its members to resign by virtue of such a decision adopted at the end of an extended procedure for debate on interpellation. The Council of Ministers is legally obliged to resign only in case of a successful vote of no confidence or if it loses the vote of confidence.

*500.* A special parliamentary sitting devoted to parliamentary control consisting in procedure for posing and answering of questions and interpellations takes place each Friday. Due to time constraints, each MP can register only two questions or interpellations which need an oral answer per week.

*501.* A relative novelty in the Bulgarian parliamentary practice has been the provision of the Regulation for the Organization and the Activity of the National Assembly adopted by the forty-third National Assembly on the holding of regular debates each second Wednesday on the general policy of the government. These debates were not preceded by exchange of formal questions in written and were supposed to serve as improvised ad hoc policy debates in the form of 'blitz' control exposing the idea competition between the government and its majority and the opposition. This novel form of parliamentary control actually did not achieve its goal to foster the controlling capacity of the National Assembly, to serve as a precursor of public deliberation and thus to compensate the decreasing belief in the Bulgarian society of the parliamentarism as 'government by discussion'.[65] It has been abolished and is not reproduced by the Regulations for the Organization and Activity of the current forty-fourth National Assembly.

*502.* The parliamentary hearings can be accomplished either in the plenary sitting of the National Assembly by its plenum or in the parliamentary committees. In

65. Georgi Bliznashki, *Principles of Parliamentary Government*, 19–33 ('St. Kliment Ohridski' University Press, 1999).

the latter case, both the standing committees and the enquiry committees may accomplish hearings. The hearings must have as an object important issue which concerns state or public interest. The hearings are accomplished on the basis of exchange of questions and answers forming a broader discussion. All state officials, office holders and civil servants are obliged to appear in front of the National Assembly or its committees, to participate in the hearing and to give information if they are requested by the Parliament to do so. They must answer the questions or give any necessary information even if it is a state or an official secret. The form in which this information has to be delivered is determined by the National Assembly.

*503.* The National Assembly and its committees can also accomplish enquiries and researches. The Constitution and the Regulation for the Organization and Activity of the National Assembly does not provide for any concrete parameters for the enquiries and researches. They may consist in hearings combined with exploration of facts, interrogation of experts and research of documentation. The only compulsory requirement posed by the Regulation for the Organization and Activity of the National Assembly is that the enquiries and researches have to concern state or public and not private interest. The capability of the Parliament and its committees to accomplish such enquiries and researches is safeguarded by the obligation of all state officials to appear in front of them and to deliver all necessary information.

### *C. Forms for Parliamentary Control Aiming at Accomplishment of the Governmental Responsibility*

*504.* There is one form of parliamentary control which aims at the accomplishment of the responsibility of the Council of Ministers – the vote of no confidence. However, the vote of confidence will also be analysed here despite the fact that it is actually a device for mobilization of the parliamentary majority by the government or for passing unpopular reforms or policies with durable and strategic consequences through the Parliament.[66] The result of an unsuccessful vote of confidence produces similar results as the successful vote of no confidence due to the fact that they both lead to the demise of the government from power. Hence the governmental responsibility may be engaged also as a consequence of the unsuccessful vote of confidence.

*505.* The 1991 Constitution has adopted the most widespread version of vote of no confidence in Europe, namely the classical or the destructive vote of no confidence. In contrast to the constructive vote of no confidence enshrined, e.g., in the German or the Spanish constitutions, the Bulgarian Constitution provides for a vote

66. According to Georgi Bliznashki, the vote of confidence is 'counter-offensive technique' aiming at 'anticipating political offensives of the opposition', 'checking whether there is coincidence between the views of the government and the Parliament on the accomplished policy' and 'mobilizing support for unpopular measures'. *See* Georgi Bliznashki, *Parliamentary Law*, 385 ('St. Kliment Ohridski' University Press, 2015).

of no confidence by virtue of which the National Assembly may remove the Council of Ministers from power without the need to elect its successor immediately. Only after the vote of no confidence is successful, the Parliament can start the procedure for the election of a new government.

*506.* The 1991 Constitution provides only for collective vote of no confidence but not for individual vote of no confidence. Hence the National Assembly may remove only the whole government from power but cannot terminate the office of a single Minister. Naturally, the Minister may be politically forced to resign or the Prime Minister can demand his or her resignation. However, the Parliament is not in possession of any legal devices by virtue of which it can compulsorily remove a single Minister from power.

*507.* The vote of no confidence can be initiated by one-fifth of the MPs by virtue of a reasoned motion introduced in the Parliament via the Chairman of the National Assembly. The debates on the motion for vote of no confidence can be accomplished between three and seven days after its introduction. This period is supposed to allow the government to avoid surprises and to be able to mobilize the support of the parliamentary groups which are supporting it. The same is the role of the provision that the voting on the vote of no confidence can take place not immediately after the debates but on the day after the day on which they have been held. The vote of no confidence is successful if it is supported by an absolute majority of the votes of all MPs.[67]

*508.* The vote of no confidence can be introduced against the Prime Minister or against the Council of Ministers. It can address specific governmental policies or the general policy of the government. In all cases, the result is the compulsory resignation of the Council of Ministers as a whole.

*509.* The vote of confidence is initiated by the Council of Ministers through the introduction of the motion by the Prime Minister in the National Assembly via its Chairman. The vote of confidence may be on the general policy of the government, on sector-specific policy or on concrete governmental measure or decision that should be adopted. The vote of confidence must be discussed at the next sitting of the Parliament and must be voted immediately at the same sitting. It is approved if a majority of the MPs who are present at that sitting vote in support of the proposal of the government. The vote of confidence could be focused on either the Prime Minister or the whole government. In any case, if the vote of confidence is not successful because the National Assembly has voted against it, the government as a whole must resign. Hence even the non-approval of the vote of confidence on concrete measure, on the policies of a distinct Minister or in the person of the Prime Minister leads to the preterm dismissal from power of the government as a whole.

67. Georgi Bliznashki stipulates that the procedures for vote of non-confidence and vote of confidence are structured in accordance with the 'rationalised parliamentarism' due to the fact that the procedural hurdles (the so-called cooling periods included) aim at stabilizing the government. *See* Georgi Bliznashki, *supra* n. 66, 382 et seq.

*D. Parliamentary Control on EU Issues*

*510.* The parliamentary control of the Bulgarian government on EU issues is constitutionally enshrined in Article 105, paragraphs 3 and 4 of the Constitution. These constitutional provisions have been introduced in 2005 in the course of the preparation of the Bulgarian membership in the EU. According to Article 105, paragraph 3 of the Constitution, the Council of Ministers informs the National Assembly on issues related to the obligations of the Republic of Bulgaria stemming out of its EU membership. Furthermore, pertaining to Article 105, paragraph 4 of the Constitution when participating in the elaboration and the adoption of EU acts, the Council of Ministers must inform in advance and also must give subsequent report of its activity to the National Assembly.

*511.* These obligations of the Bulgarian government are further developed in the Regulation for the Organization and the Activity of the National Assembly. Thus the Council of Ministers is obliged to regularly inform the National Assembly on important EU-related issues and on its participation in the legislative and other decision-making processes in the EU. In addition, the Council of Ministers must introduce at the beginning of each six months' period framing the presidency of the Council of the EU reports on the participation of the Republic of Bulgaria during the previous presidency and the Bulgarian priorities during the forthcoming presidency.

*512.* There are three main institutions which accomplish parliamentary control over the EU-related activity of the Council of Ministers and which are engaged in the observation of the principles of subsidiarity and proportionality. These are the Plenum of the National Assembly, the specialized standing parliamentary committee on EU issues and control over the EU funds and the other standing parliamentary committees in accordance with their specific competence.

*513.* The main object of the control are the activities of the Council of Ministers, the Prime Minister and the Ministers related to the adoption of EU law and the elaboration and the implementation of EU-related policy. However, the Regulation for the Organization and the Activity of the National Assembly provides also for competences related to the control for the observation of the principles of subsidiarity and proportionality, the participation in the mechanisms for evaluation of the implementation of the EU policies in the area of freedom, security and justice, and the engagement in the control over the Europol and the evaluation of the activity of Eurojust. Last but not least, the National Assembly accomplishes direct or indirect parliamentary control in the course of its participation in different other EU-related procedures, e g. in the inter-parliamentary cooperation between the Parliaments of the EU Member States or in the course of ratification of EU accession treaties or treaties for amendment of the primary EU law.

*514.* The Plenum of the National Assembly discusses the annual programme for the participation of the Republic of Bulgaria in the decision-making process in the EU which is introduced in the Parliament by the Council of Ministers within seven days after its adoption. On the basis of this programme as well as on the annual working programme of the European Commission, the National Assembly adopts the annual working programme of the Bulgarian Parliament related to EU issues.

*515.* The Council of Ministers is obliged to introduce in the National Assembly its framework position on the different draft EU legislative acts and to inform the Parliament on all changes in the initial Bulgarian position on them. The National Assembly may accomplish hearings of the Prime Minister regarding the Bulgarian position in the forthcoming meetings of the European Council.

*516.* The standing parliamentary committee on EU issues and control over the EU funds has several important competences related to the parliamentary control on EU issues. It is the central forum for elaboration and discussion of the parliamentary positions and acts related to the parliamentary involvement in the participation of Bulgaria in the decision-making processes of the EU. The standing parliamentary committee on EU issues and control over the EU funds discusses the draft legislative acts of the EU institutions and the framework positions on them. It adopts reports on them which then it presents to the Plenum of the National Assembly.

*517.* The standing parliamentary committee on EU issues and control over the EU funds accomplishes hearings of the Bulgarian candidates for different positions in the EU institutions. It has a central role in the procedures for control for observation of the principles of subsidiarity and proportionality accomplished by the National Assembly. Last but not least, the standing parliamentary committee on EU issues and control over the EU funds can impose parliamentary reserve on the Draft Legislative Act of the EU. The parliamentary reserve can be imposed on its own initiative or on a proposal of other standing parliamentary committees. In that case, the Bulgarian government is obliged not to express any view and to make no statements on that act until the pronouncement of the National Assembly.

*518.* The standing parliamentary committees support the National Assembly in the parliamentary control on EU issues and in the preparation of its annual programme related to the EU issues. They review draft legislative acts of the EU institutions with a view to the principles of subsidiarity and proportionality and can propose the imposition of parliamentary reserve to the standing parliamentary committee on EU issues and control over the EU funds, as already mentioned.

### *E. Parliamentary Control on Financial and Budgetary Issues*

*519.* Neither the 1991 Constitution nor the Regulation for the Organization and the Activity of the National Assembly provide for specific instruments for parliamentary control on financial and budgetary issues. That is why this type of control is accomplished either as part of the general procedures and via the general instruments for parliamentary control (e.g., the questions, interpellations, parliamentary debates following interpellations, hearings, enquiry committees and – as a last resort – the vote of no confidence) or in the framework of the budgetary procedure and the legislative procedures for adoption of tax and financial acts of Parliament. Usually the most important and intense parliamentary control on financial issues is performed as part of the procedures for adoption of the state budget, for adoption of the parliamentary decision for approval of the implementation of the state budget by the government and for ratification of financial loans.

*520.* Typically, the main institutions which accomplish the parliamentary control on financial and budgetary issues are the Plenum of the National Assembly and the finance and budgetary standing committee. The single MPs and the parliamentary groups can serve as initiators of different forms of parliamentary control in that domain. The standing parliamentary committee on EU issues and control over the EU funds has controlling competences which are focused on the implementation and management of the EU funds by the Bulgarian institutions and other actors disposing of EU finances.

## III. Budgetary and Financial Competences

*521.* The National Assembly is one of the most important participants in financial power. It has budgetary and financial functions which consist in the competence of the Parliament to discuss, amend and adopt the state budget, to adopt a decision for approval or rejection of the report for implementation of the annual budget by the government, to adopt the type and the amount of the state taxes and to set the type and the quantity framework for the local taxes.

*522.* The competence of the National Assembly to adopt the structure of the State Budget Act is part of its competences related to the legislative power. This is because the Structure of the State Budget Act determines the structure, the scope and the main principles that should be applied to all annual budgets which have to be adopted in the future. Thus it sets the legislative framework on which basis the annual budgets must be adopted.

*523.* Similar to many other constitutional systems, the budgetary process in Bulgaria has four main phases. These are the initiation phase, the adoption phase, the implementation phase and the report and controlling phase. These phases are logically interrelated. Although they are temporarily delimited and ordered in the just-described consecutive timely manner they may be also be partially overlapping. Thus the National Assembly can always accomplish control over the implementation of the state budget not only *ex post* with the decision for dismissing the government from responsibility for its execution but also *ex ante* in the course of the debates for the adoption of the annual budget as well as during the process of its implementation throughout the year. In addition, amendments to the annual state budget can be proposed not only in the framework of the procedure for its adoption but also during the year.

*524.* The Council of Ministers is the only institution which can propose the draft annual budget. Thus it enjoys monopoly over the agenda-setting function in the budgetary process in difference to the legislative process where also the MPs can propose draft acts of Parliament. The monopolization of the budgetary initiative by the government is justified by several reasons. The government is the most informed institution regarding the financial needs of the different policy fields and institutions funded by the state budget. Moreover, the state budget is one of the most important tools for accomplishment of the general and sectoral state policies implemented by the government. Last but not least, the concentration of the budgetary initiative in the Council of Ministers allows for the proposition of well-structured, coherent and coordinated draft budget. It does not prevent the MPs from proposing amendments to the governmental draft budget but serves as a framework and basis for their discussion.

*525.* The Minister of Finance is the initial agenda setter since it is the institution which proposes the draft annual budget to the Council of Ministers. However, the draft budged prepared by the Minister of Finance is based on the proposals of the other Ministers for the suggested revenues and spending in the departments which are governed by them. In addition, it is the government as a collegial institution which approves the draft budget and has the competence to introduce it in the Parliament.

*526.* The adoption of the state budget is the competence of the National Assembly. The whole adoption of the state budget phase is accomplished in the Parliament – either in its plenary or in its standing committees. Indeed the budgetary committee has a leading role here, but the other standing parliamentary committees are also competent to discuss the draft state budget with regard to the proposed amount and structure of the revenues and expenditures in their policy domain.

*527.* The draft budget is adopted in two parliamentary readings. The discussion and voting in the plenary of the National Assembly is preceded by the discussions and voting in its standing committees and especially in the standing committee on budget and finance.

*528.* After the Council of Ministers introduces the draft state budget in the National Assembly, it is registered in a public register. Then it is distributed by the Chairman of the National Assembly to the standing committee on budget and finance which becomes the leading committee as well as to the other parliamentary committees.

*529.* The standing committee on budget and finance discusses the draft budget and prepares a report. In this report, the standing committee on budget and finance includes its assessments and comments on the draft state budget as well as the proposed amendments in the draft budget suggested by it and by all other standing committees of the Parliament. Then the draft budget is discussed and voted on the first reading in the plenary of the National Assembly.

*530.* The first reading is devoted to the analysis of the general philosophy, logic, structure and outlook of the draft state budget. The MPs discuss the effects of the draft budget on macro and meso levels, on the financial stability, on the state deficit and the state debt and on the influence of the proposed structure of the revenues and expenditures on the strategical development of the different spheres of social governance.

*531.* If the draft state budget is adopted on first reading and thus its general structure and philosophy is approved, then it is referred back to the standing committees and especially to the standing committee on budget and finance. This is the phase of the second reading in the parliamentary committees when the parliamentary committees discuss the details of the state budget. It ends with the introduction of the draft state budget for second plenary reading together with the report of the standing committee on budget and finance. During the second reading, the MPs discuss and vote on the details of the draft state budget.

*532.* The state budget that is adopted by the National Assembly is sent to the President for promulgation and publication in SG. Formally, the President can either promulgate and publish the annual budget or can impose a suspensive veto and return it for reconsideration in the Parliament.

*533.* Until now, only one President – Rosen Plevneliev – made use of his competence to veto the annual State Budget Act. There has been a discussion whether the President has that competence. Indeed the state budget is adopted in the form of act of Parliament and the 1991 Constitution grants the competence to the President to impose veto on all acts of Parliament except the acts of the Parliament for amendment of the Constitution. However, arguments have been raised that by vetoing the budget the President gets involved in the management of the public finance which is incompatible with presidential immunity.

*534.* It is evident from the above analysis that the annual state budget is adopted by the same procedure as the procedure for the adoption of the acts of the Parliament. There are just two deviations from it – the monopoly of the government over the budgetary initiative and the central role of the standing committee for budget and finance. Moreover, the annual state budget is adopted in the form of act of Parliament. Hence the budgetary procedure can be tackled as modification of the legislative procedure while taking into account its functional and procedural specifics.

*535.* The National Assembly does not have any competences in the implementation phase of the budgetary cycle apart from the fact that the Parliament itself is a budgetary institution and has to implement its own budget.

*536.* Similar to the adoption of the state budget's phase, the National Assembly is both a key player and forum for development of the controlling phase of the budgetary cycle. The Council of Ministers introduces in the National Assembly its annual report for the implementation of the state budget. This report is based on the reports of the different budgetary institutions presented earlier to the government.

The MPs discuss the governmental report and adopt a decision for its approval or rejection. Until now, all Bulgarian National Assemblies since 1991 have approved the implementation of the state budget and thus have dismissed the government from political responsibility. Otherwise, according to the unwritten logic and rules of parliamentarism, the government should resign.

*537.* The National Assembly adopts the type and the amount of the state taxes and sets the type and the framework for the local taxes. The competence to adopt the state and the local taxes is a crossing point between the legislative and the financial–budgetary competences of the Parliament. This is because the determination of the type and the amount of the state taxes is accomplished by the Parliament via acts of Parliament. These are either the acts of the Parliament devoted to the different state taxes, e.g., the VAT Act, the Taxes on the Incomes of the Natural Persons Act etc. or the annual State Budget Act. However, the results of this legislative activity concern the financial power.

*538.* In 2007, a constitutional reform has been introduced concerning the granting of some tax autonomy for the municipalities. As a result of that reform the municipal councils are now competent to determine the local taxes. However, they may do so only under the conditions, in the framework and following a procedure adopted by act of Parliament. Hence the National Assembly is still capable of predetermining and limiting to a great extent the tax autonomy of the local self-government institutions. Thus the financial power remains largely concentrated on the national level and more precisely in the National Assembly, the Council of Ministers and the Minister of Finance.

## IV. Constitutive Competences

*539.* The National Assembly has an extensive patronage power consisting in its competence to appoint and dismiss the office holders of some of the most important state institutions. The positive patronage power of the Parliament consists in its competence to appoint and its negative patronage power in its competence to dismiss office holders. The patronage power of the Parliament is not always concentrated in it. In many cases, the National Assembly participates in schemes for separation of the patronage power with other state institutions.

*540.* The National Assembly has both the positive and the negative patronage powers with a view to the Council of Ministers. Actually it is the only institution which can elect and dismiss the Bulgarian government. The only exception is the caretaker government which is appointed and can be reorganized and dismissed by the President in case of parliamentary crisis and preterm elections for National Assembly. The positive patronage power of the National Assembly towards the Council of Ministers is accomplished via collective vote of investiture whereas its negative patronage power is effectuated via collective vote of no confidence. Hence the National Assembly cannot dismiss distinct Ministers but only the government as a whole. Moreover, it does not possess any patronage power towards the members of the cabinets of the Ministers and the Deputy Ministers. They are appointed and dismissed by the Prime Minister.

*541.* The structure of the patronage power of the National Assembly towards the Council of Ministers is predetermined by the parliamentary form of government. The lack of the contrary competence of the government to dissolve the Parliament is a deviation from the classical principles of parliamentarism. The 1991 Constitution does not provide for the competence of either the Council of Ministers or the President to dissolve the Parliament.

*542.* Another departure from the traditional institutional design of parliamentarism provided by the 1991 Constitution is the lack of patronage power of the Parliament towards the President. The Bulgarian President in contrast to the heads of state of the classical parliamentary republics is elected not by the Parliament or with the participation of the Parliament but directly by the people.

*543.* The National Assembly has full positive patronage power also towards other important state institutions. The Parliament is competent to elect the ombudsman and the Court of Auditors. Thus the National Assembly invests its democratic legitimacy as a directly elected institution for parliamentary control in these important institutions for extra-parliamentary control which themselves do not have input democratic legitimacy. Consequently, the National Assembly is in possession of the positive patronage power towards some of the key institutions for control regarding the observation of human rights and the proper management of the public finances in Bulgaria. The Parliament is deliberately deprived by the Constitution from any negative patronage power towards the ombudsman and the Court of Auditors with a view to assure the necessary degree of institutional autonomy which is needed for the proper functioning of these institutions for public control.

*544.* The National Assembly has quotas in different important state institutions. It elects parts of the members of several key collective institutions and thus participates in schemes for separation of the patronage power. The National Assembly elects one-third of the Constitutional Court's judges, members of the Electronic Media Council and the governing board of the Bulgarian National Bank as well as members in several 'next step' state agencies.

*545.* It has to be mentioned that the Parliament can only elect the office holders, but it is not allowed to influence their behaviour. Hence one can define these qualified parts of the collective institutions elected by the Parliament as 'quotas' only in the metaphorical sense. Moreover, the National Assembly does not possess negative patronage power towards the already-elected members of these institutions in order to safeguard their institutional independence.

## §5. Legal and Political Acts

*546.* The National Assembly adopts legal and political acts. The legal acts can be normative thus being a source of law and individual. The National Assembly can adopt three types of normative acts: constitutional acts of Parliament, (ordinary) acts of Parliament and the Regulation for the Organization and Activity of the Parliament.

*547.* The constitutional acts of Parliament are acts of Parliament for the amendment of the Constitution. Formally, they do not differ from the acts of the Parliament. They do not have either special title and name or specific structure. The constitutional acts of Parliament differ from the other acts of Parliament which regulate constitutional subject matter in two main aspects. First, they are adopted via special legislative procedure. The legislative initiative for constitutional acts of Parliament does not belong to the Council of Ministers and to the single MPs but to the President and to a qualified minority of one-fourth of the MPs. Moreover, the constitutional acts of Parliament are adopted not on two but on three readings. Last but not least, they are promulgated by the Chairman of the National Assembly, and the President cannot impose a veto on them. Second, the constitutional acts of Parliament do not have independent existence. Once adopted they become an integral part of the text of the Constitution.

*548.* The acts of the Parliament are the most important type of sources of law in Bulgaria. Some of the acts of the Parliament, e.g., the acts of the Parliament for ratification of international treaties and the act of the Parliament for the adoption of the annual state budget, have formal character.[68] The acts of the Parliament for ratification of international treaties are formal because they have a single article stipulating that the Republic of Bulgaria has ratified the international treaty at stake. The formality of the ratification act is a result of the use of the monist system for implementation of the international treaties in the Bulgarian legal order. The act of the Parliament for the adoption of the annual state budget consists in a composite financial plan from a substantial point of view. Its aim is to grant the hierarchical standing of act of Parliament to the state budget and to allow for a thorough preventive parliamentary control accomplished in two readings.

*549.* The Regulation for the Organization and Activity of the National Assembly is formally adopted via parliamentary decision. The decisions of the National Assembly are individual legal acts. However, the Regulation for the Organization and Activity of the Parliament is structured as a normative act. Moreover, it is an act with an extremely important normativity. It is a normative act not only because it is textually structured in provisions set as legal norms but also due to the fact that it establishes the framework for the functioning of the Parliament as well as for the accomplishment of some of the most important decision-making processes in the state. Last but not least, the Constitutional Court by virtue of Decision No. 7 of 2010

68. *See* Rosen Tashev, *supra* n. 27, 59–60.

has granted to the Regulation for the Organization and Activity of the Parliament the formal standing of an act of Parliament.

*550.* The decisions of the National Assembly, as it has just been explained, are individual legal acts. They serve as the legal form and the legal instrument for accomplishment of the non-legislative functions of the Parliament. Thus the National Assembly accomplishes its constitutive function for election of state institutions or parts of them by virtue of decisions. The most important forms of parliamentary control such as the vote of confidence and the vote of no confidence end up with and take the shape of parliamentary decision. The National Assembly adopts a decision for approval of the accomplishment of the state budget by the Council of Ministers.

*551.* The political acts of the National Assembly are the declarations and the addresses. By virtue of these acts, the Parliament participates in forms of political communication. The Constitution and the Regulation for the Organization and Activity of the National Assembly do not make a concrete distinction between these two types of political acts. Thus a dogmatic distinction can be made. The National Assembly via declarations takes a stance on issues of national importance and forms the public opinion on the issue at stake. On the contrary, the Parliament expresses its opinion on issues related to the inter-institutional dynamics by virtue of addresses to other state institutions.

# Chapter 4. The Government

## §1. General Structure of the Executive Power

*552.* The executive power in the contemporary Bulgarian constitutional model is structured in three layers. The first layer is the government (the Council of Ministers), the second layer is the 'next step agencies' (state agencies and state committees) and the third layer is the state administration.

*553.* The first and supreme layer of the executive power is the Council of Ministers which is the Bulgarian government. The Council of Ministers defines the strategic guidelines of policymaking[69] for all executive power institutions and indirectly also for the state as a whole. It has both formal and substantial supremacy in the power pyramid of the executive power.

*554.* According to the classical Westminster or Weberian ideal model of the executive power, the Council of Ministers must be party political institution. The necessary party political affiliation of the government is the typical and most important way for provision of democratic and parliamentary control. The people cannot accomplish any arbitration between the political elites and cannot influence the governmental policy[70] if the government is not elected and structured on party political basis. No functional and genetic relation between the Parliament and the government[71] and thus no parliamentary control is possible without a party government. The 1991 Constitution establishes a hybrid parliamentary system thus paving the way to the establishment of party democracy. Following the systemic logic of representative parliamentary party democracy, the Bulgarian Councils of Ministers are all party governments with the only exception of caretaker governments.

*555.* The state administration is the basis of the executive power hierarchy. According to Article 116 of the Constitution, the civil servants must be party politically neutral. They must implement their duties impartially without taking into account any party political argumentation. Moreover, the Civil Servants Act prohibits the party political membership of the civil servants.

*556.* Another aspect of the general structure of the executive power concerns its territorial dimension. The 1991 Constitution provides for unitary state with local self-government. Hence there are two main territorial levels of the executive power in Bulgaria – national and municipal, whereas the regional level has supplementary functions and is of secondary importance. The above-mentioned executive power

69. According to Georgi Bliznashki, the government has two main functions – political function (guidance for policymaking) and executive functions (accomplishment of the general policy of the state). *See* Georgi Bliznashki, *The Parliamentary Government in Bulgaria*, 83 ('St. Kliment Ohridski' University Press, 2009) (in Bulgarian),

70. For this political arbitration role of the people in a representative democracy, *see* Robert Dahl, *Democracy in the United States: Promise and Performance* (Chicago, 1972).

71. For the genetic and functional relationship between the Parliament and the government in the parliamentary form of governance *see* Vasil Kirov, *supra* n. 4, 187.

institutions – the Council of Ministers, the Prime Minister, the Ministers, the state agencies and the state committees – are allocated on national level. The different types of mayors – the municipal mayors, the rayon's mayors and the mayorship's mayors – are the most important executive power institutions on local level. The regional governor is the key institution on regional level. Many of the national administrative bodies and agencies governing different policy fields have also regional and local branches.

## §2. Constitutional Status and Structure of the Council of Ministers

*557.* The Council of Ministers is among the national institutions with a constitutional status. There is a separate Chapter V devoted to it although many important constitutional provisions related to the Council of Ministers are spread throughout other parts of the Constitution. The Council of Ministers is a constitutional institution with central importance for policymaking. Thus the Council of Ministers is among the key political constitutional institutions together with the National Assembly and the President of the Republic.

*558.* The Council of Ministers has rather simple internal structure and organization. Its composition includes three compulsory institutions: the Prime Minister, one or more Deputy Prime Ministers and Ministers. No other state institution can be part of the Council of Ministers. This can be neither the President of the Republic nor any high-ranking official, parliamentary secretary, civil servant or administrator. The Vice Ministers are also not part of the Council of Ministers. They are members of the cabinet of each of the Ministers.

*559.* Typically, each Minister covers one governmental branch, e.g., defence, finance, education etc. However, several Bulgarian governments have had also Ministers without portfolio. Usually, the Ministers without portfolio exist due to coalition-building reasons. Ministers without portfolio may be elected also in order to accomplish functional tasks, cross-cutting different branches of government.

*560.* Although the Ministers have tasks which are concentrated on a specific branch of policymaking, these branches are not enshrined in the Constitution itself. Thus they are vulnerable to extensive change leading to merger of several fields of governance in one ministry or vice versa – to separation of previously existing branches into several distinct ministries.

*561.* There is internal hierarchy in the organization and the functioning of the Council of Ministers. The Prime Minister is on top of the hierarchical pyramid of the government. He or she is followed by the Deputy Prime Ministers. The Ministers are at the bottom of the governmental pyramid. This hierarchy can be well analysed and exposed with a view to the principles for the organization and activity of the Council of Ministers. Both the internal governmental hierarchy and the principles for the organization and activity of the Council of Ministers are not explicitly proclaimed by the Constitution. However, they can be extracted from the constitutional text via systematic interpretation. It should be noted that apart from the distinction among Prime Minister, Deputy Prime Ministers and Ministers, there is no formal hierarchy among the Ministers, e.g., there are no senior or junior Ministers.

*562.* The Prime Ministerial principle consists in the leading role of the Bulgarian Prime Ministers. The constitutional factors for the strength of the Prime Ministerial principle comprise the constitutional status and powers of the Prime Minister allowing him or her to be an effective leader of the Council of Ministers and not just *primus inter pares.*[72] The most important competences of the Prime Minister include the power to set the guidelines and to determine the principles and the framework of the strategy of the Council of Ministers in the internal and external policy of the state. According to Article 108, paragraph 2 of the Constitution, the Prime Minister not only coordinates but also guides the general policy of the government. Moreover, he or she bears the political responsibility for it due to the fact that the government may be forced to resign not only due to vote of no confidence in the Council of Ministers as a whole but also due to the Prime Minister.

*563.* Seemingly, the 1991 Constitution imposes certain limitations to the Prime Ministerial principle. The Bulgarian Prime Minister is the leader of the government and usually also leader of the largest parliamentary represented political party. However, he or she is not a formal leader of the parliamentary majority due to the constitutionally proclaimed incompatibility of the ministerial and MP positions. Moreover, the Prime Minister has some limitations to his or her patronage power. The most important one is that the Prime Minister cannot appoint or dismiss the Ministers without the previous explicit consent of the National Assembly due to the principle of collective investiture. The Prime Minister can appoint and dismiss only the Vice Ministers, which is a bit problematic because it limits the personal discretion of the Ministers over the officials with which they will have to work with.

*564.* These institutional restrictions do not function as real impediments to the leadership position of the Prime Ministers from a sociolegal point of view. Typically, the Bulgarian Prime Ministers are leaders of the largest and most influential political party which wins the parliamentary elections. Most of the Bulgarian parties are in fact leadership parties which additionally reinforce the status of the Prime Minister. He or she is typically in a position to control his or her own parliamentary majority and thus to rely on its steady support for both the policy strategies that have to be approved by the Parliament and for the structural or personal reorganizations in the Council of Ministers. The National Assembly has never disapproved the appointment or dismissal of the Minister proposed by the Prime Minister.

---

72. For this status of the Prime Minister, *see* Giovanni Sartori, *Comparative Constitutional Engineering*, 102–103 (New York University Press, 1994). For the contrary opinion *see* Georgi Bliznashki, *Parliamentary Law*, 127 ('St. Kliment Ohridski' University Press, 2015), who believes that the Prime Minister according to the 1991 Constitution is *primus inter pares*.

*565.* The collegial principle determines the strength of the status of the Council of Ministers as collective and collegial body in comparison to the Prime Minister and the separate Ministers. There are three main indicators for the strength of this principle – the competences attributed by the Constitution to the government as a collegial body, the competences of the government to approve and in case of disagreement, to resist the proposals of the Prime Minister and the Ministers and the capability of the government to be collectively, politically responsible for its activity as well as for the activity of its members.

*566.* The Council of Ministers has several very important competences which it accomplishes as a collegial body. The Council of Ministers (and not the Prime Minister or the distinct Ministers) can: introduce draft acts of Parliament to the National Assembly, adopt the most important by-laws, propose the annual state budget, approach the Constitutional Court, appoint and dismiss the regional governors as well as some other important office holders (especially members of state agencies and state commissions), propose the accomplishment of national referendum, manage the state property etc.

*567.* According to Article 107 of the Constitution, the Council of Ministers can abolish the illegal or incorrect normative and individual legal acts of the Ministers. Hence the government does not only accomplish administrative control for legality of the ministerial acts; it can also abolish valid and lawful acts which may even provide for reasonable policies only on the ground that they are not in compliance with the general policy of the Council of Ministers.

*568.* This posterior control aside, the Council of Ministers accomplishes also prior control over the policy initiatives and draft proposals of the Ministers that need to get the form of governmental proposal or decision (e.g., draft act of Parliament). All such initiatives and proposals must first be previously discussed and approved by the Council of Ministers. Moreover, all sector policies accomplished by the Ministers and the administration have to be in full compliance with the governmental priorities and strategy.

*569.* Last but not least, the political destiny of the Ministers is fully dependent on the political destiny of both the Prime Minister and the Council of Ministers. Successful vote of no confidence or failed vote of confidence in the government leads to immediate resignation of all Ministers.

*570.* The ministerial principle consists in the predominant position of the Ministers in the sphere of government they head. The Ministers are on top of the sector hierarchy of the respective governmental domain. They can set the policy guidelines and determine the strategy of their political cabinet and administration. The Ministers may adopt normative acts that determine the legal background for the accomplishment of sector policies. They possess also patronage power over some parts of the administration as well as the members of their political cabinet with the exception of the Vice Ministers. The Ministers can abolish legal acts of the office holders which have subordinate positions in the power hierarchy of the respective policy domain.

*571.* Consequently, the Prime Ministerial principle prevails over the collegial principle and the collegial principle over the ministerial principle in the contemporary Bulgarian constitutional model. This hierarchy is additionally reinforced in the political practice in comparison to the normative model.

## §3. Election and Dismissal of the Government

*572.* The procedure for election and dismissal of the Council of Ministers is predetermined by the parliamentary form of government provided by the 1991 Bulgarian Constitution. In that regard, the 1991 Constitution follows the mainstream solutions offered by the parliamentary constitutions in Europe. In brief, the 1991 Constitution provides for election and dismissal procedures with decisive and almost exclusive role of the Parliament structured around collective investiture, collective vote of no confidence and collective vote of confidence.

*573.* The general aim of both the procedures for election and dismissal of the government is to keep the National Assembly in general and the parliamentary majority in particular the guardian of the destiny of the government thus allowing both *ex post* and *ex ante* parliamentary dependence of the Council of Ministers. In practice, the logic of dependence is reversed – it is the parliamentary majority and thus to certain extent also the Parliament which is dependent on the Council of Ministers and the Prime Minister. This power constellation is typical for the systems with majoritarian parliamentarism especially the South European systems.

*574.* The comparative historical analysis demonstrates that such system of enhanced patronage power of the Parliament over the government may lead to either the establishment of durable and reliable parliamentary control fostering the parliamentary democracy or domination of the will of the oligarchical elites concentrated in and around the Parliament over the government. The disadvantages of the latter situation have been demonstrated by the Third French Republic, the Weimar Republic in Germany and in some periods of the Italian constitutional history. However, in the Bulgarian context, the government is neither sufficiently well controlled by the Parliament nor a hostage of the parliamentary oligarchy. Usually the Prime Minister is also the leader of the largest parliamentary represented political party thus controlling also the parliamentary majority.

*575.* The procedures for election and dismissal of the Council of Ministers seem to be effective and to function well in the contemporary Bulgarian constitutionalism. They are not factors for governmental and parliamentary instability. On the contrary, they are functional devices that contribute for the sufficiently swift election or (in theory) the dismissal of a new government.

*576.* The governmental election procedure has been inspired predominantly by the 1975 Greek Constitution. The Bulgarian government has parliamentary provenance based on collective and explicit vote of investiture. The role of the head of state is nominal until the eventual last (third) attempt for election of government whereas the key actors in the procedure are the National Assembly in general and the parliamentary groups in particular.

*577.* The procedure for election of Council of Ministers includes the activity of the National Assembly, the President of the Republic, the parliamentary groups and the nominees for Prime Minister. It has two phases – pre-parliamentary and parliamentary phases.

*578.* In the pre-parliamentary phase, the President of the Republic, after consultation with the parliamentary groups, assigns to the largest parliamentary group a mandate for forming a government. This group has seven days upon assignment to present to the President of the Republic a proposal for Prime Minister and Ministers as well as for the structure of the government encompassing the number of Ministers and their departments. The first attempt will be unsuccessful if the parliamentary group cannot make a proposal for the structure and personal staff of the government or if its proposal is rejected by the National Assembly. If the proposal for Council of Ministers is approved by the Parliament, then this is the successful end of the procedure.

*579.* In the former case, when the first attempt is not successful, there are two additional attempts (or eventual rounds) for forming the government. They follow the same logic and procedure as the first attempt. If the first two attempts at forming the government have failed, then during the third attempt, the President of the Republic has the discretion to choose to assign the mandate to one of the remaining parliamentary groups.

*580.* In other words, in the first two attempts the President of the Republic is obliged to assign the government formation mandate to the first and then to the second largest parliamentary group. On the contrary, during the third attempt the head of state is obliged not to give the mandate again to the first or the second largest parliamentary group. In fact, the President of the Republic has a choice only if there are more than three parliamentary groups. The impact of the presidential discretionary choice increases if the Parliament is fragmented into many parliamentary groups which are not extremely hostile to each other and might be akin at forming a coalition government.

*581.* In general, the President of the Republic has no discretionary power in the procedure of forming and electing a government. Thus usually his or her influence on that procedure is rather nominal. This general logic aside, the President of the Republic has two types of discretionary powers by virtue of which he or she can influence the procedure.

*582.* First, the President of the Republic, as already mentioned, can choose to which parliamentary group to assign the mandate in the third attempt for forming a government. Thus he or she can serve as a mediator for forming a coalition government or eventually but very unlikely, a minority government. Hence the nominal role of the President of the Republic actually may turn to be real and active in the third round by producing a coalition government. Clear example of such presidential activity is the key role that the President Georgi Parvanov played in forming the so-called triple coalition in 2005.

*583.* Second, the President of the Republic has some discretion regarding the timing. The 1991 Constitution provides for a term of seven days for presenting a proposal for new government by the nominee for Prime Minister launched by the respective parliamentary group. This term commences with the assignment of the mandate by the head of state. However, the Constitution does not provide for a specific term during which the President of the Republic should accomplish the preceding consultations with the parliamentary groups.

*584.* Moreover, there is also no explicit and fixed term for the dissolution of the National Assembly and appointment of caretaker government in case the third attempt for forming a government has also been unsuccessful. Usually the Bulgarian Presidents are rather fast in starting the emergency procedure leading to preterm parliamentary elections with the exception of President Plevneliev who had postponed the procedure for a longer period of time.

*585.* The parliamentary phase of the government election process commences with the proposal that the President of the Republic makes to the National Assembly for election of Council of Ministers. It is clear that the pre-parliamentary and parliamentary phases are not monolithic and isolated from each other. They are ordered as consecutive elements in the procedure, and they follow one after the other. Thus if the Parliament is incapable of electing a government during all three attempts, there might be three pre-parliamentary and three parliamentary phases followed by an extraordinary post-parliamentary phase resulting in the appointment of a caretaker government by the President and scheduling preterm parliamentary elections after the dissolution of the National Assembly.

*586.* The 1991 Constitution provides for explicit collective investiture meaning that the National Assembly must approve by explicit and formal voting not only the Prime Minister but also the Council of Ministers as a whole. In both cases, absolute majority of more than half of all MPs is required. In addition, there are two separate votes for two separate decisions – the first for the election of the Prime Minister and the second one for the election of the government. According to Decision No. 20 of 1992 the Constitutional Court, in case the Prime Minister is elected but the Parliament rejects the proposal for structure and personal composition of the government, the whole procedure is not successful. Such situation emerged in 2005 when during the first attempt at forming the government the National Assembly elected Sergey Stanishev as Prime Minister but rejected his proposal for Council of Ministers.

*587.* The Council of Ministers is elected immediately as of the second vote in the Parliament – the vote on the decision approving the structure and the composition of the government. The newly elected government does not need to get appointed by the President of the Republic. This is another example of the desire of the constitutional legislator to limit as much as possible the influence of the head of state on the government-formation process. The President of the Republic does not have any real and substantial positive patronage power over the government. He or she can serve only as a facilitator, broker and eventually as power reserve leading the state out of a governmental crisis that has turned itself into parliamentary crisis. The President of the Republic is deprived of the symbolic function to appoint the government after it is elected by the Parliament.

*588.* There are several grounds for preterm termination of the term of office of the Council of Ministers. These are the death of the Prime Minister, the resignation of the Prime Minister or the government, the successful vote of no confidence in the Prime Minister or the government or the unsuccessful vote of confidence in the Prime Minister or the government. It is clear that the destiny of the government is neatly bound to the destiny of the Prime Minister. The death, the resignation, or the formal expression of no confidence in the Prime Minister automatically leads to the dismissal of the Council of Ministers.

*589.* On the contrary, the preterm termination of the office of individual Ministers does not produce any legal effect on the office of the Prime Minister or the government. The Ministers are dependent on the Prime Minister and not on the National Assembly for their stay in office. This is because there is no individual vote of no confidence by virtue of which the Parliament can remove from power particular Ministers against the will of the Prime Minister. Moreover, the resignation of key Ministers has never led the political practice to preterm termination of the governmental mandate.

*590.* The dismissal procedure of the government is organized as collective vote of no confidence. The 1991 Constitution provides for the classical version of the vote of no confidence according to which the government should first be dismissed and only then the procedure for election of a new government commences. Hence the Bulgarian constitutional legislator did not opt for constructive vote of no confidence which exists, e.g., in Germany and Spain.

*591.* Only the collective vote of no confidence is available. This means that the National Assembly may dismiss via vote of no confidence only the government as a whole but not the distinct Ministers. Even if the vote of no confidence is directed towards the Prime Minister, it leads to preterm termination of the office not only of the head of the government but of the Council of Ministers as a whole.

*592.* The vote of no confidence can be initiated by one-fifth of the MPs and is approved only if an absolute majority of all MPs have voted in favour. This would be the case when the typical Bulgarian majority government has lost its parliamentary support turning into a minority government. There are procedural hurdles aiming at stabilization of the government in power. The vote of no confidence can be discussed not earlier than three and not later than seven days after its introduction in Parliament. It cannot be voted on the same day on which the discussion has been held, but on the next day.

*593.* As a matter of fact, no Bulgarian government during the post-communist period has been removed from power due to successful vote of no confidence. However, the reason for that is not the high procedural hurdles set by the procedure for vote of no confidence but the sociopolitical dynamics and the fact that most of the Bulgarian governments are majority governments. Hence the typical reason for the preterm termination of their office is the resignation and not the vote of no confidence. The resignation is usually triggered by public pressure and civic protests, e.g., in the Videnov, the first Borisov and the Oresharski governments. Other triggers may be some party political or other political considerations which are frequently not sufficiently public. Only one government – the second government of Boyko Borisov – has resigned considering the loss of presidential elections by the ruling party as an indicator for diminishing popular support.

*594.* One Bulgarian government has been removed from power as a consequence of an unsuccessful vote of confidence. The government of Philip Dimitrov lost the vote of confidence initiated by him in 1992 with the intent to strengthen the unity of his parliamentary group and to enhance its fragile parliamentary support. One of the main institutional reasons why Philip Dimitrov lost the vote of confidence is the fact that his Council of Ministers was a minority government which relied on the support of 110 out of 240 MPs.

*595.* The President has no role in the procedure for the dismissal of a government. He or she cannot dismiss either the Prime Minister, or single Ministers or the government. Thus the Council of Ministers is dependent only on the will of the Parliament, or in fact on the will of the parliamentary majority, for staying in power.

## §4. Functions and Competences

*596.* The Council of Ministers accomplishes the strategic policy determination of the external and internal policy of the state. It sets the general policy guidelines in cooperation with the National Assembly relying on its legislative and budgetary support as well as its support for ratification of key international treaties. The government provides the strategic leadership in the external relations and the defence in cooperation with the President of the Republic. Hence the Council of Ministers participates in inter-institutional cooperation with the other national political institutions – the Parliament and the head of state, with regard to the determination of the political strategy needed for the governance of the Republic of Bulgaria.

*597.* The Council of Ministers also sets the political and to some extent the normative framework for the strategic and most important sectoral policies accomplished by the Ministers and the state administration. The Council of Ministers adopts normative acts that determine the legal basis for the provision of sectoral policies and decisions which are legally binding for the Ministers and the administration. Moreover, it can abolish the legal acts of the Ministers. Last but not least, some of the most important policy initiatives of the Ministers, e.g., those related to the proposal of draft acts of Parliament, need the approval of the Council of Ministers.

*598.* The Council of Ministers is not only strategic policy centre and generator of key political decisions; it accomplishes also administrative functions concerning important tactical governance.[73] The Council of Ministers may adopt decisions on concrete but important issues. It provides leadership in situations of crisis management related to the internal and external defence as well as for the maintenance of public order. The Council of Ministers is responsible for maintaining public order and national security and for responding to natural disasters. It accomplishes the general governance of the state administration.

*599.* The Council of Ministers guides the implementation of the annual state budget and is responsible for the preservation and proper management of the state property. The Council of Ministers is the agenda setter and key policymaking institution in the sphere of public finance and economy. It sets the guidelines and the framework for the most important policy sectors. The 1991 Constitution provides for the welfare state principle. Hence the state has additional and extended functions in the spheres of economy, labour market, social affairs, healthcare, education and culture. The normative basis for the accomplishment of the enhanced functions of the welfare state is set by the National Assembly and the Council of Ministers. The implementation of welfare state policies is strategically guided by the government.

*600.* The intermediate conclusion is that the executive power in its diversity of social relations and manifestations is the topical centre of the functions and competences of the Council of Ministers. Indeed the government is the main holder of the executive power in Bulgaria. It is central, collective and collegial institution of the executive power. However, the Council of Ministers has competences also in the other branches of state power.

*601.* Two players that may propose the adoption of acts of Parliament are the government and every single MP. However, it is the Council of Ministers which is the main proactive veto player in the legislative power. It must be noted that it is the Council of Ministers as collegial institution, and not the Prime Minister or the Ministers, that can introduce draft acts of Parliament in the National Assembly.

73. *See* Georgi Bliznashki, *The Parliamentary Government in Bulgaria*, 83 ('St. Kliment Ohridski' University Press, *2009) (in Bulgarian).*

Indeed it is the Ministers who are the initiators of the draft acts of Parliament. However, the Ministers propose them to the Council of Ministers who then decides whether to initiate the parliamentary legislative procedure, to introduce amendments in them or to reject them.

*602*. There are several reasons for the clear predominance of the government over the MPs as initiators of draft acts of Parliament. The Council of Ministers has overwhelming organizational capacity, expert support and sectoral policy knowledge in comparison to the MPs. Moreover, it is the driving force behind the policymaking. Thus it possesses focused information and strengthened motivation for adoption of its legislative background. Last but not least, the European integration has produced executive federalism.[74] It enhances the capacity of the government to serve as a binding unit between the two-track legislative processes in the EU in the case of implementation of EU directives which comprise EU and nation state level of legislative activity.

*603*. Article 62, paragraph 1 of the 1991 Constitution ascribes the legislative function to the National Assembly. However, in the political practice, the legislative function of the state is performed predominantly by a composite power unit comprising the Council of Ministers as key legislative policy initiator and the governmental majority in the National Assembly as a factor that drives the governmental draft acts of Parliament through the parliamentary phase of the legislative process.

*604*. This does not mean that the National Assembly is just a rubber-stamping institution. The parliamentary majority may modify and in some rare cases also oppose the governmental projects. The opposition may also have a role in the parliamentary legislative process by proposing alternative legislative ideas that may have a chance to influence the final outlook of the act of Parliament. In most of the cases however, the informal power unit composed of the Council of Ministers and its parliamentary majority dominate the legislative function of the National Assembly and thus the core of the legislative power.

*605*. Moreover, the Council of Ministers and individual Ministers may adopt normative acts. Indeed they are allocated below the acts of the Parliament in the Bulgarian hierarchy of sources of law. However, they have a huge impact on the way the acts of the Parliament are further developed. Thus the governmental normative acts may influence to an important extent the legal basis of key policy domains especially if the acts of the Parliament contain not exhaustive but framework, abstract, principle and vague provisions.

*606*. Last but not least, the Ministers as members not only of the Bulgarian government but also of the Council of Ministers of the EU have key role in the legislative decision-making. They participate in the adoption of supranational normative

---

74. *See* Andreas Maurer, *Parlamentarische Demokratie in der Europäischen Union* (Nomos, 2002); and Jurgen Habermas, *On the Constitution of Europe*, 68 et seq. (Kritika i humanizam, 2011) (in Bulgarian).

acts which enjoy primacy over the acts of the National Assembly. Thus indirectly the Bulgarian government is able to frame and influence the national parliamentary legislation.

*607.* The Council of Ministers has no competence in the judicial power. Even the Minister of Justice and the Minister of Interior as institutions that in comparative and historic perspective may have a role in the administration of the courts' system and the state prosecution and investigation system accordingly have a rather limited role. The Minister of Justice chairs the sittings of the Supreme Judicial Council and has some competences regarding the property management of the judiciary and the education of the magistrates. However, the key role for the administration of the judiciary belongs to the Supreme Judicial Council. The Minister of Interior has influence over the education and the career development of the investigative police officers but not over the state prosecutors and the state investigators, which are part of the judiciary and thus fall into the jurisdiction of the Supreme Judicial Council.

*608.* The Council of Ministers directly as composite institution and indirectly via its members – the Prime Minister and the Ministers – has important functions in the external power of the state. The external power comprises the functions and competences related to the participation of the state in the international relations. The Council of Ministers possesses a huge part of the patronage power over the diplomatic positions. It elaborates and implements the strategic and the most important tactical decisions in the foreign policy. It safeguards the coherency of the Bulgarian policy in the international relations as well as in the EU.

*609.* The Prime Minister and the Ministers have an important role in representing Bulgaria in both the international relations (in front of other states and in the different international organizations) as well as in the European Council and the Council of Ministers of the EU respectively. Two Ministers have a special role in the external power. The Minister of Foreign Affairs plays a key proactive role in the symbolic, substantive and personal policy of Bulgaria with regard to the traditional international relations and to the participation of the state in the EU. A Minister of the European integration existed in the Stanishev government which ruled Bulgaria in the pre-accession period and during the first years of the EU membership. Since the EU accession of Bulgaria there is only a Minister of Foreign Affairs without a separate Minister for EU issues. However, the competence to govern the EU matters in general (e.g., the second Borisov government) or some specific EU-related issues such as the finances provided by the European funds (e.g., the caretaker governments of Marin Raykov, Georgi Bliznashki and Ognyan Gerdjikov) have been ascribed to a Deputy Prime Minister. The third Borisov government includes also a special Minister who is responsible for the Bulgarian Presidency of the EU.

*610.* The Council of Ministers and the Minister of Finance are the most important participants in the financial power together with the National Assembly, the Bulgarian National Bank and the Court of Auditors. The Minister of Finance and the Council of Ministers prepare the draft state budget, implement it after its adoption by the Parliament and give an account of its implementation in front of the National Assembly.

*611.* It has already been mentioned that the Council of Ministers has important patronage power. In some cases, the patronage power is concentrated in the Council of Ministers. An example of such concentration is the appointment and dismissal of the regional governors. In most of the cases however, the Council of Ministers participates in schemes for the sharing of patronage power. There are two such schemes. These are the consecutive and the simultaneous separation of patronage power.

*612.* The government participates in consecutive separation of the patronage power with regard to the diplomats and the high-ranking officials in the armed forces and the police. This means that the proposals for appointment or dismissal of diplomats are made by the Minister of Foreign Affairs to the Council of Ministers which then launches the proposal to the President of the Republic. The same is the scheme with high-ranking officers from the police and the army with the only difference that the initial proposal is made not by the Minister of Foreign Affairs but by either the Minister of Interior or the Minister of Defence. The Council of Ministers can reject the proposal of the Ministers.

*613.* The simultaneous separation of patronage power concerns institutions whose office holders are appointed on the basis of quotas assigned to different state institutions. The Council of Ministers has such quotas in different state agencies and commissions. Actually, these institutions could have been appointed exclusively by the government but the Bulgarian legislator granted quotas also to other state institutions – in most of the cases to the National Assembly – in order to safeguard some form of checks and balances.

## §5. Relationship Between the Government and the Subnational Institutions of the Executive Power

*614.* Bulgaria has always been a unitary state. Thus the whole system of inter-institutional relations between the Council of Ministers as the national institution of the executive power, the regional governors as institutions of the executive power in the regions and the mayors in the municipalities, districts and mayorships as institutions which combine the executive power with the local self-government is built upon the institutional logic of the unitary state.

*615.* The Council of Ministers has patronage power only over the regional governors. This is because they are institutions which are responsible for the implementation of the national policy on a regional level. The government appoints and dismisses the regional governors. However, it does not have any patronage power over the municipal mayors, the mayors of the rayons or the mayors of mayorships who are directly elected by the people. The direct election of the mayors is the reason why they can be conceived as local self-government institutions which possess executive power competences.

*616.* The same is true for the power of the Council of Ministers to determine the policy accomplished by the subnational institutions of the executive power. The Council of Ministers sets the policy guidelines via adoption of normative or individual legal acts. It massively influences the parliamentary legislation as well as the state budget. Thus it determines the legislative and financial framework and sets the general policy guidelines for the subnational institutions of the executive power. However, the Council of Ministers can directly influence the policy only of the regional governors by assigning concrete tasks to them. The government cannot intervene directly in the sphere of discretionary competences of the mayors.

*617.* The Ministers interact with the institutions for regional government and local self-government directly or via the regional or local level units which are a subordinated part of their ministerial domain. Thus apart from the general political interaction between the national and the subnational institutions for political government, there is also cooperation between the different levels of the state and local, general and specialized administrations.

## §6. Types of Governments

*618.* The 1991 Constitution provides for three institutionalized types of governments. These are the Council of Ministers, the Council of Ministers in resignation and the caretaker Council of Ministers. Both the Council of Ministers in resignation and the caretaker Council of Ministers are instruments for prevention of the interregnum. In Bulgarian legal terminology, Council of Ministers is synonymous to government so these two terms are used in parallel. Apart from these three institutionalized governmental types, one can also distinguish types of Councils of Ministers with regard to their party political composition.

*619.* The regular government is the Council of Ministers. Its structure, functions and competences have been explained in the above sections. It has to be mentioned that the other two types of government – the Council of Ministers in resignation and the caretaker Council of Ministers formally have the same competences and powers as the regular Council of Ministers. However, from a political viewpoint it is recommendable that they should refrain from taking strategic decisions due to their limited legitimacy although the adoption of such decisions is not explicitly prohibited by the Constitution.[75] Moreover, the caretaker Council of Ministers cannot accomplish these governmental competences for which a parliamentary cooperation is required due to the lack of National Assembly in the predominant part of its term of office.

75. Plamen Kirov, *supra* n. 4, 222.

*620.* The second type of government is the Council of Ministers in resignation. The regular Council of Ministers turns to be the Council of Ministers in resignation in two cases. The first case is the situation when a governmental crisis has produced the need for election of new government or for preterm elections. Such governmental crisis can be a result of: resignation of the Prime Minister or the government as a whole, death of the Prime Minister, a successful vote of no confidence or an unsuccessful vote of confidence. The Council of Ministers in resignation governs the country until the election of new regular Council of Ministers or the appointment of a caretaker government. The second case of government in resignation is not a consequence of governmental and parliamentary crisis. It is a result of the accomplishment of regular elections. In that situation, the Council of Ministers submits its resignation to the newly elected Parliament and from that moment until the election of new government the old government turns to be the Council of Ministers in resignation.

*621.* The third type of government is the caretaker Council of Ministers. This is a government which is appointed by the President of the Republic in case of governmental crisis which has escalated into a parliamentary crisis. In this situation, the National Assembly is incapable of electing a new regular Council of Ministers after three consecutive attempts. In that case, the President dissolves the National Assembly, schedules preterm parliamentary elections and appoints a caretaker government.

*622.* There are three main differences between the Council of Ministers and the caretaker Council of Ministers: the source of its mandate, the main functions and tasks that it has to perform and the duration of its mandate. The caretaker government has not a parliamentary provenance but is the result of the will of the head of state. It is the President via decree and not the Parliament via decision who determines the structure of the government, the type and the number of the Ministers and the concrete persons who will be appointed as Prime Minister, Deputy Prime Ministers and Ministers. The President may use the structure of the previous government or can amend the number of Ministers and their cabinets.[76]

*623.* Moreover, the caretaker Prime Minister is an appointee of the President, and he or she should serve as a first aid of the head of state and not as a political leader. Although not explicitly stipulated by the Constitution, the caretaker Prime Minister is *primus inter pares* with his or her colleagues – the Ministers –who are also usually chosen by the head of the state and not by the head of the government. In contrast to that situation, the (regular) Prime Minister is a high-profile political leader who presides over the informal governance unit composed by the government and the parliamentary majority. The (regular) Prime Minister is typically the leader of the government and usually the Ministers are selected by him or her before being approved by the National Assembly.

---

76. Plamen Kirov, *supra* n. 4, 223–224.

*624.* The caretaker government has two main tasks. First, it has to accomplish free and fair preterm parliamentary elections. Second, it has to accomplish the everyday government of the different policy fields and safeguard the normal functioning of the state.[77]

*625.* The scope of activities concerning the accomplishment of free and fair preterm elections for National Assembly may vary. Its core concerns the organizational support that the caretaker government has to deliver to the Central Electoral Commission.

*626.* The caretaker Council of Ministers is supposed to accomplish only day-to-day politics and to perform only minimal activity which is necessary for the maintenance of normal functioning of the state institutions and the society. There is no explicit constitutional prohibition for taking strategic decisions with long-lasting effect by the caretaker government. However, the adoption or even the preparation of such decisions seem to be problematic with a view to the spirit of the Constitution that provides for the caretaker government only as an institution for prevention of a short-term interregnum.

*627.* The third difference between the regular and the caretaker government is their term of office. The regular government does not have a fixed term of office. However, its term of office is coordinated with and dependent on the four-year term of office of the Parliament. Hence the regular Council of Ministers can have approximately four-year term of office.

*628.* The caretaker government has much more limited time frame. According to Article 64, paragraph 3 of the Constitution, the elections for a new National Assembly must be accomplished within two months after the dissolution of the previous National Assembly by the President of the Republic. Furthermore, according to Article 75 of the Constitution, the newly elected National Assembly has to be summoned on its first sitting by the President of the Republic within a month. The National Assembly does not have fixed term in which to elect the new regular Council of Ministers. However, usually this is one of the first tasks of the Parliament. Hence the term of office of the caretaker government can vary between two and five months depending on the date on which the new parliamentary elections are scheduled and the expediency of the newly elected National Assembly in electing a new regular Council of Ministers. The term of office of the five caretaker governments that have ruled Bulgaria so far has been approximately three months.

*629.* In case the newly elected Parliament is incapable of electing a new government after three consecutive attempts, the President again dissolves it, schedules preterm parliamentary elections and appoints the caretaker government. In such a situation, the head of state may appoint a new caretaker government or reappoint

77. Emilia Drumeva, *supra* n. 31, 478.

the same caretaker government. In the latter case, the term of office of the caretaker government may exceed half a year. However, such situation has never occurred in the Bulgarian constitutional history.

*630.* There have been five caretaker governments so far. These are the caretaker governments with Prime Ministers Reneta Indjova (October 1994–January 1995) appointed by President Jelju Jelev, Stefan Sofianski (February 1997–May 1997) appointed by President Petar Stoyanov, Marin Raikov (March 2013–May 2013) appointed by President Rosen Plevneliev, Georgi Bliznashki (August 2014–November 2014) appointed by President Rosen Plevneliev and Ognyan Gerdjikov (January 2017–May 2017) appointed by President Rumen Radev. Thus the only Bulgarian President who has never appointed a caretaker government is Georgi Parvanov although he had two terms of office. This is because he has been President during one of the most stable phases of the post-communist Bulgarian constitutional history.

*631.* It is not easy to define the character of the Bulgarian governments apart from the clear institutional distinction between the (regular) Council of Ministers, the Council of Ministers in resignation and the caretaker Council of Ministers. The differentiation between single party and coalition governments with regard to the party political composition of the Council of Ministers is vague and obscure in the contemporary Bulgarian context. One of the reasons is the fact that some of the political parties are established as framework structures encompassing different parties and having the character of formal or informal coalition. Thus the Union of Democratic Forces which was the dominant centre–right Bulgarian party during the first years of transition to democracy was actually a party coalition composed of different parties. The same holds true for its semi-informal successors – the Blue Coalition and the Reformist Block. The government of Jean Videnov has been de facto single-party government of the Bulgarian Socialist Party which formally has to be defined as a coalition government due to the fact that it included also Ministers of some small and marginal coalition partners of the Bulgarian Socialist Party.

*632.* Notwithstanding these classification issues, most of the Bulgarian Council of Ministers which ruled the country after the adoption of the 1991 Constitution are coalition governments. This is the case with the governments of Prime Ministers Jean Videnov (1995–1997), Ivan Kostov (1997–2001), Simeon Saxe-Coburg-Gotha (2001–2005), Sergey Stanishev (2005–2009), Plamen Oresharski (2013–2014) and the second and third governments of Boyko Borisov (2014–2017 and 2017–present).

*633.* Two of the post-1991 Bulgarian Councils of Ministers have been single-party governments. These are the government with Prime Minister Philip Dimitrov (1991–1992) (although the Union of Democratic Forces over which he presided was much more a coalition than a coherent party) and the first government of Boyko Borisov (2009–2013). There are also two quasi-expert governments namely the Councils of Ministers with Prime Ministers Dimitar Popov (1990–1991) and Ljuben Berov (1992–1994). They may be perceived as non-party expert governments due to the lack of party political affiliation of their Prime Ministers and the fact that they have been composed predominantly of experts and not of high-profile politicians governing the state in times of political turbulence and crisis. However, they have been elected on the basis of the mandate of some of the political parties represented in the National Assembly and have enjoyed overt or hidden party political support.

*634.* Except for the Philip Dimitrov's and the first Boyko Borisov's governments, all other Bulgarian Councils of Ministers are majority governments. This is because they had the support of the majority of the MPs in the National Assembly. The first government of Boyko Borisov was formally a single-party minority government of the political party GERB which needed the situational support of some independent MPs and other parties. In fact, it is hard to define that government as real minority cabinet since it missed just one MP to become a majority government.

## Chapter 5. The Judiciary

### §1. Constitutional Principles of the Judicial Power

*635.* There are several principles of the judicial power provided by the 1991 Constitution. All of them are elements of the general constitutional principle of rule of law proclaimed by Article 4, paragraph 1 of the Constitution. The constitutional principles of the judiciary can be ordered into three groups: first, principles safeguarding the autonomy and independence of the judicial power; second, principles which provide for the due process of law and the right to fair trial; and third, principles addressing the need to balance the principle of democracy with the principle of rule of law.

*636.* The first group includes principles safeguarding the autonomy and the independence of the judicial power. They concern the organizational, personal and financial autonomy of the judicial power. Article 117, paragraph 2 proclaims the full independence of the judicial power from other branches of state power. It provides that the magistrates must obey only the law. Thus they should not follow any illegal instructions or attempts at influencing the due process of law. The judicial power has a distinct budget. There is a special institution – the Supreme Judicial Council – which belongs to the judicial power and accomplishes the administration of the judiciary, the state prosecutors' office and the state investigator's office in cooperation with the administrative directors of the courts, the state prosecutors' offices and the state investigators' offices. These are the main ways in which the Bulgarian constitutional law tries to emancipate as much as possible the judicial power in general and the judiciary in particular from the direct influence of the political institutions.

*637.* In fact, the judiciary cannot be absolutely isolated from the influences of state institutions belonging to the different branches of state power. Eleven of the members of the Supreme Judicial Council are elected by the National Assembly. The National Assembly must vote and approve the annual budget of the judiciary. The Minister of Justice presides over the Supreme Judicial Council although not having a right to vote. Anyway, full encapsulation of the judiciary is also undesirable because it will foster the establishment of judicial oligarchies that will remain totally uncontrollable and unaccountable. Thus the above-mentioned instruments for influence of the Parliament and the Minister of Justice can be defined as part of the mechanisms for checks and balances provided by the 1991 Constitution.

*638.* The second group of principles of the judicial power encompasses principles aiming at ensuring the due process of law and the right to fair trial. It includes: the prohibition of the extraordinary courts, the prohibition of retroactive criminal justice (*nullum crimmen nulla poena sine lege praevia*), the prohibition of the double sentencing for the same crime (*non bis in idem*), the public character of the process, the equality of the citizens in front of the institutions of the judiciary, the competitive character of the judicial process, the principal aim of the judicial process to establish the truth, the right to defence, the right to appeal judicial decisions, the obligatory motivation of the judicial acts and the establishment of the structure of the state prosecutors' offices in accordance with the structure of the courts.

*639.* The third group of constitutional principles of the judicial power is an attempt in balancing the principle of democracy with the principle of rule of law. It includes: the delivering of justice in the name of the people and the use of court with lay judges for delivering justice in first instance criminal cases for grave criminal offences.

*640.* Article 1, paragraph 2 of the 1991 Constitution proclaims the people to be the source of all state power thus enshrining the principle of people's sovereignty. The delivering of justice in the name of the people – an imperative which has its particular reflection in the fact that all judicial decisions and verdicts commence with that formula – tries to establish a link between democracy as a constitutionally enshrined form of government in Bulgaria and the elitist activity of delivering justice via professional judges.

*641.* This formula, however, has just symbolic meaning and no substantial impact on the judicial procedure or on its outcome. This is because the constitutional and the ordinary legislator give preference to the principle of rule of law to the principles of people's sovereignty and democracy in the context of the judicial power. The reason is that a 'democratized judiciary' based on elective magistrates, recall of magistrates or direct influence of the popular opinion on the delivering of justice is actually incompatible with the requirements of the rule of law.

*642.* There is one exception from the general predominance of the rule of law over people's sovereignty and democracy in the institutional design of the judiciary in Bulgaria. It consists in the citizen's participation in the judicial process through court with lay judges.

*643.* The jurisdiction of the Bulgarian court with lay judges includes first instance criminal cases for major criminal offences. The court with lay judges in Bulgaria belongs to its European version and is closer to the French Assize Court or the German Court of Lay Assessors (Schöffengericht) than to the US Jury Court. This is because the lay judges form a part of the court, participate in the whole procedure that develops in front of the court and are competent to pronounce on all elements of the verdict on equal footing with the professional judge or judges. The lay judges may even decide the case against the will of the professional judge since they prevail as votes. This is due to the fact that the court with lay judges in Bulgaria is composed of one judge and two lay judges (or in some cases two judges and three lay judges) – and the lay judges vote before the professional judge.

*644.* The jury court aims at introducing 'practical reasoning' and 'public sense of justice' corresponding to the prevailing legal culture and the apprehension of justice in the society. The right to be judged and sentenced 'by equals' is an element of the due process of law and thus of rule of law since Magna Carta. However, the Bulgarian version of the jury court is rather an obsolete institution. It neither increases the democratic legitimacy of the judiciary in general and the verdict in particular nor has really anything in common with the initial idea of being judged by equals. This is due to three main reasons.

*645.* First, the lay judges are not selected via lot on the basis of coincidence. They are not a representative sample of the society. The procedure for their appointment is administrative, bureaucratic and does not have anything in common with democracy and people's sovereignty or with the predominant public morality. The lay judges are appointed by the general assembly of the higher court (e.g., the Court of Appeal for the lay judges of the district court) on a proposal of the municipal council. The municipal council makes its proposal on the basis of the application of the candidates for lay judges. The argument that lay judges selected via such procedure can reflect the public morality and the feeling of justice predominating in the society is hardly convincing.

*646.* Second, the lay judges are 'equals' to the defendant in the very broad sense that they are all Bulgarian citizens. However, this is no reasonable argument why the lay judges will increase the chances for more just and lawful verdict in comparison to a verdict pronounced only by a professional judge.

*647.* Third, the lay judges are not really qualified. They have undergone a brief instruction which is absolutely insufficient in order to allow them to competently participate in the judicial process on an equal footing with the professional judge. Despite that fact, they are full members of the court who can even determine the verdict against the will of the professional judge. As a matter of fact, this is actually an infringement of the fair trial and not a safeguard for it. In practice, the lay judges have a nominal presence and accomplish self-restraint in intervening with the work of the professional judge in the course of the judicial trial.

## §2. ORGANIZATION OF THE JUDICIARY

### I. General Structure of the Judiciary

*648.* The VII Grand National Assembly has been preoccupied with safeguarding the full political independence of all state institutions performing conflict resolution and delivering of judicial functions. The reason has been the frequent attempts at asserting political influence over the courts, the state prosecutors and the institutions for criminal investigation during both constitutional monarchy and communist periods. Such influence has been asserted especially by the Minister of Justice (with regard to the courts) and the Minister of Interior (with regard to the state prosecutors and the state investigators). That is why until 2006 not only the courts but also the state prosecutors and the state investigators have been part of the judiciary. This legal status of the state prosecutors and state investigators allocates them in the administrative jurisdiction of the Supreme Judicial Council instead of the Ministers of Justice and the Interior.

*649.* After a constitutional amendment accomplished in 2006, a large part of the investigation of criminal offences is now assigned to investigative police officers. They are part of the Ministry of Interior and fall under the administrative jurisdiction of the Minister of Interior. However, all courts and state prosecutors as well as the state investigators remain part of the judiciary.

*650.* The 1991 Constitution explicitly allocates the Constitutional Court outside of the scope of the judicial power. The Court of Auditors is also an institution which is not part of the judiciary. In Bulgaria, there is no specialized court for public finance matters distinct from the Supreme Administrative Court. The Court of Auditors is an administrative body which does not accomplish judicial power.

*651.* There are also several courts of arbitration in Bulgaria. They are private jurisdictions which neither belong to the system of the institutions of public power nor are part of the judiciary and the judicial power in Bulgaria.

## II. Structure and System of the Courts

*652.* There are two types of courts in Bulgaria – ordinary courts and specialized courts. The extraordinary courts – courts which deliver retroactive criminal justice and are established *ex post* and frequently ad hoc – are constitutionally banned. The Bulgarian theory and positive law defines as ordinary courts the courts that deliver justice and have jurisdiction over civil law and criminal law matters.

*653.* There are three types of specialized courts in Bulgaria. Two of them deliver criminal law justice. The specialized courts are: the specialized courts for organized crime, the specialized military (criminal) courts and the administrative courts. It has to be noted that the first type of specialized courts are not explicitly defined as courts for organized crime. However, their proper function as organized crime courts can be outlined via interpretation of the jurisdiction which is granted to them by the Criminal Code and the Criminal Procedure Code. Here the term 'specialized criminal courts' will be used due to the fact that this is the term provided by the Bulgarian legislation. However, it should be borne in mind that the military courts are also specialized criminal courts which are competent to deliver justice in criminal cases which have reference to the military as specified by the legislation.

*654.* The criminal and civil justice in Bulgaria is delivered in three instances whereas the administrative justice is accomplished via two procedures. The Courts of First Instance are the rayon courts and the district courts. The main Courts of First Instance are the rayon courts. They deliver criminal justice on non-grave criminal offences and civil justice in cases with lower public or material interest. The district courts function as Courts of First Instance for grave criminal offences and for civil law issues with high public or material interest. There are also specialized Courts of First Instance. These are the administrative courts, the military courts and the specialized criminal courts.

*655.* If the rayon court has served as First Instance Court, then the second instance court to which its decisions and verdicts can be appealed is the district court. In case the district court has been the Court of First Instance, then the second instance court is one of the five Courts of Appeal in Bulgaria. In other words, the rayon court is always first and the Court of Appeal is always appellate instance whereas the district court can be either first or appellate instance court depending on the type of civil or criminal law case. There are also second instance specialized courts. These are the military courts of appeal and the specialized criminal Court of Appeal. The Supreme Court of Cassation is the third instance court in all criminal and civil law cases whereas the Supreme Administrative Court is the second and final cassation instance court in administrative matters.

*656.* The intermediate conclusion is that there is a separate system of specialized administrative justice which comprises the administrative courts as first and the Supreme Administrative Court as cassation instance. On the contrary, the two types of specialized criminal courts – the military courts and the specialized courts for organized crime – have separate courts on first and appellate instance. However, the Supreme Court of Cassation serves as third and final instance for both the ordinary and the specialized criminal courts. The idea behind the institutional design of the two types of specialized criminal courts is to allow a focused jurisprudence on the first two instances delivered by separate and specialized courts while allowing the Supreme Court of Cassation to perform unifying and standard setting functions as universal Court of Cassation in Bulgaria in the criminal law domain.

## III. Structure and System of the State Prosecutor's Office and the State Investigator's Office: Functions of the State Prosecutor's Office and the State Investigator's Office

*657.* Pertaining to Article 126 of the Constitution, the system and structure of the state prosecutors' offices is in accordance with the system and structure of the courts. Consequently, the state prosecutors' offices are allocated on three levels according to the three levels of the criminal courts.

*658.* The first level of the state prosecutors' offices comprise the rayon and the district state prosecutors' offices. The latter can perform functions in the first instance or appeal criminal trial depending on the fact whether the district court has served as first or as second instance court. The military state prosecutors' offices and the specialized state prosecutors' offices for organized crime are also allocated on the first level.

*659.* The second level state prosecutors' offices comprise the state prosecutors' offices of appeal, the military state prosecutors' offices of appeal and the specialized state prosecutors' offices of appeal for organized crime. The third level of state prosecutors' offices include the Supreme State Prosecutors' Office of Cassation, the Supreme Administrative State Prosecutors' Office and the State Prosecutor General.

*660.* Consequently, there is a state prosecutor's office related to the administrative justice which is institutionally delimited only on the third level of the structure of the state prosecutor's office in Bulgaria. On the lower levels, there are administrative branches which are part of the district state prosecutors' offices. The existence of the supreme administrative state prosecutors' office as well as of the administrative branches within the district state prosecutors' offices is predetermined by the functions of the Bulgarian state prosecutor's office in the administrative justice.

*661.* Since 2009, the state investigators are part of the state prosecutor's office. Previously they have been institutionally independent third pillar of the judicial power which existed in parallel to the courts and the state prosecutor's office. The main purpose of the merger of the state investigators into the state prosecutor's office has been to enhance the efficiency of the cooperation between the two institutions. This institutional reform became possible due to the assignment of the predominant part of the criminal investigation concerning the most common and frequently accomplished crimes to the investigating police officers. Thus the activity of the state investigators has been limited to the investigation of cases with factual or legal complexity, for some types of criminal offences which expose increased public interest (e.g., state treason), for crimes which are committed abroad and for international legal aid cases.

*662.* There are currently three types of state investigator's institutions. These are the National Office of Investigation, the investigation branches within the district state prosecutors' offices and the investigation branch within the specialized state prosecutor's office for organized crime. The National Office of Investigation is directed either by the State Prosecutor General or by a director who is deputy to the State Prosecutor General responsible for the state investigation.

*663.* The State Prosecutor General is a single and supreme institution at the top of the hierarchy of the state prosecutor's office in Bulgaria. He or she has enhanced competences which allow him or her to serve as indisputable leader of the state prosecutor's office and to have a major impact on the outlook of the state function for the accomplishment of prosecution for criminal offences. The State Prosecutor General can influence also key administrative processes and phenomena such as privatization deals due to the state prosecutor's office function to safeguard the legality of administrative acts which concern major public interest. The State Prosecutor General may give compulsory instructions to all state prosecutors in Bulgaria influencing the way they should resolve the case. Moreover, he or she can accomplish actions which fall into the competence of the different state prosecutors. Last but not least, the State Prosecutor General can abolish acts of all state prosecutors.

*664.* Thus the state prosecutor's office in Bulgaria is very centralized and hierarchical. Not only the State Prosecutor General but also all superior state prosecutors can issue binding instructions and can abolish or amend the acts of the inferior state prosecutors. On the one hand, this high degree of centralization allows for better control and theoretically for increased efficiency of the state prosecutors' offices in the course of the accomplishment of coordinated functions as prescribed by the Constitution and the legislation. On the other hand, such emphasis on hierarchy and subordination definitely diminishes the autonomy and discretion of the different state prosecutors (especially of those who are at the lower levels of the hierarchy). It vests huge and to a great extent uncontrollable power to the State Prosecutor General and to the state prosecutors of the two supreme state prosecutors' offices.

*665.* Article 127 of the Constitution provides that the main function of the state prosecutor's office is to safeguard the legality by virtue of several activities which are supposed to be different dimensions of the just-mentioned broader function. The state prosecutor's office directs the state investigation of criminal offences and exercises supervision as to the legality of the procedural actions undertaken by the state investigations, carries out investigations, indicts the perpetrators of criminal offences and prosecutes criminal cases for publicly prosecutable offences, exercises supervision over the implementation of the criminal sanctions and other coercive measures, takes action for the revocation of illegal acts and participates in civil and administrative cases and proceedings which involve huge public interest.

*666.* The main tasks of the state prosecutors are to guide the preliminary investigation on criminal offences, to accomplish the most important activities of the preliminary investigation and to introduce and prove convictions against criminal offenders in front of the criminal courts. That is why the state prosecutors participate in both the preliminary investigation of criminal offences and in the judicial trial.

*667.* Apart from this central function of the state prosecutors which is focused on the delivering of criminal justice, there are also several other tasks that they perform. The control over the legality of administrative acts which concern major public interest without constituting a crime is a peculiarity of the Bulgarian state prosecutor's office. It has been inherited from the Soviet type of state prosecutor's office. In this model, the state prosecutor's office is supposed to serve the function of general control for legality of the activity of the state officials and the citizens and not only to conduct criminal prosecution in the prejudicial and the judicial phases of the criminal process. For example, the state prosecutors in Bulgaria have accomplished such control over major privatization deals.

*668.* Last but not least, the state prosecutor's office in Bulgaria accomplishes control for the legality of the conditions for serving different criminal sentences as well as compulsory medical and administrative measures. The state prosecutors can visit the penitentiary institutions and can issue binding instructions to the administration of these institutions regarding the lawful implementation of the conditions for serving the punishment or the compulsory measure provided by the court's verdict.

*669.* Thus the state prosecutors actually serve the function of penitentiary ombudsman in parallel to the general competence of the national ombudsman to accomplish similar control over the detention facilities and the hospitals. However, there is also a difference between the competences of the state prosecutors and the national ombudsman. The state prosecutors may impose binding instructions on the directors of the detention facilities and other penitentiary institutions and can even amend their acts. The ombudsman can only issue recommendations to these administrative institutions without the competence to either impose instructions or abolish and amend administrative acts. Thus the protection offered by the state prosecutors is higher and more intense than the protection rendered by the national ombudsman.

## §3. System for Administration of the Judiciary

*670.* The administration of the judiciary in Bulgaria is accomplished by the Supreme Judicial Council, the Minister of Justice and the administrative directors of the courts, the state prosecutors' offices and the National Investigation Office. The 1991 Constitution vests controlling functions for the proper functioning of the institutions of the judiciary with both the Supreme Judicial Council and the Inspectorate to the Supreme Judicial Council.

*671.* Hence the 1991 Constitution provides for the most widespread system of administration of the judiciary in Europe. It is structured around a specialized and autonomous institution for the administration of the judiciary – the Supreme Judicial Council – supported by Inspectorate and Chairmen of the different institutions belonging to the judicial power. All these institutions, which are a part of the judicial power, cooperate with the Minister of Justice as specialized executive power institution having competences for administration of the justice.

*672.* In fact, the 1991 Constitution is the first Bulgarian Constitution which provides for specific institution for the administration of the judiciary independent from the political branches of the state power and more precisely from the Parliament, the head of state and the Council of Ministers. The Supreme Judicial Council is independent also from the Minister of Justice who chairs its plenary sittings but without the right to vote.

*673.* The Supreme Judicial Council in Bulgaria has been constructed following mostly the models of the Italian and the French Supreme Judicial Councils in the institutional design they had in 1990–1991. Thus the Supreme Judicial Council is a body selected by institutions belonging to different branches of state power – the

Parliament and the magistrates. This model safeguards the separation of the patronage power and provides for polycentrism of the influences on the personal policy regarding the central institution for administration of the judiciary. The Supreme Judicial Council is chaired by the Minister of Justice as a key institution, which is both an agenda setter of legislative initiatives and driving force behind the judicial policy of the state. Initially, the Bulgarian Supreme Judicial Council has had a monolithic structure without internal subdivisions such as colleges or branches. Naturally, there have been committees on different functions performed by the Supreme Judicial Council such as career development of the magistrates and the disciplinary procedures.

*674.* The Supreme Judicial Council consists of twenty-five members. Three of them – the Chairman of the Supreme Court of Cassation, the Chairman of the Supreme Administrative Court and the State Prosecutor General – are ex lege members. Eleven of the members of the Supreme Judicial Council are elected by the National Assembly and eleven by the magistrates (six by the judges, four by the state prosecutors general and one by the state investigators). The Minister of Justice participates in the Supreme Judicial Council's sittings and chairs them but without a right to vote.

*675.* The Chairman of the Supreme Court of Cassation, the Chairman of the Supreme Administrative Court and the State Prosecutor General have seven-year term of office whereas the rest of its members have five-year term of office. They cannot be immediately re-elected for another term of office. The members of the Supreme Judicial Council must be lawyers with high moral and professional qualities and must have at least fifteen years of service as a magistrate, university professor, attorney-at-law or any other legal profession which counts as official legal practice.

*676.* Hence both the normative and the factual composition of the Supreme Judicial Council reflect the concept of internal separation of the patronage power among different institutions. It aims at safeguarding internal checks and balances and at blocking lobbyist interests hidden behind one of the quotas in this important institution. It allows for mutual control between the different types of magistrates and for a balance between the judicial independence and the indirect public control via the parliamentary quota.

*677.* Major constitutional reform of the judiciary was accomplished in 2015. It introduced four important novelties with regard to the Supreme Judicial Council. It changed its structure, assigned some of the functions which previously were given to the Council in general to its colleges, introduced the direct election of the members of the Supreme Judicial Council by the judges, the state prosecutors and the state investigators and provided for qualified majority for the election of the members of the parliamentary quota.

*678.* One of the main aspects of this reform was to restructure the previously unified Supreme Judicial Council that possessed equal jurisdiction over all magistrates (the judges, the state prosecutors and the state investigators) by dividing it into two colleges. As a consequence, the Supreme Judicial Council currently encompasses plenum and two colleges – judicial college and state prosecutors' college.

*679.* The plenum of the Supreme Judicial Council consists of the abovementioned twenty-five magistrates, and it is chaired by the Minister of Justice. It reflects the previous monolithic and unified structure of the Supreme Judicial Council.

*680.* The judicial college consists of fourteen members. Two of them – the Chairman of the Supreme Court of Cassation and the Chairman of the Supreme Administrative Court – are members as of right. Six of the members are elected directly by the judges and six by the National Assembly.

*681.* The sittings of the judicial college are chaired by the Chairman of the Supreme Court of Cassation. This fact reflects the implicit suggestion of the constitutional legislator that the general jurisprudence has higher, substantial importance than the administrative jurisprudence despite the fact that there is no hierarchy between the Supreme Court of Cassation and the Supreme Administrative Court as well as between their Chairmen and they are both formally coequal.

*682.* The state prosecutors' college consists of eleven members. The State Prosecutor General is a member as of right. Four of its members are elected directly by the state prosecutors, one is elected directly by the state investigators and five are elected by the National Assembly. The sittings of the state prosecutors' college are chaired by the State Prosecutor General.

*683.* The main idea behind the structural and functional reform of the Supreme Judicial Council was to increase the institutional autonomy of the different types of magistrates and especially to limit the influence of the state prosecutors and state investigators on the career development of the judges. The previous system which allowed the plenum of the Supreme Judicial Council to have equal jurisdiction and uniform competences over all types of magistrates has been perceived by the MPs that have introduced the constitutional reform as an unjustified influence of the state prosecutors which are parties in the judicial process over the judges as main institutions which should impartially deliver justice.

*684.* However, the new structure of the Supreme Judicial Council allows for the encapsulation of the different types of magistrates, limits the internal separation of powers, thus may eventually lead to decrease in transparency and accountability. The power of the State Prosecutor General to determine the career development of the judges has been limited. However, the instruments for control and transparency over the organization, activity and career development of the state prosecutors and state investigators have been also definitely curtailed. Thus the courts and the state prosecutor's office may turn to be 'semi-independent realms' in the judicial power with limited channels for mutual influence.

*685.* The 2015 constitutional reform has also introduced asymmetry in the structure of the Supreme Judicial Council. It is demonstrated by the fact that the judicial college consists of fourteen members whereas the state prosecutors' college consists of eleven members. This asymmetry is a result of the fact that any additional restructuring of the Supreme Judicial Council consisting in increase or decrease of its members would require the need for the summoning of the Grand National Assembly which was practically impossible at the moment of the introduction of the 2015 constitutional reform.

*686.* The reform of the functions of the Supreme Judicial Council is a consequence of the reform of its structure. This is because the 2015 constitutional amendment neither provided for new functions nor abolished any of the existing functions of the Supreme Judicial Council. It has just internally reallocated the functions of the Supreme Judicial Council by preserving some of them to its plenum while assigning others to the two colleges – the judicial college and the state prosecutors' college.

*687.* Since 2015, the plenum of the Supreme Judicial Council possesses limited competences. They address issues, which according to the constitutional legislator, concern all institutions belonging to the judicial power. The most important of them comprise the adoption of the draft budget of the judicial power, the organization of the qualification of the magistrates, the decision of organizational issues which are common to all branches of the judicial power, the management of the property of the judicial power and the adoption of the annual reports on the functioning of the judicial power.

*688.* Some of the competences which previously belonged to the Supreme Judicial Council are, since 2015, assigned to the judicial college and the state prosecutors' college. These competences concern the career development and the attestation of the magistrates (including the adoption of decision for granting irremovability of the magistrates), the imposition of disciplinary penalties on the magistrates (including their removal from power), the appointment and dismissal of the administrative directors and the decision on issues which are of special importance for the specific branch of the judicial power. Hence the main result of the 2015 constitutional reform has been the separation of the career development of the judges from the career development of the state prosecutors and the state investigators.

*689.* The direct election of the members of the magistrates' quotas in the Supreme Judicial Council by the judges, the state prosecutors and the state investigators is also an important novelty introduced by the 2015 constitutional reform. Previously, the representatives of the magistrates in the Supreme Judicial Council have been elected by magistrates' delegates. Thus until 2015, the predominant part of the judges, the state prosecutors and the state investigators could only indirectly influence the election of the members of the Supreme Judicial Council belonging to the magistrates' quotas. This reform has to be welcomed since it increases the internal checks and balances and the transparency of the selection process and limits the power of lobbyist and elitist groupings in the judiciary to predetermine the composition of the magistrates' quotas in the Supreme Judicial Council.

*690.* The last element of the 2015 constitutional reform of the Supreme Judicial Council is the requirement for election of the members of the parliamentary quota by two-thirds qualified majority of all MPs. The main idea is to allow for the election of experts with broadly recognized professional capacity and moral integrity. The same qualified majority is constitutionally required also for the election of the members of the Inspectorate to the Supreme Judicial Council.

*691.* The competences of the Minister of Justice related to the administration of the judiciary have been constitutionally enshrined by virtue of a previous constitutional reform, which was accomplished in 2006. Many of these provisions have been again modified or amended by virtue of other constitutional reforms in 2007 and 2015. This is one of the clear examples of the semi-permanent reform of the judiciary in Bulgaria which is believed to magically transform the functioning of the judiciary and the mentality of the magistrates but actually leads to normative inflation and further constitutional stalemates and tangles.

*692.* Since the 2015 reform, the Minister of Justice has three main competences regarding the administration of the judiciary. First, he or she proposes a draft budget of the judicial power to the Supreme Judicial Council and later introduces it in the National Assembly together with the suggestions made by the Supreme Judicial Council. Second, he or she can make proposals for career development of the magistrates consisting in their appointment, dismissal, promotion, demotion and displacement. The Minister of Justice can make such proposal, but the decision is made by the Supreme Judicial Council. Third, the Minister of Justice in cooperation with the Supreme Judicial Council organizes the qualification of the magistrates.

*693.* The administrative directors have organizational and budgetary competences. They organize the activity of the courts and the state prosecutors' offices. Moreover, they appoint and dismiss the state servants working in their administrations. The administrative directors have to deliver different types of reports and information to the Supreme Judicial Council for the functioning of the court or the state prosecutor's office they direct.

*694.* The control over the proper functioning of the institutions of the judicial power is accomplished not only by the Supreme Judicial Council and the administrative directors but also by a special body – the Inspectorate. The Inspectorate is attached to the Supreme Judicial Council. It consists of eleven members – chief inspector and ten inspectors. The chief inspector and the inspectors are elected by the National Assembly with two-thirds majority of all MPs. The chief inspector has five-year term of office whereas the inspectors have four-year term of office which cannot be immediately renewed after its expiration.

*695.* The Inspectorate inspects the activity of the magistrates without interfering in the way they tackle the cases. The Inspectorate may also perform inspections regarding the magistrates' decency as well as conflict of interest. The Inspectorate acts on its own initiative as well as on the initiative of citizens, legal persons or state institutions. The Inspectorate presents an annual report to the Supreme Judicial Council and adopts signals, proposals and reports to other state institutions.

## §4. Constitutional Status of the Magistrates

*696.* The constitutional status of the magistrates comprises several main elements. They may be systematized as follows: preconditions and procedure for appointment as magistrate, incompatibilities with the magistrate's position, procedure and grounds for termination of the office, attestation and acquiring of irremovability and magistrate's immunity. The specific rights and duties of the magistrates provided by the Judicial Power Act, which are different from the magistrate's immunity, and the magistrate's irremovability will not be discussed here due to space constraints.

*697.* All judges, state prosecutors and state investigators as well as all administrative directors of the courts, state prosecutors' and state investigators' offices are appointed and dismissed by the Supreme Judicial Council. The only exceptions are the Chairman of the Supreme Court of Cassation, the Chairman of the Supreme Administrative Court and the State Prosecutor General. They are appointed and dismissed by the President of the Republic on a proposal by the Supreme Judicial Council which itself elects a candidate out of proposals made by either one-fifth of its members or of the Minister of Justice. The head of the National Investigation Office is elected by the state prosecutors' college of the Supreme Judicial Council on a proposal made alternatively by three members either of the state prosecutors' college, or the State Prosecutor General or the Minister of Justice.

*698.* There are several requirements for the appointment of the magistrate. The candidate must be a Bulgarian citizen with no dual citizenship. He or she must be in possession of a law degree, must have accomplished compulsory practical training at the judicial power provided by the state and must have acquired legal qualification as lawyer after passing a compulsory practical and theoretical exam at the ministry of justice. The candidate should possess the necessary moral and ethical qualities as defined by the Ethical Code of the Bulgarian Magistrates, should not be a dismissed member of the Supreme Judicial Council on disciplinary grounds and must not have been sentenced to imprisonment for intentional crime. The candidate must also not suffer from any mental illness for which he or she provides a medical certificate. After winning a competition for magistrate's position the candidate has to undergo additional magistrate's education at the National Institute for Justice.

*699.* There are also requirements regarding the necessary minimal length of service as a lawyer in order for the candidate to be appointed as a magistrate in the different courts or state prosecutors' offices. The Bulgarian legislation imposes the following minimal requirements regarding the length of service: three years for appointment as a judge in the rayon court or as a rayon state prosecutor; eight years for appointment as a judge in the district court or as a district state prosecutor or as a judge in the administrative court; ten years for a judge at the Court of Appeal; ten years for a judge or state prosecutor at the specialized criminal court, five of which as a criminal law judge or state prosecutor; twelve years for a judge or state prosecutor at the specialized criminal court, eight of which as a criminal law judge or state prosecutor; and twelve years for a judge at the Supreme Court of Cassation or the Supreme Administrative Court or as state prosecutor at the Supreme State Prosecutors' Office of Cassation or at the Supreme Administrative State Prosecutors' Office. The Judicial Power Act provides also for terms of the length of service with regard to the eligibility as an administrative director of the different courts and state prosecutors' offices. According to Decision No. 3 of 2018 of the Constitutional Court, the administrative directors of the courts, state prosecutors offices and state investigators offices can be elected only for two terms of office.

*700.* The procedure for dismissal of magistrates is similar to the procedure for their appointment. The judges, the state prosecutors and the state investigators are dismissed by the respective college of the Supreme Judicial Council. The grounds for termination of the office are death, retirement at the age of 65 years, resignation, entering into force of an imprisonment sentence for intentional crime, severe infringement or systemic dereliction of professional duties, activity infringing the moral integrity and the prestige of the judiciary, durable factual incapacity to perform the duties for more than one year, disciplinary dismissal from power by the Supreme Judicial Council, refusal of the judges or the state prosecutors' college of the Supreme Judicial Council for granting irremovability, incompatibility with positions or activities provided by law and reinstatement in previous job from which the magistrate had been fired illegally.

*701.* The Chairman of the Supreme Court of Cassation, the Chairman of the Supreme Administrative Court and the State Prosecutor General are dismissed by the President of the Republic on a proposal of the plenum of the Supreme Judicial Council. The President of the Republic can reject such proposal only once.

*702.* The magistrates who have acquired irremovability can be dismissed only on the grounds of death, retirement at the age of 65 years, resignation, entering into force of an imprisonment sentence for intentional crime, severe infringement or systemic dereliction of professional duties, activity infringing the moral integrity and the prestige of the judiciary, durable factual incapacity to perform the duties for more than one year and incompatibility with positions or activities provided by law. The irremovability is acquired after serving five years as a judge, state prosecutor or state investigator. It is acquired not automatically but only after a positive complex note of the attestation assigned by the Commission for Attestation of the judicial or the state prosecutors' college of the Supreme Judicial Council. The irremovability is granted by the respective college of the Supreme Judicial Council.

*703.* Article 195 of the Judicial Power Act provides for an extensive list of incompatibilities with the magistrate's position. The magistrates cannot take in parallel to his or her job as a judge, state prosecutor or state investigator any other position in the system of state institutions. Moreover, the magistrate must refrain from all commercial, economic and financial activities in the private sector. The magistrate cannot be a member of a political party or trade union with the exception of trade unions in the framework of the judiciary. A peculiarity of the Bulgarian legal system is the incompatibility of the position as a judge, state prosecutor or state investigator with a permanent position in the universities and the academia.

*704.* The 1991 Constitution in its initial variant provided for absolute immunity of the judges, state prosecutors and state investigators. The desire of the constitutional legislator was to fully safeguard the independence of the judiciary and to prevent any possible attempts at asserting pressure on the magistrates.

*705.* However, in the course of the transition to rule of law and democracy, these enhanced standards for judicial independence began to be perceived by the civic society as unjustified privileges and as an undue escape for corrupt magistrates. This is the reason why in 2003 the absolute immunity of the magistrates consisting in prohibition of criminal persecution for any form of presumed criminal activity has been reduced to functional immunity.

*706.* The functional immunity protects the magistrate against convictions for committing a crime in the course of the accomplishment of his or her professional functions. However, it does not impede criminal prosecution for offences committed outside of the scope of his or her professional activity. Article 132 of the Constitution in its current version after the 2003 and 2007 constitutional reforms provides that in the course of the accomplishment of the judicial power the judges, the state prosecutors and the state investigators should not bear any criminal or civil liability for their official activity or for the acts that they issue except if they constitute an intentional criminal offence prosecuted by the state.

# Chapter 6. The Constitutional Court

## §1. Constitutional Status and Place in the System for Separation of Powers

*707.* The Constitutional Court is not included in the judicial power. There are two main reasons for that conclusion – formal and substantial. Formally, the Bulgarian Constitutional Court is not provided by Chapter VI 'Judicial Power' of the 1991 Constitution but by separate Chapter VIII 'Constitutional Court'. Substantially the Constitutional Court is neither in administrative nor in hierarchical relations with the other courts in Bulgaria. There is no court's decision which can be appealed in front of the Constitutional Court. Hence the Constitutional Court is no superior instance of the system for the delivering of justice in Bulgaria. It is no final instance of appeal either for the ordinary or for the specialized courts.

*708.* Administratively the Constitutional Court is a separate state institution which is fully independent from the institutions belonging to the judicial power according to the 1991 Constitution – the courts, the state prosecutors and the state investigators offices. The system for administration of the judiciary whose main institution is the Supreme Judicial Council is not applicable to the Constitutional Court. The Constitutional Court has full institutional independence from all state institutions. It determines its budgetary, administrative, organizational and personal staff issues in full autonomy.

*709.* The 1991 Constitution provides for Constitutional Court which has formally coequal standing with the other key national constitutional institutions – the Parliament, the government, the President, the Supreme Administrative Court, the Supreme Court of Cassation, the State Prosecutor General and the Supreme Judicial Council. It is collective and collegial constitutional institution due to its composite nature and the majoritarian decision-making.

## §2. Structure and Composition

*710.* The Bulgarian Constitutional Court has a simple unicameral structure. It is the result of the lack of direct constitutional complaint and the fact that most of the Constitutional Court cases concern control for constitutionality of sub-constitutional acts, control for conformity of the legislation to the international treaties and abstract interpretation of the Constitution. That is why there is no need for specialization of the Constitutional Court's judges which is reflected in the existence of a monolithic structure of the Constitutional Court making all of them competent to participate in the deliberation and decision of all types of Constitutional Court's cases.

*711.* Most of the Constitutional Court's decisions are prepared by single judge-rapporteur. However, the Constitutional Court is competent to appoint more than one judge-rapporteur in the cases which are of special importance or present greater difficulty. The only instance in which the Constitutional Court Act provides for compulsory preparation of the decision by three judge-rapporteurs concerns the cases for impeachment of the President of the Republic.

*712.* The Bulgarian Constitutional Court is composed of twelve judges coming from three quotas. One-third of the Constitutional Court judges are elected by the National Assembly, one-third are appointed by the President of the Republic and one-third are elected by the general assembly of the judges of the Supreme Court of Cassation and the Supreme Administrative Court. The idea of the constitutional legislator is to prevent the concentration of the patronage power over the Constitutional Court in a single institution. This tripartite separation of patronage power over the Constitutional Court is supposed to allow for mutual control and restraint between the judges coming from different quotas.

*713.* In addition, the involvement of the Parliament in the procedure for recruitment of the staff of the Constitutional Court aims at investing some form of input democratic legitimacy in the Constitutional Court and at mitigating the tension stemming out of the declaration of unconstitutionality of the acts of the Parliament. The competence of the two supreme courts to elect one-third of the judges of the Constitutional Court implies an indirect form of linkage with the judiciary. Last but not least, the competence of the President of the Republic to appoint another one-third of the judges of the Constitutional Court allows the head of state to have reinforced status in the constitutional system without possessing leading function that competes with the Prime Minister.

*714.* The Constitutional Court's judges have nine-year term of office which is non-renewable. This is the longest mandate of a state institution according to the 1991 Constitution. Every three years there is rotation for partial renewal of the seats in the Constitutional Court. This means that on each third year one-third of the judges in the Constitutional Court are replaced with new judges. Due to the fact that one-third of the judges means four judges, this replacement functions on the basis of a formula that provides for the renewal of two judges from one of the quotas and one judge from each of the other two quotas. The allocation of judges who have to be replaced shifts accordingly on the next rotations thus allowing the general number of judges per quota to remain the same.

*715.* It must be noted that the judges of the Constitutional Court are not delegates or representatives of the institution or institutions that have elected or appointed them. The Constitutional Court's judges enjoy full independence and any binding instructions which are given to them are null and void. Consequently, the just-described scheme for separation of powers aims at preventing the concentration of influence in one electing or appointing institution only at the initial moment of the election or appointment of the judges. It does not concern the later functioning of the Constitutional Court which has to be free of any institutional, personal or political influence of the constituting factors.

§3. Functions and Competences

*716.* It has already been mentioned that the gravity centre of the functions of the Constitutional Court is set on its quality as 'court for the state' while its human rights' dimension definitely has subordinate status. In fact, the intent of the VII Grand National Assembly has been to establish an institution which can provide for the smooth functioning of the constitutional model during the transition to democracy and which can dynamically clarify the meaning of the constitutional provisions thus safeguarding their contextual adequacy.

*717.* Indeed the Bulgarian Constitutional Court has served well the intent of the constitutional legislator. It has established itself as an authoritative interpreter of the 'open texture' of the 1991 Constitution. The Constitutional Court has contributed to the stability of the governmental process. Last but not least, it has paved the way to the EU integration of Bulgaria allowing the accomplishment of timely constitutional amendments.

*718.* At the same time, the Bulgarian Constitutional Court became an activist constitutional jurisdiction. In some limited but important occasions, the Constitutional Court even subrogated itself in the role of quasi-constituent power through extensive constitutional interpretation and ascription of meaning to the constitutional texts. This tendency gave rise to concerns regarding the democratic legitimacy of the activist interpretative jurisprudence of the Constitutional Court in parallel to the problems with a view to the consistency of its case law.

*719.* The competences of the Constitutional Court can be classified into several groups: first, general interpretation of the 1991 Constitution; second, hierarchical norm control; third, competence conflict resolution with regard to the horizontal and vertical separation of powers; fourth, safeguarding the Constitution against anti-system factors; fifth, decision for legality of elections.[78]

*720.* Hence the Constitutional Court accomplishes the following main functions. It is the institution which provides for the adaptation of the 1991 Constitution to the current sociopolitical context through interpretation of the constitutional texts. It safeguards the normative hierarchy in the Bulgarian legal order via its normative control decisions. The Constitutional Court is supposed to guarantee the normal functioning of the institutional system and the smooth development of the inter-institutional dynamics by virtue of its competence to resolve disputes regarding the horizontal and vertical separation of powers. Moreover, the Constitutional Court is the safeguard of the 1991 Constitution against anti-systemic factors due to its competence to impeach the President and to prohibit political parties as unconstitutional. Last but not least, the Constitutional Court serves as a safeguard also for the legality of the elections as central instruments for the establishment and the maintenance of the representative democracy in Bulgaria.

78. *See* Emilia Drumeva, *supra* n. 31, 578–598.

*721.* The Bulgarian Constitutional Court has the relatively rare competence in comparative perspective to adopt decisions for abstract interpretation of the Constitution. The immediate aim of these decisions is to allow the court to clarify the meaning of unclear constitutional provisions. The 1991 Constitution is not a product of continuous development of the national constitutional tradition. It is a result of massive legal borrowing from European democracies. Thus it is evident that many of the ideas, concepts, values, principles and institutions enshrined in the 1991 Constitution may have been initially unclear for the Bulgarian politicians and citizens. They may have proved to be dysfunctional in the Bulgarian sociopolitical context without some adjustment to both the Bulgarian constitutional tradition and the current state of art in the ideal and the factual constitution.[79]

*722.* That is why the Constitutional Court seemed as an appropriate institution that may adapt the transplanted and receipted legal texts to the existing social context without the need of formal constitutional amendment. The founding fathers and mothers of the last Bulgarian Constitution believed that by giving the Constitutional Court the competence to abstract constitutional interpretation they guarantee the longevity of the 1991 Constitution due to the establishment of a mechanism for its dynamic evolution and gaining of adequate meaning adjusted to the Bulgarian reality.

*723.* In fact, the Constitutional Court is almost unrestrained in its activity for abstract interpretation of the Constitution. It is not truly bound to the parameters of concrete case because it is not focused on the clarification of the constitutionality or the unconstitutionality of specific legislative provision as in the cases of the abstract or concrete control for constitutionality or in the rare occasions of indirect constitutional complaints. The Constitutional Court frequently functions as a creative interpreter of the Constitution by using teleological interpretation and by implying new meaning in the 'open texture' of the Constitution.

*724.* There are only three theoretical limitations to the interpretative activity of the Constitutional Court in the procedure for giving abstract interpretation of the Constitution. The first limitation consists in the fact that the Constitutional Court does not act *ex officio*. It has to be approached by the competent institutions in order to be able to give interpretative decision. Indeed this is the most important limitation of the interpretative expansion of the Constitutional Court. However, the plurality of the subjects that can approach the Constitutional Court with the demand to give interpretative decisions of the Constitution limits the restrictive role of the ban on *ex officio* activity of the court in practice. Moreover, this restriction cannot frame the interpretative activity of the Constitutional Court once it has been approached.

*725.* The second limitation is the issue with which the Constitutional Court has been approached. The Constitutional Court can give interpretative decisions only regarding the constitutional provision targeted by the institution that has approached

---

79. For the concepts of ideal and factual constitution, *see* Evgeni Tanchev, *supra* n. 20, 112.

the court and only with a view to the questions raised by it. However, there are several factors which diminish the restrictive character of that limitation. Usually, the questions are formulated very broadly thus giving the Constitutional Court the chance to imply a broad meaning in them and to use them as a starting point of activist jurisprudence which is not really framed by the demand of the institution that has approached it. Moreover, there are instances in which the approaching of the Constitutional Court serves as a pre-negotiated point for creeping informal constitutional amendment based on the inter-institutional dialogue between the subject that has initiated the case and the court. In addition, the variations of the wording of the question allow for intentional broadening of the scope of the discretion of the Constitutional Court to accomplish de facto virtual amendment of the Constitution. Last but not least, the Constitutional Court sometimes uses arguments based on the systemic linkage between the interpreted provision and other constitutional values, principles or institutions. Thus it spreads its interpretation also to these issues which were not an immediate object of the demand of the institution that has initiated the proceedings.

*726.* The third limitation is that the Constitutional Court is supposed to maintain the consistency of its jurisprudence. The Constitutional Court can deviate from its constant practice only in exceptional occasions after the lapse of sufficient time and only in case of drastic change in the situation. In fact, the Bulgarian Constitutional Court tries to stick to that requirement which is actually related to the principle of legal predictability and stability that is itself part of the rule of law. However, there are important instances in which the Constitutional Court was not able to provide consistent and continuous jurisprudence. Paramount examples are Decision No. 3 of 2003 and Decision No. 3 of 2004, which are fundamentally controversial. They serve as a clear example of radical conceptual shift in the Constitutional Court's jurisprudence accomplished in a period of less than a year.

*727.* It has to be mentioned that the interpretative decisions of the Constitutional Court are the second largest group in its case law after the decisions for norm control. Hence it seems that the competence of the Constitutional Court to adopt binding abstract interpretation of the Constitution has been in the focus of the interest of the constitutional institutions during the past twenty-six years. The number and the importance of these interpretative decisions predetermine the fact that the 1991 Constitution cannot be properly understood without taking them into account.

*728.* Undoubtedly, the most important competence of the Bulgarian Constitutional Court is the control for the abidance of the normative hierarchy at the top of the domestic pyramid of sources of law. The Bulgarian Constitutional Court is granted the competence to control the constitutionality of the legal acts of Parliament as well as the legal acts of President. Moreover, it can accomplish preliminary control for the compliance of the international treaties with the 1991 Constitution before their ratification. The Constitutional Court can accomplish also control of the compliance of the legal acts of the Parliament and the President with the international treaties to which Bulgaria is a part as well as with the generally recognized principles of international law.

*729.* The Parliament adopts two types of legal acts which can be an object of the control accomplished by the Constitutional Court. These are the acts of the Parliament and the decisions. The acts of the Parliament are the primary target of the control accomplished by the Constitutional Court. The President of the Republic can adopt only one type of legal acts. These are the presidential decrees which are individual administrative acts. Hence, in practice, it is very unusual that decrees of the President may become an object of control for constitutionality. The lack of normative character of the presidential decree can make the control to some extent obsolete. If the President adopts an unconstitutional decree it might be not just reason for control of constitutionality but also a cause for initiation of procedure for his or her impeachment.

*730.* The 1991 Constitution does not provide for control of the constitutionality and of compliance with the international treaties and the generally recognized principles of international law of the legal acts of the government. They can be controlled for such compliance with the superior legal acts in the Bulgarian normative hierarchy by the Supreme Administrative Court. The reason of the constitutional legislator to avoid granting such controlling competence to the Constitutional Court with regard to the governmental acts is to prevent the overload of the Constitutional Court. However, the workload of the Bulgarian Constitutional Court during the decades after its establishment is definitely low. Thus it is regrettable that the Constitutional Court has no competence to pronounce also on the constitutionality and the compliance with the international treaties of the governmental acts.

*731.* The 1991 Constitution provides for centralized control for constitutionality which is concentrated in the Constitutional Court. The ordinary courts may accomplish diffuse control for constitutionality by disregarding unconstitutional legislative provisions only with a view to the pre-constitutional legislation (the acts of the Parliament which have entered into force before 13 July 1991 – the date of entering into force of the new Constitution).

*732.* The 1991 Constitution has rather an unclear standing on the issue whether they are allowed to apply its supremacy and the direct derogative effect on the post-constitutional legislation. It seems that the constitutional legislator expects that in the latter case the ordinary courts will address the issue to the Supreme Court of Cassation or to the Supreme Administrative Court which while serving as a filter may then decide to approach the Constitutional Court. This is the procedure for concrete control of constitutionality. The control is concrete because the Constitutional Court is approached with a view to, and on the occasion of, a concrete instance of presumed unconstitutionality of an act of Parliament detected in the context of a pending lawsuit in an ordinary Court of First, Appellate or Cassation Instance.

*733.* In the context of the concrete control for constitutionality, the Constitutional Court both clarifies the issue with binding force for all legal subjects and helps the ordinary court to solve the concrete case by declaring the constitutionality or the unconstitutionality of the legislative provision which is under scrutiny. Hence the concrete control for constitutionality differs from the abstract control for constitutionality not with regard to the consequences of the Constitutional Court's decision – in both cases it is legally binding for all subjects of the Bulgarian constitutional law, but with a view to the procedure for initiation of the case and approaching the court with a demand for pronouncement of unconstitutionality.

*734.* The Constitutional Court can also accomplish an abstract control for constitutionality. It consists in the declaration of unconstitutionality of legislation which is not provoked by a pending lawsuit in front of the courts. The abstract control for constitutionality is driven by the belief of one of the institutions that may initiate control for constitutionality that some legislative provisions are unconstitutional and have to be officially declared as such by the Constitutional Court.

*735.* Both the abstract and the concrete controls for constitutionality accomplished by the Constitutional Court are forms of *ex post* control for constitutionality. This means that the Bulgarian Constitutional Court can accomplish control only on acts which have been already adopted and entered into force. Thus the 1991 Constitution has provided for the *ex post* centralized control for constitutionality which is the predominant version of constitutional control in Europe.

*736.* The only instance of preventive or *ex ante* control concerns the control for the constitutionality of the international treaties. This control is accomplished by the Constitutional Court before their ratification. The aim is to avoid a situation in which either the Constitution or the principle *pacta sunt servanda* will be infringed.

*737.* In many cases in the Constitutional Court's practice, the court has been approached and accepted for decision demands for simultaneous unconstitutionality and contravention of acts of Parliament to the international treaties. This is especially true with regard to cases concerning contravention to international human rights' treaties. The international treaties which are most frequently used as criteria for invalidation of contravening provisions of acts of Parliament are the EConvHR, the ICCPR and the ICESCR.

*738.* The case law of the Constitutional Court related to norm control serves two main functions. First, it guarantees the normative hierarchy provided in the 1991 Constitution. More precisely, it is a safeguard for the supremacy of the Constitution and the primacy of the international treaties over the sub-constitutional legislation. Second, in the course of declaring the constitutionality or the unconstitutionality of the international treaties, the legal acts of the Parliament or the President, the Constitutional Court also interprets the Constitution. The interpretations of the 1991 Constitution given by the Constitutional Court in the framework of the procedures for abstract and concrete controls for constitutionality are numerous, binding and a very important source of law containing crucial information regarding the proper meaning of the constitutional provisions.

*739.* The Constitutional Court safeguards the constitutionally enshrined institutional design and the abiding of the model for horizontal and vertical separation of public power through its competence to decide on competence conflicts and disputes by the state institutions. With regard to the horizontal separation of powers, the Constitutional Court is competent to resolve conflicts between the National Assembly, the President of the Republic and the Council of Ministers. The Constitutional Court can decide also on conflicts for vertical separation of powers between the Council of Ministers and the municipal councils.

*740.* It has to be noted that these two competences of the Constitutional Court are very rarely used. The office holders of the Bulgarian institutions prefer to solve the inter-institutional conflicts either by political means or by approaching the Constitutional Court with the demand to issue an interpretative decision for clarification of the disputed competence. Hence the role of the Constitutional Court as an arbiter between the state institutions is clearly overshadowed by its functions as a safeguard for the supremacy of the Constitution and the international treaties as well as authoritative interpreter of the constitutional texts.

*741.* The Constitutional Court possesses two competences which grant it the status of a guarantor of the constitutional model against anti-systemic factors.[80] These are the Constitutional Court's competences to declare the unconstitutionality of political parties and to pronounce on the impeachment of the President of the Republic. There are two alternative grounds for the unconstitutionality of the political parties according to the 1991 Constitution. A Bulgarian political party is unconstitutional if it is established on ethnic, religious or race basis or if it pursues violent assent to the power. The grounds for unconstitutionality of the political parties serve as qualitative limitations to the political pluralism aiming at the assurance of the republican, liberal and democratic character of the state and the public sphere in Bulgaria.

*742.* Until now, the Constitutional Court has been approached twice with the demand to declare the unconstitutionality of a political party. In both cases, the presumed unconstitutionality concerned the suggestion that the political party is established on ethnic origin. In the first case, the Constitutional Court was not able to make a decision on the unconstitutionality of the Movement for Rights and Freedoms due to the fact that there was a split in the votes of the Constitutional Court's judges (six judges were in favour and six judges were against), while seven votes were needed for the assertion of either the constitutionality or the unconstitutionality of this party. In the second case, the political party OMO 'Ilinden' was declared unconstitutional and thus prohibited because the Constitutional Court decided that it is a party established on ethnic background.

*743.* There are two alternative grounds for impeachment of the President of the Republic. The President can be removed from power if he or she has committed state treason or violation of the Constitution. The impeachment procedure is analysed in the paras 284–295 which are devoted to the President of the Republic.

---

80. Emilia Drumeva, *supra* n. 31, 591–592.

§4. Constitutional Court's Procedure

*744.* The Constitutional Court's procedure is defined by the 1991 Constitution but especially by the Constitutional Court Act and the Rules for the Organization and the Activity of the Constitutional Court. These Rules are adopted by the Constitutional Court and are an expression of its organizational autonomy.

*745.* Six institutional players have the competence to approach the Constitutional Court with demands for the issuing of interpretative decisions, decisions for normative control and decisions for the unconstitutionality of political parties. These are one-fifth of the MPs in the National Assembly, the President of the Republic, the Council of Ministers, the Supreme Court of Cassation, the Supreme Administrative Court and the State Prosecutor General. Hence these institutions may be defined as initiators of Constitutional Court's cases with general competence.

*746.* In addition, there are several institutions which have the right to approach the Constitutional Court with regard to a specific competence. The municipal councils may approach the Constitutional Court with regard to competence conflicts with the Council of Ministers. The ombudsman and the Supreme Attorneys Council may approach the Constitutional Court with the demand to declare the unconstitutionality of provisions of acts of Parliament if they infringe constitutionally provided human rights.

*747.* At a first glance, it may seem that the range of institutions that may approach the Constitutional Court and initiate cases in front of it is rather wide. Indeed the 1991 Constitution establishes wide options for different public power institutions to approach the Constitutional Court. Many of these institutional opportunities constitute elements of the right to opposition. This is due to the fact that the predominant part of the Constitutional Court's cases are initiated by either the opposition in the Parliament (via the one-fifth quota of MPs) or the President when he or she does not share political affiliation of the governing majority in the Parliament and in the government. Moreover, the key institutions of the judicial power – the Supreme Court of Cassation, the Supreme Administrative Court and the State Prosecutor General are also granted direct access to the Constitutional Court which they use rather frequently in practice.

*748.* However, there are two actors of special importance which unfortunately have indirect and thus very limited or even fictitious access to the Constitutional Court. These are the citizens and the ordinary courts and state prosecutors.

*749.* There is no direct constitutional complaint in Bulgaria. This fact deprives the Bulgarian citizens from the chance to have important remedy to human rights violations accomplished by public power institutions. Moreover, the lack of constitutional complaint essentially limits the occasions on which the Constitutional Court can develop intense and broad human rights jurisprudence. Thus human rights' dimension of the activity of the Bulgarian Constitutional Court remains incremental and is overshadowed by the other functions of the court.

*750.* The citizens have four theoretical options to trigger a case for human rights violations in front of the Constitutional Court. The most clear and direct path is to inform the ombudsman regarding such issue who can then approach the Constitutional Court if he or she considers that there is indeed human rights violation. The ombudsman serves as a filter thus making the citizens' complaint indirect. Furthermore, the ombudsman himself has limited options because he or she can approach the Constitutional Court only if human rights are infringed by act of Parliament and not by any other source of law. Another important limitation is that only human rights as provided by the 1991 Constitution can be protected via that procedure for indirect constitutional complaint. Human rights which are provided by the international or EU law cannot be subject to this procedure.

*751.* The Bulgarian ombudsman tries to make use of the right to approach the Constitutional Court with demands for declaration of unconstitutionality of acts of Parliament which infringe constitutionally provided human rights. However, the number of these indirect constitutional complaints remains limited and is not able to fully remedy the lack of direct constitutional complaint.

*752.* The second option is available only in case of a lawsuit which is pending in front of a court. The parties to the lawsuit can raise the issue of unconstitutionality of legislative provision or international treaty which is applicable in the case. If the court considers the demand to be reasonable, it can approach the Supreme Administrative Court or the Supreme Court of Cassation depending on the type of the court and the procedure. The Supreme Administrative Court or the Supreme Court of Cassation is then competent to reject that motion or to approach the Constitutional Court. It is clear that this is rather a lengthy procedure. It is unlikely to be used by the citizens due to the fact that it will additionally slow down the process and will impede the timely solving of their case which will reflect also on the protection of the pretended rights. The ordinary courts also systematically avoid using that procedure because it hampers the process and has very low chances to end up with successful result in a timely manner.

*753.* The citizens may also ask their attorneys to raise a demand in front of the Supreme Attorneys Council to approach the Constitutional Court with the issue whether a constitutionally enshrined human right is infringed by an act of Parliament. However, this procedure seems fictitious in practice. It meets high motivational and organizational impediments concerning both the attorney that would initiate it as well as the Supreme Attorneys Council which is supposed to approach the Constitutional Court. Moreover, the Supreme Attorneys Council has the same limitations as the ombudsman. It can approach the Constitutional Court only with regard to acts of Parliament that infringe human rights provided by the 1991 Constitution.

*754.* Finally, the citizens may expose the presumed infringement of their human rights to the institutions with general competence to approach the Constitutional Court. These institutions are not obliged in any way to consider such complaint. This is rather an exotic opportunity which has never triggered any procedure in front of the Constitutional Court.

*755.* There are two main phases of the procedure in front of the Constitutional Court. These are the admissibility phase and the discussion on the merits of the case phase. The first phase starts with the initiation of the case by the subjects that may approach the Constitutional Court. It ends with a resolution for admission or for rejection of the case. During the admissibility phase, the Constitutional Court decides whether all formal and procedural requirements have been successfully met and whether it is the competent institution to discuss and resolve the issue. The discussion on the merits phase commences with the just-mentioned resolution with which the Chairman of the Constitutional Court determines the judge–rapporteur. It consists in elaboration, discussion and adoption of the Constitutional Court's decision.

*756.* The Constitutional Court decides whether it is competent to adjudicate on the issue with which it has been approached. However, the Constitutional Court cannot initiate itself any procedures. It has to be approached by a competent institution with a demand for initiation of the case in written form. The Constitutional Court may constitute as interested parties different state institutions, NGOs or public institutions. The Court decides alone which should be these interested parties. The interested parties have the right but not the duty to present written statement on the case. The Constitutional Court is not obliged to take into account the written statements presented by the interested parties. They serve only as additional source of information and argumentation and may be cited by the Constitutional Court in the motives to the decision, may be used without explicit referral or may be left aside.

*757.* The procedure in front of the Constitutional Court is usually written. It is typically accomplished in a closed session without the presence of the institutions that have approached the Constitutional Court, the interested parties or any other institutions, organizations and persons other than the Constitutional Court judges themselves. In principle, the Constitutional Court takes into consideration only written evidence. The Court may demand the presentation of additional evidence and may appoint different types of expertise.

*758.* An important exception is the procedure for impeachment of the President or the Vice President of the Republic. The impeachment procedure includes oral hearings in which several office holders must participate. These are the President or the Vice President in person or via their attorneys as well as an MP or MPs who are determined by the National Assembly to sustain the accusation in front of the Constitutional Court. The impeachment procedure is exceptional also with a view to the fact that not only written but also oral and material evidence may be presented to the Constitutional Court. The other procedures in which such types of evidence may be gathered and used by the Constitutional Court are the procedures for the declaration of the unconstitutionality of political parties as well as the procedures for control of the legality of the parliamentary and presidential elections.

*759.* The claims to the Constitutional Court must be motivated and must contain all written evidence. Demands for declaration of the unconstitutionality of acts of Parliament or presidential decrees can be made as of the day of their publication in SG. The Constitutional Court Act provides that conflicts of competence between state institutions can be addressed to the court only after initial attempts have been made at their resolution by the involved institutions through discussion. The claims for declaration of illegality of the elections for President and Vice President, for MPs in the National Assembly and for MPs in the European Parliament have to be made not later than the fifteenth day after the decision of the Central Electoral Commission.

*760.* The Chairman of the Constitutional Court constitutes the case, appoints one or more judge–rapporteur and determines the date for hearing the case. The judge–rapporteur prepares the case and presents the draft decision to the other judges of the Constitutional Court. Usually, there is only one judge–rapporteur for each case. The exception is the procedure for the impeachment of the President or the Vice President of the Republic when the draft decision of the Constitutional Court is prepared by three judges–rapporteurs. In some cases concerning the issuing of interpretative decisions or decisions for control of the constitutionality of sub-constitutional legislation, the Constitutional Court has also decided to appoint more than one judge–rapporteur due to the complexity and the importance of the case.

*761.* The Constitutional Court is not bound by concrete terms for admission, consideration and decision of the case. An exception is the procedure for the impeachment of the President or the Vice President which has to be accomplished within a month after the introduction of the motion in the Constitutional Court. Further terms which have to be observed by the court concern the determination of the date for discussion of the case by the Chairman of the Constitutional Court as well as the two-month term for adopting the decision of the case once the Constitutional Court considers the case to be sufficiently clarified. However, in both cases the Chairman of the Constitutional Court or the Constitutional Court itself actually set the initial moment of the term. Thus these two terms are relatively open to their discretionary judgement with regard to the timing.

*762.* The Constitutional Court's decisions are adopted with absolute majority of the votes of the judges. The Constitutional Court consists of twelve judges. This means that the absolute majority amounts to seven judges. In case of parity of the votes (six votes in favour and six votes against the decision), the decision is considered as being not adopted. The only exception is the procedure for impeachment of the President and the Vice President. The decision for impeachment should be adopted not by absolute but via qualified two-thirds majority of the votes of the Constitutional Court's judges. In both cases, the presence of at least two-thirds of the Constitutional Court's judges is needed for the successful adoption of a Constitutional Court's decision. The same quorum applies for all proceedings and for all sessions of the Constitutional Court.

*763.* The Constitutional Court's decisions are adopted by open voting. The Constitutional Court's judges who disagree with the decision and have voted against it can present a dissenting opinion. The Constitutional Court's judges who have voted in favour of the decision but disagree with some of its motives can present concurring opinion. Both the dissenting and the concurring opinions are published and are available for consideration to the public.

## §5. Constitutional Court's Acts

*764.* The Constitutional Court adopts two types of legal acts – decisions and rulings. The rulings are acts which concern procedural issues. The Constitutional Court by virtue of rulings rejects or admits the cases for further consideration on their merits.

*765.* The decisions are the acts on the merits of the case. There are three types of Constitutional Court's decisions: first, interpretative decisions, second, decisions for norm control and third, individual (non-normative) decisions on concrete matters.

*766.* The interpretative decisions are decisions for abstract interpretation of the Constitution. They have the same rank as the Constitution itself and form a part of a normative complex, which consists of the interpreted constitutional provision and the interpretative decision. Indeed there is no explicit provision of the 1991 Constitution which deliberately clarifies the hierarchical rank of the interpretative decisions of the Constitutional Court. However, the interpretative decision clarifies the meaning of the interpreted constitutional provision. The constitutional provision should then be understood with the new meaning extracted and defined, but it should also be frequently further developed by the Constitutional Court. Thus both the interpreted constitutional provision and the interpretative decision of the Constitutional Court should possess the same hierarchical status.

*767.* The decisions for norm control are adopted by the Constitutional Court as a result of its competence to control the compliance of the international treaties, the legal acts of the National Assembly and the decrees of the President of the Republic with the 1991 Constitution as well as the compliance of the above-mentioned acts of the Parliament and the President with the international treaties and the generally recognized principles of the international law.

*768.* Similar to the interpretative decisions, the decisions for norm control are sources of law which have the same hierarchical status as the safeguarded act. Again, there is no explicit constitutional provision stipulating the hierarchical rank of these decisions. Hence this rank is defined on the basis of the logic that the norm control decisions, in order to have the derogative effect of blocking the contravening legal provision due to unconstitutionality or non-compliance with international law, should possess the rank of the controlled superior norm. The specificity here is that there are different sources of law which are safeguarded by the Constitutional Court through its norm control decisions. Thus the decisions for declaration of unconstitutionality should possess constitutional rank or at least rank that is above the international treaties whereas the decisions for non-compliance with the international treaties and the generally recognized principles of international law should have their rank.

*769.* The third category of the Constitutional Court's decisions encompasses all other decisions of the Constitutional Court which do not possess the character of a source of law. These are the decisions for impeachment of the President, for prohibition of political parties due to unconstitutionality, for control of the legality of elections and for the solving of conflict of competences regarding the horizontal and the vertical separation of powers. It has to be taken into account that the last type of decisions – the decisions for resolution of conflicts of competences – may also have normative character. This is because they may contain important interpretation of the constitutional provisions regarding the scope of competence of some of the most important state institutions thus giving additional idea about the meaning of the constitutional texts.

*770.* The Constitutional Court's decisions are published in SG within fifteen days after their adoption. They enter into force three days after the day of their publication. In fact, these are the same requirements for entering into force which are applicable also to the acts of the Parliament. The Bulgarian Constitutional Court publishes its decisions and rulings also on its web page: www.constcourt.bg.

## §6. Status of the Constitutional Court's Judges

*771.* The judges of the Constitutional Court have nine years of non-renewable mandate. This means that the judges have a fixed term of office whereas the Constitutional Court is a permanently functioning institution with partial renewal of the staff which is accomplished every three years. One-third of the Constitutional Court's judges are elected by the National Assembly, one-third are elected by the general assembly of the judges of the Supreme Court of Cassation and the Supreme Administrative Court and one-third are appointed by the President of the Republic.

*772.* The 1991 Constitution and the Constitutional Court Act establish system of safeguards for the independence of the Constitutional Court's judges. It comprises the requirements for election or appointment as a judge in the Constitutional Court, the incompatibilities with other offices and activities, the immunity of the judges, the irremovability of the judges until the lapse of their term of office and the safeguards for their material status.

*773.* The Constitution provides for rather broad requirements for the election or appointment as a judge in the Constitutional Court. The candidates must be lawyers with at least fifteen years of legal practice and should possess high professional and moral qualities. The service as a judge, state prosecutor, state investigator, attorney-at-law, in-house lawyer of a company, state notary, executive magistrate and legal scientist in the universities or the scientific institutes counts as qualified legal practice as one of the requirements for election or appointment as a judge in the Constitutional Court. However, in practice, most of the Constitutional Court's judges are either law professors or former judges. Some of the Constitutional Court's judges have also experience as politicians.

*774.* There is no explicit age requirement for the election or appointment as a judge at the Constitutional Court. Most law students finish their university education at the age of 24–25 years. If they immediately get a job which counts for the legal practice requirement, then they should meet that requirement at the age of 40.

*775.* The status as Constitutional Court's judge is incompatible with the representative mandate, with the position in any state institution or with the accomplishment of public service, with membership in a political party or trade union and with the accomplishment of any paid professional activity either in the public or in the private sector. The only exception is the academic activity in the universities and the scientific institutes. In the latter case, the Constitutional Court's judge should take an unpaid leave from the university or the scientific institute.

*776.* According to Article 147, paragraph 6 of the Constitution, the Constitutional Court's judges enjoy the same immunity as the MPs in the National Assembly. The immunity of the MPs has already been analysed in the chapter related to the National Assembly. According to Article 148, paragraph 2 of the Constitution, the Constitutional Court lifts the immunity of a judge and establishes the actual inability of a judge to discharge the duties thereof by a secret ballot and by a majority of at least two-thirds of all judges.

*777.* According to Article 148 of the Constitution, the term of office of a Constitutional Court's judge ends in case of expiry of the term of office, resignation, entry into force of a sentence whereby a penal sanction of deprivation of liberty has been imposed for an intentional offence, actual inability to discharge the duties thereof for a period exceeding one year, incompatibility with the above-mentioned offices and activities and death. This means that the only instance in which a Constitutional Court's judge may be removed from office concerns the case when the Constitutional Court has lifted his or her immunity and he or she has been sentenced to deprivation of liberty for intentional offence. All other grounds for pre-term termination of the office of a Constitutional Court's judge are either objective phenomena such as the death or the actual inability to perform its duties or a result of his or her will as in the case of the resignation. Hence the judges in the Constitutional Court are partially irremovable from office with the only exception of imprisonment sentence.

*778.* Last but not least it has to be mentioned that the Constitutional Court judges enjoy the status of the Chairman of the National Assembly. The Chairman of the Constitutional Court receives a salary amounting to the medium salary of the President of the Republic and the Chairman of the National Assembly whereas the Constitutional Court's judges receive 90% of the salary of the Chairman of the Constitutional Court. The Constitutional Court's judges, if they wish so, may get retired immediately after the end of their term of office.

# Chapter 7. The Institutions for Extra-Parliamentary Control of the Activity of the State Institutions

## §1. The Court of Auditors

*779.* The Court of Auditors became constitutional institution – an institution with a status provided by the Constitution itself – with the adoption of the 1991 Constitution. Consequently, although the Court of Auditors is not a novelty for the Bulgarian institutional design and tradition, its constitutional status is a novelty for the Bulgarian constitutional law.

*780.* According to Article 91 of the Constitution, the National Assembly elects a Court of Auditors which controls the implementation of the state budget. The Constitution just briefly provides for the existence of this institution and refers to a special act of Parliament to determine the status, functions and competences of the Court of Auditors.

*781.* The purpose of vesting constitutional status in the Court of Auditors through the just-mentioned laconic provision is a result of the awareness of the constitutional legislation of the importance of the public finance and the need for safeguarding the independence of the institution which controls the public finance management. The granting of constitutional status to the Court of Auditors is an institutional reflection of the emancipation of the financial power from the executive power of the state. Thus the 1991 Constitution reflects the emergence of financial constitution, financial power and financial constitutionalism as durable elements of the modern constitutional law.[81]

*782.* The Court of Auditors is a collective constitutional institution of the financial power which is allocated on national level. The Court of Auditors enjoys increased independence from the other constitutional institutions. Its institutional autonomy consists in its separate budget, in the long seven-year term of office of its members which exceeds the four-year term of office of the National Assembly as an institution which elects it and in its freedom of judgment and activity in performing its constitutionally and legislatively ascribed functions.

*783.* The Court of Auditors is composed of Chairman, two Vice Chairmen and two members. They are all elected by the National Assembly with seven-year term of office. The Chairman cannot be re-elected whereas the Vice Chairmen and the members can be re-elected for an unlimited number of terms of office.

*784.* The National Assembly elects separately the Chairman, the Vice Chairmen and the members of the Court of Auditors. Candidates for Chairman can be proposed by the MPs whereas the candidates for Vice Chairmen are proposed by the

81. For the concepts of financial constitution, financial power and financial constitutionalism, *see* Martin Belov, *Financial Constitutionalism*, 1–109 (Sibi, 2015).

elected Chairman of the Court of Auditors. The candidates for members of the Court of Auditors are proposed by the Institute of Licensed Expert Auditors and by the Institute of Internal Auditors. Thus the Court of Auditors Act introduces a complex scheme for separation of patronage power regarding the Court of Auditors. It mixes political influences accomplished by the Parliament and expert-corporatist influences ascertained by the Institute of Licensed Expert Auditors and by the Institute of Internal Auditors.

*785.* According to Article 23 of the Court of Auditors Act, the auditing activity of the Court of Auditors is organized in directorates which are headed by directors. The directorates may be structured into branches, sectors and temporary territorial structures.

*786.* The broad constitutionally proclaimed task of the Court of Auditors is to accomplish control over the implementation of the state budget. This constitutional task is further developed in more detail by the Court of Auditors Act. According to the act, the Court of Auditors accomplishes several types of audits – financial audits, conformity and compliance audits, execution audits and specific audits. The Court of Auditors by virtue of these audits controls the legality and the due administration of the public finance.

*787.* More precisely, the scope of the object of the auditing activity of the Court of Auditors includes: the state budget, the budget of the state social assurance, the budget of the National Health Assurance Fund, the municipal budgets and other budgets which are adopted by the National Assembly. The Court of Auditors accomplishes auditing activity also over the public service providers, the public finance stemming out of EU funds, the issuing and management of public debt, the implementation of the budgets of various important state institutions as well as private sector actors which dispose of budgetary funding etc.

*788.* The central part of the activity of the Court of Auditors is the control over the implementation and management of the state budget by the Council of Ministers. The Court of Auditors adopts a special report which summarizes and analyses its finding on this important activity of the government. The report is presented to the National Assembly who adopts decisions regarding the dismissal of the Council of Ministers from responsibility for the implementation of the state budget based on the suggestions of the Court of Auditors. The Court of Auditors introduces in the National Assembly similar reports for the implementation of the different budgets which have been presented above.

*789.* The Court of Auditors accomplishes its activity on the basis of annual auditing programme. In addition, the National Assembly may assign to the Court of Auditors up to five extraordinary audits per year, which are not included in this annual programme.

§2. THE OMBUDSMAN

*790.* The national ombudsman has been established for the first time in the Bulgarian history by the Ombudsman Act in 2004 (the act was adopted in 2003 but entered into force on 1 January 2004). It has gained a constitutional status in 2006 by virtue of the provision of Article 91a of the Constitution. According to this act, the National Assembly elects an ombudsman who defends human rights and freedoms. Moreover, the Constitution delegates to the Parliament to further develop the status, functions and competences of the ombudsman. This task has been already accomplished by the Parliament two years in advance before the adoption of this constitutional provision. In addition, the 2006 constitutional amendment has granted the ombudsman the competence to approach the Constitutional Court with the demand to declare unconstitutional acts of Parliament which infringe constitutionally provided human rights and freedoms.

*791.* The ombudsman is an independent national institution which is an important safeguard of the constitutional rights of the citizens as well as of the non-citizens in Bulgaria. There are only two elements of semi-dependence of the national ombudsman from the Parliament. First, the rules for the organization of the activity of the ombudsman have to be approved by the National Assembly via parliamentary decision. Second, the National Assembly adopts the budget of the ombudsman.

*792.* Apart from the national ombudsman, there are also other types of ombudsmen in Bulgaria. There are many local ombudsmen on different levels of the territorial structure of the state. There are also specialized ombudsmen attached to different public organizations such as the state-owned heating provider, many universities. However, there is no other ombudsman with general or special competence on national level in Bulgaria. It should be mentioned again that some of the functions of the ombudsman are traditionally performed in Bulgaria by the state prosecutors. This is especially true for the oversight for the implementation of the penitentiary, detention and compulsory medical measures which is typically and much more frequently performed by the state prosecutors than by the ombudsman.

*793.* The ombudsman is elected by the National Assembly with five-year term of office on a proposal of the MPs, the parliamentary groups or the NGO's working in the sphere of human rights via open voting and with the majority of the MPs who have participated in the voting. The National Assembly elects also vice ombudsman who supports the ombudsman in the accomplishment of his or her tasks. The ombudsman and the vice ombudsman must be Bulgarian citizens and must possess the requirements necessary for election as an MP. They must have high moral qualities, university education and proven experience in the sphere of human rights protection. The vice ombudsman is elected by virtue of the same procedure as the ombudsman and has to meet the same requirements for election. The only difference is that the vice ombudsman is elected on a proposal of the ombudsman. Both the ombudsman and the vice ombudsman may be re-elected for only one additional term of office.

*794.* In general, the status of the ombudsman is comparable to the status of the MPs. The Ombudsman Act explicitly refers to the requirements for election of the MPs and determines them as core requirements for the election as an ombudsman. Moreover, the ombudsman enjoys similar rights and privileges as the MPs. For example, the ombudsman has the immunity of an MP with the same salary.

*795.* The Bulgarian ombudsman performs one main function – a human rights' protection function, which can be divided into five main sub-functions. These are protection against already accomplished human rights violations, mediation, prevention, policy initiation in the human rights domain and the normative control function for the compliance with higher human rights standards.

*796.* The ombudsman safeguards human rights by virtue of check-ups for their violation by the state institutions as well as by the public service providers. The ombudsman may issue recommendations to these institutions for discontinuation or for prevention of human rights violations. He or she can mediate between the state institutions and the citizen for remedying human rights infringements. Furthermore, the ombudsman may prepare and present recommendations for protection of human rights violated or threatened by private subjects. This novel competence of the ombudsman, introduced in the Ombudsman Act in 2018, puts special emphasis on the horizontal dimension of the human rights related to their protections from violations accomplished by non-governmental, private entities. This is one of the rare examples of explicit provision of 'horizontal' or 'societal' dimension of the human rights in the Bulgarian constitutional law. Last but not least, the Ombudsman Act grants the ombudsman the competence to safeguard the rights of the child.

*797.* The ombudsman may also present his or her opinion on draft legislative acts as well as on draft normative acts of the government which concern human rights. He or she may recommend to the Parliament and to the government the ratification of international treaties concerning human rights. The ombudsman observes and takes measures for support and encouragement of the efficient application of human rights provided by international treaties that are ratified by the Republic of Bulgaria. The ombudsman can also inform the state prosecutor's office for human rights violations which constitute criminal offence.

*798.* The ombudsman can approach the institutions that are competent to approach the Constitutional Court with demand for giving an interpretation of constitutional texts as well as for accomplishing control for the compliance of the international treaties with the Bulgarian Constitution and for the compliance of the acts of the Parliament with the international treaties and with the generally recognized principles of international law. The ombudsman can start a procedure for control of the compliance of the Bulgarian legislation with human rights standards set in the international law only via this indirect path. This is because the ombudsman can directly approach the Constitutional Court only for infringement of the constitutionally enshrined human rights by virtue of an act of Parliament.

*799.* The ombudsman cannot directly approach the Constitutional Court for violation of human rights provided by the international treaties or by the EU law. Moreover, the ombudsman cannot safeguard constitutional rights against infringement via international treaties or normative acts of the government. This restrictive constitutional background is rather problematic. It has been adopted due to the fear of the constitutional legislator that the Constitutional Court might have to address an increased workload.

*800.* However, this argument is rather weak due to three main reasons. First, the ombudsman is a state institution which can use its competence to approach the Constitutional Court with reason and moderation. So far, the ombudsman has served very well his or her role to safeguard the constitutional rights against infringements via acts of Parliament. The ombudsman has approached the Constitutional Court on key issues and only in very important cases. Second, the extension of the ombudsman's competence to approach the Constitutional Court may compensate the lack of direct constitutional complaint and may partially enhance the role of the court as a safeguard for human rights in Bulgaria. Third, the Bulgarian Constitutional Court has currently very low workload with an average of ten to twenty cases per year.

*801.* The ombudsman serves also as national preventive mechanism in accordance with the UN Convention against Torture and Other Cruel, Inhuman or Degrading Treatment or Punishment. The ombudsman's competences as a national preventive mechanism are provided in a separate Chapter IV of the Ombudsman Act. This chapter has been adopted in 2012.

# Part III. The Form of Territorial Distribution of State Power

## §1. General Characteristics of the Unitary State with Local Self-Government

*802*. The unitary state with local self-government is among the most durable and profound characteristics of the Bulgarian statehood since its re-establishment in 1879. The four Bulgarian constitutions have provided for three forms of government – constitutional monarchy, Soviet type of people's democracy and hybrid parliamentary republic. However, all of them have provided for the unitary nature of the territorial model of the state power and have preserved, although to a different extent, the local self-government. Thus the unitary form of the statehood is an element of the Bulgarian constitutional tradition and eventually may be determined also as a part of the Bulgarian constitutional identity.[82]

*803*. There are three main issues of the local self-government which impede its effective and proper functioning. They have emerged in the context of the transition to democracy since 1989–1991.

*804*. First, there is a clear tendency for fragmentation of the Bulgarian municipalities. The permanent emergence of new municipalities splitting out of existing ones is predominantly motivated and driven by economic reasons such as investment interest in municipalities possessing natural, cultural, tourism, production or other resources. The drive to control these resources produce tensions which sometimes culminate in secession and establishment of new municipalities. The fragmentation of the municipalities diminishes the economic and financial sustainability of some of them and produces complicated structure of the administrative–territorial division of the state.

*805*. Second, the Bulgarian state in the context of the post-1989 democratization fostered the local self-government. In many cases, however, the increase of the institutional, economic and tax autonomy of the municipalities does not lead to the establishment of vital local democratic communities but strengthens and consolidates local oligarchic elites. These elites became factors mediating the regulative influence of the state and its reformist attempts and frequently playing an important

82. Martin Belov, *The Bulgarian Constitutional Identity*, 164 (Sibi, 2017).

role in the political life of the local communities by controlling the local business and dominating the investment and the management of the public procurement. In fact, the establishment of local patronage and nepotism schemes is central impediment for the real establishment of rule of law and democracy in Bulgaria.

*806.* Third, the decrease of the centralized policymaking influence of the state has produced the emergence of 'winners and losers' among the municipalities. According to Article 20 of the 1991 Constitution, the state safeguards the balanced development of the different regions of the country and aids the territorial institutions through its financial, credit and investment policy. However, this is one of the most fictive provisions of the current Bulgarian Constitution. The very uneven development of the Bulgarian municipalities is a result not only of the difference in the investment interest but also in the lack of durable and rational regional policy of the state. Clear example is the fact that the capital city of Sofia is among the most rapidly developing cities in Europe having welfare comparable to the European average whereas the municipalities in North Western Bulgaria are the poorest in the EU.

*807.* Article 2, paragraph 1 of the 1991 Constitution prohibits the establishment of territorial autonomies. This provision should be read in systematic and teleological conjunction with Article 2, paragraph 2 of the 1991 Constitution which proclaims the inviolability of the territorial unity and integrity of the Republic of Bulgaria. The constitutional legislator tries to provide remedies against eventual separatist tendencies and definitely believes that federalism or territorial autonomy enhances such risks. The Bulgarian constitutional legislator does not go that far as the Romanian, which prohibits any federalization of Romania and provides for the unitary state as an unamendable clause of the 1992 Romanian Constitution. However, the 1991 Constitution imposes the unitary form as an entrenched clause. It provides for safeguards for it as well as for the territorial integrity of the state.

## §2. The Territorial Structure of the Public Power

### I. The Administrative–Territorial Structure of the State

*808.* The territorial structure of the public power in Bulgaria consists of two main levels and one intermediary level. The two main levels are the national and the local level whereas the regional level serves intermediary functions and is of secondary importance. Moreover, the local level itself is not a homogeneous category since it is additionally divided into further levels of public power.

*809.* Such conclusion does not immediately stem out of Article 135 of the Constitution. According to this article, the territory of the state is divided into regions and municipalities. The territorial structure of the capital city of Sofia and the establishment of other administrative–territorial units can be provided by an act of Parliament. The lack of explicit mentioning of the national level is because the Constitution implicitly presumes its existence. Moreover, the Constitution delegates the further development of the territorial structure of the public power to the National Assembly. Hence the territorial structure of the public power and the different types of the administrative–territorial units can be properly understood via systematic reading of the Constitution in conjunction with the parliamentary legislation.

*810.* Two acts of Parliament have been adopted by the National Assembly as a result of the just-mentioned legislative delegation. These are the Local Self-Government and Local Administration Act and the Administrative and Territorial Structure of the Republic of Bulgaria Act. According to both the Constitution and these two acts of Parliament, the administrative–territorial units are the regions and the municipalities. The municipality is the main administrative–territorial unit of the state. Composite administrative–territorial units in the framework of the municipality are the rayons and the mayorships. The region, the municipality and the mayorship have their administrative centre, boundaries, territory, population and name whereas the rayon has all these components except the administrative centre. The procedure for the establishment of administrative–territorial units and for their reform is provided by the Administrative and Territorial Structure of the Republic of Bulgaria Act.

*811.* The region is composed of one or more municipalities. The name of the municipality is the name of the city which serves as its administrative centre. The territory of the Republic of Bulgaria is divided into twenty-eight regions. The capital city of Sofia has the quality of both region and municipality. Moreover, there are two regions related to Sofia – the Sofia City region and the Sofia region. The first coincides with the city of Sofia and comprises the Sofia municipality. The second comprises the municipalities around Sofia. The region is an administrative–territorial unit in which only state institutions on regional level but no regional self-government institutions are allocated. Thus Bulgaria remains within the category of the classical unitary states without any form of federal-like devolution of state power.

*812.* The municipality is composed of one or more cities and villages. It is named after the city which is its administrative centre. Currently, there are more than 260 municipalities in Bulgaria. The municipality is the main administrative–territorial unit in which the self-government of the people is accomplished. The local self-government on municipal or lower levels can be accomplished via direct, participatory or representative democracy. In the municipalities, there are both institutions for local self-government and for local administration. Some institutions, e.g., the municipal mayor, combine the characteristics of institution for both local government and local self-government.[83]

*813.* Rayons must be established in the capital city of Sofia and in cities with population above 300,000 inhabitants. In the cities with population above 100,000 inhabitants, rayons may be established on the basis of a decision of the municipal

83. Tsvetan Sivkov, *The Municipality. Main Public Law Aspects*, 137 (Sibi, 2002).

council. Currently, there are three cities – Sofia, Plovdiv and Varna – which have rayon subdivision of their municipality. The rayons are established in order to facilitate the administration of big cities with their complex communal management and large number of inhabitants.

*814.* The mayorship consists of one or more towns or usually of one or more villages. The mayorship is not a compulsory administrative–territorial unit. It can be established via a decision of the municipal council. Usually, mayorships are created for small and remoted villages which need a small but always present administration available in close proximity to the inhabitants.

*815.* An intermediary conclusion can be made that the 1991 Constitution and the Bulgarian legislation provide for relatively simple territorial structure of the public power which is predetermined by the relatively small territory and population of Bulgaria. The administrative–territorial structure of the power reflects the unitary form of the state with local self-government and the need to provide for institutional design capable of addressing the administration and self-government needs of big cities such as Sofia, medium-sized and small cities as well as remoted towns and villages. Thus the administrative–territorial structure of Bulgaria is adequate to its social, demographic, geographic, economic and political conditions and is a central part of the Bulgarian constitutional tradition.

## II. The Territorial Structure of the Judiciary

*816.* The territorial structure of the judiciary (including the territorial structure of the courts and the state prosecutors' offices) may coincide with the territorial structure of the administration. However, this is just an option and not a necessary requirement. Thus the seats and the territorial jurisdictions of the courts and the state prosecutors' offices are determined by the plenum of the Supreme Judicial Council on proposal of its judicial or state prosecutors' colleges respectively or on proposal of the Minister of Justice. The seats and territorial jurisdictions of the military courts are determined in coordination with the Minister of Defence.

*817.* There are three compulsory requirements provided by the Judicial Power Act which must be respected by the Supreme Judicial Council while determining the territorial structure of the judiciary. First, the structure and thus the seats and the territorial jurisdictions of the state prosecutors' offices parallels and coincides with seats and the territorial jurisdictions of the courts. Second, the seats and the territorial jurisdictions of the administrative courts must coincide with the seats and the territorial jurisdictions of the district courts. Third, the seats of the two supreme courts – the Supreme Court of Cassation and the Supreme Administrative Court, the seats of the Supreme State Prosecutors' Office of Cassation and the Supreme Administrative State Prosecutors' Office as well as of the Specialized Criminal Court and the Specialized Criminal Court of Appeal are in Sofia. However, these institutions have jurisdiction over the whole territory of the Republic of Bulgaria.

§3. THE REGIONS AND THE STATE INSTITUTIONS FOR REGIONAL GOVERNMENT

*818.* The number and the allocation of the regions are determined by the Administrative and Territorial Structure of the Republic of Bulgaria Act. The boundaries and the administrative centres of the regions are determined with a decree by the President on a proposal of the Council of Ministers. The region comprises one or more municipalities. The territory of the Republic of Bulgaria is divided into twenty-eight regions ('oblast', „област' in Bulgarian). The capital city of Sofia has the status of both municipality and region. The name of the region is the name of the city which is its administrative centre.

*819.* The region is an administrative unit of the territorial structure of the state for a decentralized state government. Thus the region is governed only by a regional governor as an institution of the executive power appointed by the Council of Ministers while there is no elective, collective institution for regional self-government. The central state institutions, e.g., in the domains of police, maintenance of the public order, healthcare, finance, education etc., may have their regional substructures for accomplishment of their competences and tasks on regional level.

*820.* The regional governor accomplishes the state policy in the region. He or she serves as an intermediary institution between the national and the local levels of public power. The regional governor accomplishes administrative control over the acts of the municipal mayors and the municipal councils.

§4. THE LOCAL SELF-GOVERNMENT IN THE MUNICIPALITIES

## I. The Mayors

*821.* There are three types of mayors: mayors of municipality, mayors of rayons and mayors of mayorships. All mayors are elected by the people by virtue of a majority voting system with absolute majority. They are elected for four-year term of office. There is no limitation for the re-election of the mayors. The right to stand as a candidate for mayor belongs to Bulgarian citizens older than 18 years who are not under custody, do not serve an imprisonment sentence and have lived for at least six months in the place in which they apply for being elected.

*822.* The term of office of the mayors can be terminated before the lapse of the four-year period in case of: death, resignation, permanent inability to perform the duties for more than six months due to illness, unjustified absence from work for more than one month, putting under custody, sentencing to imprisonment for intentional crime or sentencing to deprivation of the right to accomplish the profession as state office holder, lack of preconditions for election as mayor which has been discovered after the election, incompatibility with offices or activities provided by the Local Self-Government and Local Self-Administration Act, conflict of interests, change in the mayor's permanent address with one which is outside of the municipality, rayon or mayorship and discontinuation of the existence of the municipality, rayon or mayorship.

*823.* The competences of the municipality mayors are enlisted in Article 44 of the Local Self-Government and Local Self-Administration Act. This list is not exclusive since additional competences are provided by other acts of Parliament. The municipality mayor: guides the activity of all executive power institutions in the municipality, coordinates the policy of the specialized administration in the municipality, implements the legislation as well as the acts of the municipal council, appoints and dismisses the vice mayors as well as the municipality office holders, organizes the implementation of the municipal budget and the different financial or planning programmes.

*824.* The municipal mayor may delegate some of his or her competences to the rayon mayors and the mayors of the mayorships. The municipal mayor coordinates and supervises the activity of the rayon mayors and the mayors of the mayorships and accomplishes control for legality and appropriateness of their activity and the legal acts that they adopt.

*825.* The municipality mayor has specific competences in the field of urban planning, public construction works, maintenance of public order and security, issuing of acts related to the civic status of the inhabitants of the municipality etc. Last but not least, the municipality mayors have representative and disciplinary competences. They represent the municipality in front of the state institutions, the other municipalities and the civic society. They may impose disciplinary sanctions on the office holders who belong to the municipal administration.

*826.* The municipality mayors issue orders. The orders are the individual administrative acts by virtue of which the municipality mayors accomplish their competences. They are subject to control for legality in front of the administrative courts. The regional governors may control the orders of the mayors with regard to both their legality and appropriateness.

*827.* The municipality mayor is accountable to the municipal council. He or she must give regular account on the implementation of the legislation and the acts of the municipal council, on the implementation of the municipal budget and the other programmes and plans adopted by the municipal council.

*828.* The competences of the rayon mayors and the mayors of mayorships are enlisted in Article 46 of the Local Self-Government and Local Self-Administration Act. According to this article, they are competent to: implement these parts of the municipal budget which are related to the rayon or the mayorship, organize, undertake and coordinate measures related to public services and municipal undertakings, provide for public services, implement policies related to ecology, culture, development of the public infrastructure, protection of the public order etc.

*829.* The rayon mayors and the mayors of mayorships issue orders. They are individual administrative acts which are subject to control by the municipality mayors, the municipal councils and the administrative courts.

## II. The Municipal Council

*830.* According to Article 138 of the Constitution, the municipal council is the institution for local self-government in the municipality. It is elected directly by the citizen of the municipality on the basis of proportional representation system for four-year term of office.

*831.* The municipal council is the only representative and collective institution which is elected by the people on subnational level. Together with the National Assembly, it forms the range of institutions for proportional representation of the social interests and party affiliations in the system of public power. There are no such collective representative bodies either on regional level or in the rayons or the mayorships. In these administrative–territorial units, in contrast to the municipality, there are only institutions of the executive power which may be appointive by the central government (in the case of the regional governor) or elective by the people (in the case of the mayors of the rayons and the mayorships).

*832.* The municipal council is composed of municipal councillors. Their number differs in accordance with the number of the population in the municipality. Article 19 of the Local Self-Government and Local Administration Act defines the number of the municipal councillors in the different type of municipalities with a view to their inhabitants. Thus the municipal councils in the least populated municipalities are composed of eleven municipal councillors whereas the Sofia municipal council comprises sixty-one municipal councillors.

*833.* The municipal council has wide-ranging functions. They may be structured into five main groups: norm-setting function, controlling function, constitutive function, financial and budgetary function and policy determination function. Apart from these legal functions, the municipal council accomplishes also political functions. These are the representation, legitimation and integration functions.[84]

*834.* The municipal council adopts normative acts – regulations and decrees – which are valid in its territorial jurisdiction. They are allocated at the lowest level of the normative hierarchy in Bulgaria and are subordinated to all sources of law adopted by the institutions on national level. Furthermore, the municipal council adopts also instructions which may possess in some cases normative character. The decisions of the municipal council are individual administrative acts. Last but not least, the municipal council adopts also political acts such as the declarations and the addresses.

---

84. For more about the functions of the municipal council, *see* Tsvetan Sivkov, *ibid.*, 139 et seq.

*835.* The municipal council accomplishes political control over the mayors of the municipality, rayon and mayorship. It accomplishes administrative control over the just-mentioned mayors as well as over the municipal administration. The municipal council accomplishes preventive and posterior control for the due implementation of its acts.

*836.* The municipal council elects the municipal ombudsman. It constitutes its own standing or temporary committees and elects its Chairman and Vice Chairmen. It determines the structure of the municipal administration as well as the number of office holders and civil servants in it.

*837.* The municipal council adopts the annual budget of the municipality. It approves the annual report of the municipal mayor for its implementation. Since the 2007 constitutional reform, the municipal council is allowed to determine the municipal taxes in accordance, in the framework and on the basis of procedure determined by the acts of the Parliament. This constitutional amendment has introduced a degree of financial decentralization in Bulgaria.

*838.* Last but not least, the municipal council participates in the framing and determining the main principles and trends of the different policies in the municipality. This is done not only via its legal and political acts but also through the approval of different strategies, programmes and plans for the development of the municipality.

# Part IV. Constitutional Status of the Citizens

## Chapter 1. Bulgarian Citizenship

### §1. Acquisition of Bulgarian Citizenship

*839.* Bulgarian citizenship is acquired either *ex lege*, automatically and without the expression of any will by virtue of the birth of the person, or as a result of his or her will through naturalization or via restoration of Bulgarian citizenship. There are two ways for acquisition of Bulgarian citizenship by birth – *ius sanguinis* and *ius soli*.

*840.* The main method for acquisition of Bulgarian citizenship is *ius sanguinis*. That is, a person whose parents or at least one of them is a Bulgarian citizen gets Bulgarian citizenship automatically. Article 9 of the Bulgarian Citizenship Act provides that a person becomes a Bulgarian citizen via *ius sanguinis* also if he or she is recognized as a child by Bulgarian citizen or if his or her origin from a Bulgarian citizen is recognized through judicial decision.

*841.* The other method for acquisition of Bulgarian citizenship is *ius soli*. *Ius soli* consists in the fact that a person who is born on Bulgarian territory gets Bulgarian citizenship if he or she does not acquire Bulgarian citizenship via *ius sanguinis*. Hence *ius soli* is an alternative and subsidiary method which is of secondary importance in Bulgaria. The typical case of acquisition of Bulgarian citizenship through *ius soli* is regulated by Article 11 of the Bulgarian Citizenship Act. It provides that a child who is found without any information regarding its parents is supposed to be born on the Bulgarian territory and thus acquires Bulgarian citizenship via *ius soli*.

*842.* Chapter II, Section III of the Bulgarian Citizenship Act provides for several procedures for naturalization. The main procedure is provided in Article 12 whereas Articles 12a to 16 determine the conditions for ‘privileged naturalizations’.

*843.* The main procedure for naturalization provided by Article 12 of the Bulgarian Citizenship Act is based upon the several preconditions that must be fulfilled by the applicant. These requirements are: coming of age of maturity; acquisition of permanent or long-term residence permit not earlier than five years before the moment of filing of the application; lack of criminal verdict for intentional crime issued by a Bulgarian court and lack of initiated criminal proceedings for such criminal offence except if the person is rehabilitated; possession of an income or profession which allows the person to make his or her own living in Bulgaria; sufficient command of the Bulgarian language and release of his or her current citizenship or sufficient evidence that the person has already initiated such procedure for release of previous citizenship.

*844.* The 'privileged naturalizations' differ from the general procedure for naturalization with regard to the omission of some or even all prerequisites needed for naturalization. They are available to different types of persons who in the view of the legislator deserve special treatment and eased procedures for naturalization. The scope of such persons includes: persons who are married to or adopted by Bulgarian citizens; persons who are born in Bulgaria; persons who have acquired their permanent or long-term residence permit before the age of 18; persons who have received asylum, status of refugee or humanitarian status before certain number of years; stateless persons; huge investors; persons from Bulgarian origin and persons whose parent is a Bulgarian citizen. Last but not least, Article 16 of the Bulgarian Citizenship Act does not impose any requirements for the naturalization of persons who have special merits to the Republic of Bulgaria or whose naturalization aims at satisfying special interest of the Republic of Bulgaria.

*845.* The restoration of Bulgarian citizenship is provided for in Chapter IV of the Bulgarian Citizenship Act. The restoration is a method for acquisition of Bulgarian citizenship by persons who have previously been released from it. However, such restoration is not automatically granted because it is preconditioned upon several requirements. These requirements are as follows: first, the applicant should not have been sentenced for intentional crime in the state in which he or she lives or in Bulgaria; second, the person must not pose a threat to the national security, the public order, the public health and the public moral; third, the person should be in possession of permanent or long-term residence permit in Bulgaria. Moreover, according to Article 27 of the Bulgarian Citizenship Act, the Bulgarian citizenship may be restored to persons who are deprived of Bulgarian citizenship without a valid legal ground or on the basis of ground for deprivation of citizenship which has lost its importance.

## §2. Loss of Bulgarian Citizenship

*846.* There are three main procedures for loss of Bulgarian citizenship. These are the release from Bulgarian citizenship, the abolition of the naturalization and the deprivation from Bulgarian citizenship. The first is a voluntary method for termination of the relationship between the citizen and the Bulgarian state, whereas the second and the third procedures possess the characteristics of a sanction, and they are imposed by the state against the will of the Bulgarian citizen. Moreover, the release from Bulgarian citizenship may be used as a method for loss of all kinds of citizenship – either acquired by birth (via *ius sanguinis* or *ius soli*) or by virtue of naturalization. On the contrary, the abolition of the naturalization and the deprivation from Bulgarian citizenship are applicable only to cases of citizenship acquired through naturalization. In other words, the methods for loss of citizenship which have the characteristics of a sanction are applicable only to naturalized citizens but not to Bulgarian citizens by birth.

*847.* The release from Bulgarian citizenship is an option which is available only to Bulgarian citizens who live permanently abroad and have acquired the citizenship of another state or are in the process of such acquisition.

*848.* The abolition of naturalization is a procedure for loss of citizenship due to defects in the procedure for its acquisition. It is applicable in the following three cases of improper acquisition of Bulgarian citizenship by naturalization. The first case consists in filing documents or presenting data and facts required by law for the acquisition of citizenship which have later been proved to be false via a judicial decision. The second case concerns the concealing of data and facts that, if revealed, would have been a ground for refusal of granting of citizenship. The third case concerns only the granting of privileged naturalization due to investment in Bulgaria. It consists in non-maintenance of the volume of the investments necessary for acquisition of Bulgarian citizenship for a period of at least two years.

*849.* The deprivation from Bulgarian citizenship is applicable only to naturalized Bulgarian citizens who have been sentenced via a judicial verdict, which has entered into force for grave criminal offences against the Republic of Bulgaria. However, the deprivation from citizenship can be activated only if the citizen is living abroad and will not become a stateless person.

## §3. Procedure for Acquisition or Loss of Bulgarian Citizenship

*850.* The Bulgarian citizenship is granted to people applying for naturalization, Bulgarian citizens are released from Bulgarian citizenship and they lose citizenship via abolition of the naturalization and the deprivation from Bulgarian citizenship with a decree of the President of the Republic. The President of the Republic may delegate this competence to the Vice President of the Republic. The decree of the President or the Vice President of the Republic enters into force as of the day of its issuing.

*851.* The procedure for acquisition of Bulgarian citizenship via naturalization commences by filing of application by the interested person. The application must be filed either in the Ministry of Justice or in the Bulgarian embassies abroad. In the latter case, the Bulgarian ambassador or some of the civil servants at the embassy must give an opinion on the application. Proposals for granting citizenship to persons who have special merits to the Republic of Bulgaria or from whose naturalization the state has special interest should be made by the Minister who is in charge of the respective field of social relations. Proposals for abolition of the naturalization and for deprivation from Bulgarian citizenship are made by the State Prosecutor General although in some cases such a proposal can be made also by the Minister of Justice.

*852.* The President and the Vice President of the Republic act on a proposal of the Minister of Justice who himself or herself acts on the advice of the Citizenship Council attached to the Ministry of Justice. The Citizenship Council is chaired by a Vice Minister of Justice. Its members are representatives of the Minister of Justice, the Minister of Interior, the Minister of Foreign Affairs, the Minister of Regional Development, the Minister of Labour, the Minister of Health, the State Agency for National Security, the State Agency for the Bulgarians Living Abroad and the State Agency for Refugees. A representative of the President of the Republic may also participate in the meetings of the Citizenship Council. The Citizenship Council issues advisory opinions which are not compulsory for either the Minister of Justice or the President or the Vice President of the Republic.

# Chapter 2. Fundamental Rights and Liberties

## §1. General Issues

### I. Terminological Issues

*853.* The 1991 Constitution uses a range of terms for denomination of human rights. The most frequently used term is simply 'right' either in combination with its specific character, e.g., property right, right to information etc., or as a plain expression. In the latter case, the term 'right' is used in different contexts, e.g., as a limitation to other human rights or to the activity of the state institutions, as peculiar expression of the universality of human rights and of the equality of the citizen in front of the law (Article 6) etc.

*854.* The preamble of the Constitution proclaims, among others, that the 'rights of the person' are supreme principle of the Bulgarian constitutional order. The same expression is used by Article 4, paragraph 2 which provides that the Republic of Bulgaria safeguards the life, dignity and the rights of the person and creates conditions for the free development of the person and the civil society.

*855.* The third term which is used by the Bulgarian Constitution is 'basic rights'. The very title of Chapter II devoted to human rights is 'basic rights and obligations of the citizen'. In addition, Article 24, paragraph 2 provides that basic rights and freedoms are among the main aims of the Constitution. Furthermore, according to Article 31, paragraph 5 the state safeguards the realization of all basic rights of the people sentenced to imprisonment which are not restrained by the judicial sentence. Last but not least, Article 57, paragraph 1 declares that the basic rights are irrevocable whereas Article 85, paragraph 1, point 6 provides that all international treaties related to the basic rights must be ratified by the National Assembly.

*856.* The term 'constitutional right' is not used by the Constitution. Also the terms 'human rights' and 'citizens' rights' are not immediate part of the constitutional vocabulary. However, the Constitution frequently distinguishes between rights belonging to all people and rights reserved to the Bulgarian citizens.

*857.* In fact, the 1991 Constitution does not use very precise terminology while differentiating between citizens' rights and human rights. It defines as citizens' rights not only rights which are usually reserved for the citizens due to their relation to state sovereignty (e.g., election rights) or to welfare state redistribution (e.g., social security rights) but also many other rights which should be provided also to foreigners because they possess universal value.

*858.* Examples of proclaiming of universal human rights as citizens' rights are the protection of the private life, the freedom of assembly, the freedom of association, the right to petition and the right to defence. The very nature of these rights and freedoms, their provision in international treaties to which Bulgaria is a part as well as the comparative analysis of their provision in the modern constitutional systems demonstrate that they should be proclaimed as universal human rights and not rights limited to the Bulgarian citizen. Moreover, the Bulgarian legislation allows the enjoyment of these rights to be granted also to foreigners.

*859.* Consequently, the Bulgarian Constitution does not use very precise terminology. Indeed the constitutional legislator intended to reserve some of the constitutional rights only to Bulgarian citizens. This is the case of the election rights, the right to be elected or appointed as an office holder of state institution and many of the social rights. However, this is not the case with the above-mentioned universal rights incorrectly (and eventually not deliberately) defined as citizens' rights.

*860.* Finally, the logic on which basis the constitutional legislator uses the terms 'right' and 'freedom' is also not very clear. The term 'freedom' is used usually in conjunction with the political freedom. In that regard, the 1991 Constitution not only provides for freedom of correspondence and communications (Article 34) but for right to information. Moreover, the freedom of opinion is defined as a right to opinion. Other constitutionally enshrined freedoms are the freedom of conscious, thought and religion and the freedom of scientific, art and technical creativity. Last but not least, the competence of the people to form and join associations and to organize and join assemblies and manifestations is neither explicitly defined as a right or as freedom.

*861.* Conclusion can be made that it is recommendable for the constitutional legislator to set a more clear delimitation between the terms 'rights' and 'freedoms', to define the above-mentioned rights as universal and not as citizens' rights and to establish more uniform use of the terms related to rights. Hence a reform of the wording of human rights provisions of the 1991 Constitution may be recommended. However, this is not a pressing issue because the concern is indeed the constitutional wording and not the way the 1991 Constitution provides the substance of human rights.

## II. Classification of the Human Rights Provided by the Bulgarian Constitutional Law

*862.* The 1991 Constitution systematizes human rights according to the predominant classification scheme provided by the Bulgarian constitutional theory[85] and enshrined in the Bulgarian constitutional tradition. It is applicable to the Tarnovo Constitution but is decisive and directly visible in the 1947 and the 1971 constitutions. According to that classification scheme, the constitutional provisions related to human rights commence with the civil rights, continue with the political rights and finish with the social, economic and cultural rights.

85. *See* Stefan Stoychev, *supra* n. 30, 231 et seq., Evgeni Tanchev, *supra* n. 20, 388.

*863.* The 1991 Constitution provides for human rights and constitutional duties which encompass all four statuses of man and citizen according to the theory of Georg Jellinek.[86] The civil rights are part of the negative status; the political rights, of the active status; the social, economic and cultural rights, of the positive status; and the constitutional duties, of the passive status. Moreover, the 1991 Constitution provides for human rights belonging to all three generations of human rights as defined by K. Vasak[87] as well as for human rights that serve as a constitutional basis for both negative and positive freedom according to the theory of I. Berlin.[88]

## III. National and Supranational Sources of Law Providing for the Human Rights as Valid Law in Bulgaria

*864.* There are four main types of sources of law which contain human rights provision and form the legal basis of human rights protection in Bulgaria. These are the 1991 Constitution, the EU law, the international law and the acts of the Parliament. Other sources of law also may contain human rights provisions. These are the Constitutional Court's decisions and the normative acts of the government. However, they are frequently much less relevant in the human rights domain.

*865.* One of the reasons is that the Bulgarian Constitutional Court is much more 'state court' than 'human rights court'. Its competences, but especially its jurisprudential activities, are focused predominantly on safeguarding and interpreting the institutional design than on human rights protection. The main reason is the lack of direct constitutional complaint by virtue of which the citizen can protect their constitutional rights in front of the Constitutional Court. Hence the Constitutional Courts' decisions are very important sources of law, but there are not many such decisions which are directly related to human rights and their protection.

*866.* Moreover, the normative acts of the Council of Ministers and the Ministers rarely provide for human rights. There is no explicit parliamentary reserve for exclusive provision of human rights by acts of Parliament. However, it is usually the Parliament which adopts human rights related provisions. One of the reasons is the fact that the 1991 Constitution on several occasions requires acts of Parliament regarding distinct constitutional rights to be adopted without prohibiting their further concretization via governmental acts.

*867.* Bulgaria has ratified all-important human rights international treaties. Being a Member State of the UN and the CE, Bulgaria is a high contracting party

86. *See* Georg Jellinek, *System der subjektiven öffentlichen Rechte* (Mohr, 1905), Robert Alexy, *Theorie der Grundrechte*, 229 et seq. (Suhrkamp, 1994).
87. *See* Karl Vasak, *Pour une troisième generation des droits de l'homme, Etudes et essais sur les principes de la Croix-Rouge en l'honneur de Jean Picte*, 837–850 (Geneve, 1984).
88. *See* Isaiah Berlin, *Four Essays on Liberty*, 1–286 (Oxford University Press, 1990).

to the UDHR, the ICCPR, the ICESCR, the EConvHR and many of the conventions of the UN system of international organizations such as International Labour Organization (ILO), United Nations Educational, Scientific and Cultural Organization (UNESCO).

*868.* Since 2007, Bulgaria is Member State of the EU. Thus human rights provided by the primary and secondary EU law and especially by the CFREU enjoy primacy over the Bulgarian legal order.

*869.* The 1991 Constitution provides for an extensive catalogue of human rights. Human rights belonging to all human rights generations are provided in its Chapter II. The Bulgarian Constitution complies with the international and supranational standards for human rights protection.

*870.* There are many important acts of Parliament in human rights domain. Some of them provide for different human rights whereas others establish institutional safeguards for human rights. The most important acts of Parliament belonging to the first category comprise the Direct Participation of the Citizen in the State Power and in the Local Self-Government Act, the Assemblies, Rallies and Manifestations Act, the Bulgarian Citizenship Act, the Refugees and Asylum Act, the Foreigners in the Republic of Bulgaria Act, the Religious Denominations Act, the Political Parties Act, the Electoral Code, the Access to Public Information Act, the Personal Data Protection Act, the Child Protection Act, the Consumer Protection Act, the Protection Against Discrimination Act etc. The most important acts of Parliament falling into the second category are: the Judicial Power Act, the Attorneys-at-Law Act, the Legal Aid Act, the Ombudsman Act, the Constitutional Court Act, the Code of Administrative Procedure, the Code of Civil Procedure, the Code of Criminal Procedure, the Liability of the State and the Municipalities for Damages Act etc.

## IV. Outline of the Development of the Human Rights in the Bulgarian Constitutional History

*871.* The 1879 Tarnovo Constitution provided for a wide range of human rights. All classical civil and political human rights have been proclaimed by the first Bulgarian Constitution. The proclamation of full political equality of all citizens independent of their sex, ethnicity, religion and race and the lack of any census on the political rights should be underlined. The provision of free and universal electoral suffrage as well as the proclamation of the freedom of expression, freedom of assembly, freedom of association and the prohibition of the censorship is of special importance. Last but not least, the Tarnovo Constitution proclaimed also some welfare rights such as the right to free initial education.

*872.* Unfortunately, this liberal and democratic constitutional design of human rights has been massively infringed by the sub-constitutional legislation comprising unconstitutional acts of Parliament, governmental decrees and decrees of the monarch. The Bulgarian electoral legislation introduced a gender census prohibiting women to have the right to vote and to stand as candidates for elections. The Bulgarian elections were generally not free and were marked by huge human rights infringements. In addition, the political practice was also deviated from the spirit and the text of the Tarnovo Constitution.

*873.* The 1947 Constitution did provide for a wide range of human rights. Although the initial period of the establishment of the communist regime in Bulgaria was marked by severe human rights violations concerning both the civic and the political rights, the 1947 Constitution itself was actually moderately authoritarian. It provided for a wide range of civic, political, social, economic and cultural rights, permitted the private property and its inheritance and did not explicitly prohibit the freedom to form and join different political parties and associations and the freedom of expression.

*874.* In contrast to the 1947 Constitution, the 1971 Constitution explicitly prohibited the private property and the political pluralism proclaiming the unity of state power and the leading role of the Bulgarian Communist Party. However, it formally proclaimed for many civic, political, social, economic and cultural rights.

*875.* Consequently, a conclusion can be made that the issues related to human rights in Bulgaria have not been related so much to the constitutional provisions, but typically concerned two main groups of problems. First, the legislation typically infringed human rights even if they have been enshrined in the Constitution. Second, the political practice deviated even further from the constitutional human rights provisions.

## V. General Structure of the Constitutional Status of the Man and Citizen

*876.* The constitutional status of man and citizen comprises five main elements.[89] These elements are first, the citizenship or its alternative status – the foreigner, second, the principles of the constitutional status, third, the constitutional rights and freedoms, fourth, the constitutional duties and fifth, the safeguards for the constitutional status of man and citizen in general and for the constitutional rights and freedoms in particular.

*877.* The Bulgarian Constitution provides for the first four elements of the constitutional status of man and citizen in Chapter II devoted to the constitutional rights although some provisions are contained also in other constitutional chapters. The fifth element, the constitutional safeguards for the constitutional rights are provided especially in Chapter VI 'Judicial Power' and in Chapter VIII 'Constitutional Court' but again some provisions, e.g., concerning the ombudsman, are allocated in other parts of the 1991 Constitution.

---

89. *See* Evgeni Tanchev, *supra* n. 20, 368.

*A. Circles of Human Rights Provided for Different Categories of People*

*878.* The civil rights are universal human rights which should be provided for all people independent of their citizenship. The 1991 Constitution follows that important principle and provides the civil rights as rights available to all human beings on the Bulgarian territory as well as for the Bulgarian citizens living abroad.

*879.* Some of the political rights as well as the social, economic and cultural rights are preserved for Bulgarian citizens only. There are two main justifications for that. First, some of the political rights are directly related to state sovereignty allowing for influence on the Bulgarian policymaking. Second, the social, economic and cultural rights allow for participation in the national wealth redistribution, for gaining of benefits stemming out of national solidarity with citizens at risk or for inclusion in the labour market and the social welfare as components of the national security in the wider sense.

*880.* There are four categories of political rights according to their holders. These are: first, political rights belonging to Bulgarian citizens without dual citizenship, second, political rights granted to Bulgarian citizens with dual citizenship, third, political rights of the EU citizens without Bulgarian citizenship and fourth, political rights granted to foreigners without either Bulgarian or EU citizenship (including *apatrides*).

*881.* It should be mentioned again that the wording of the 1991 Constitution makes the impression that the political rights are reserved for Bulgarian citizens only. However, this is an incorrect interpretation not just with a view to the reasons mentioned above. The National Assembly has interpreted on several occasions the constitutional text rather extensively so as to allow the EU citizen to possess not only electoral rights for EU Parliament and for local self-government institutions but also the right to form and join Bulgarian political parties.

*882.* The 1991 Constitution grants several political rights as exclusive rights of the Bulgarian citizens without dual citizenship. These are the right to stand for elections as President, Vice President, MP in the National Assembly and mayor of municipality, rayon or mayorship, the right to be elected as Prime Minister, Deputy Prime Minister or Minister or to be elected or appointed as a judge in the Constitutional Court. The appointment as a judge, state prosecutor and state investigator is also reserved to this category of Bulgarian citizens without dual citizenship.

*883.* The Bulgarian citizens with dual citizenship do not possess the above-mentioned group of constitutional rights. However, they enjoy some additional political rights in comparison to the foreigners. These are rights to vote in elections for President and Vice President of the Republic, for National Assembly and for mayors.

*884.* The EU citizens who do not possess Bulgarian citizenship have extended political status in comparison to the foreigners who are neither Bulgarian nor EU citizens. The EU citizens can vote and stand as candidates in elections for MPs in the European Parliament and in elections for municipal councillors. They can also vote for the different types of mayors in Bulgaria and can participate in the forms of deliberative and participatory democracy. Thus they can participate in national or local citizens' initiatives and can form or join Bulgarian political parties.

*885.* The fourth group of political rights is granted to all people no matter what citizenship they possess. The foreigners enjoy the freedom of opinion, the right to information, the freedom of assembly, the freedom of associations different from political parties and the right to petitions.

*886.* The foreigners enjoy also some social, economic and cultural rights in Bulgaria. These are the right to marriage and divorce, the right to raise and educate their children, the right to join trade unions and employers organizations, the right to education, the right to make use and enjoy the national and world cultural heritage and to develop their culture in accordance with their ethnic origin, the intellectual and industrial property rights, the freedom of scientific, technical and creative activity and the right to healthy environment.

*887.* Finally, it should be mentioned that some specific constitutional rights are granted only to foreigners. These are the right to asylum and the right to acquire Bulgarian citizenship.

### *B. Restrictions on the Human Rights*

*888.* The human rights restrictions are usually classified in the theory of human rights into two main groups: legal restrictions (provided by the law) and natural restrictions (stemming out of the objective, factual determinants of the human right). Furthermore, the legal human rights restrictions can be systematized and divided into supranational, international, constitutional, legislative restrictions as well as restrictions defined by the acts of the government, the courts and the Constitutional Court.[90] This classification is based on the source of law which imposes human rights restrictions. Here only the constitutional restrictions on the constitutional rights are going to be presented due to space constraints.

*889.* The Bulgarian Constitution imposes one general restriction which is valid for all human rights as well as special restrictions related to some of the constitutional rights. The general restriction is provided by Article 57, paragraph 2 of the Constitution which prohibits the misuse of constitutional rights resulting in behaviour infringing the rights or the legal interests of other persons. This provision serves as a legal basis for the horizontal effect of the constitutional rights in Bulgaria. Despite the lack of real debate on the horizontal effect of the human rights in the Bulgarian constitutional theory and the inexistence of deliberate case law on it,

90. For a thorough and comprehensive presentation of the different types of human rights' restrictions *see* Robert Alexy, *supra* n. 86, 249 et seq.

Article 57, paragraph 2 of the Constitution can be used as a general clause for their development by the doctrine and the courts.

*890.* The special restrictions concern predominantly the political rights. This is because the political rights are related to the civic participation and engagement in the political discourse. Some of them concern the accomplishment of important state policies occasionally related to state sovereignty.

*891.* There are also some constitutional limitations to the civil rights. Important examples are the provision of Article 34, paragraph 2 of the Constitution imposing some limitations to the freedom and secret of correspondence and other communication means and the provision of Article 35, paragraph 1 of the Constitution proclaiming the national security, public health and rights and freedoms of the citizen as limitations to the freedom of movement and settlement of people on Bulgarian territory. In addition, Article 37, paragraph 2 of the Constitution defines national security, public order, public health, public moral and rights and freedoms of the citizen as limitations to the freedom of conscience, thought and religion.

*892.* It has to be mentioned that in some cases the 1991 Constitution directly provides for some limitations of the constitutional rights. In other cases, however, it delegates that task to the Parliament allowing it to determine either concrete limitations or conditions and procedure for accomplishment of the constitutional rights which in some cases serve as a limitation to human rights. For example, Article 30, paragraphs 2 and 3 of the Constitution empower the National Assembly to determine the conditions and the procedure for detention, search and other activities restraining the personal freedom and inviolability of the person. Article 32, paragraph 2 of the Constitution allows the National Assembly to determine the instances in which the people may be filmed, photographed or taped without their knowledge and consent.

*893.* There are also hypotheses in which the Constitution indirectly allows the Parliament to determine limitations of constitutional rights. These are the hypotheses in which the Constitution makes use of specific concepts and terms, the content of which is clarified and further developed by acts of Parliament. An example is Article 33, paragraph 2 of the Constitution providing for the concept of extreme necessity as a limitation of the inviolability of the home which is defined by the Criminal Code and not by the Constitution itself.

*894.* Here are some of the most important limitations to the political rights provided by the 1991 Constitution. Typically, the constitutional legislator proclaims the political rights in the first paragraph of the respective constitutional article and then sets the constitutional limitations to it in the subsequent paragraph or eventually paragraphs.

*895.* Thus the first paragraphs of Articles 39 and 40 provide for the information and communication rights and freedoms. Then their second paragraphs define the constitutional limitations to these rights. Article 41 is grounded on the same logic apart from the fact that the right to search, distribute and acquire information and its limitations are provided in the same paragraph. The Constitution provides for the rights and the good name of the people, the prohibition of proclamation of violent replacement of the constitutionally established public order, the prohibition of accomplishment of crimes and inciting hatred and violence on people as limitations to the freedom of opinion, the freedom of press and the prohibition of censorship. The constitutional limitations to the right to information are the national security, the public order, the rights and the good name of the people, the public health and the public moral. In addition, Article 41 of the Constitution provides for the classified information or the information that may infringe the rights of other citizens as a limitation to the right of the citizen to acquire information from the state institutions.

*896.* There are no constitutional limitations to the freedom of assembly apart from the requirement that the assemblies must be peaceful and the participants in them must not carry any weapons. Article 43, paragraph 2 outsources to the Parliament the competence to determine further limitations to that constitutional right by providing for the conditions and procedure for its accomplishment.

*897.* The constitutional legislator sets a concrete range of limitations to the freedom of association. Article 44, paragraph 2 defines the limitations to the general freedom of association whereas Article 11, paragraph 4 determines the limitations to the freedom of association in political parties. These two sets of limitations are applied distinctly and alternatively to the two types of the general freedom of assembly – the freedom of assembly in NGOs and the freedom of assembly in political parties.

*898.* Article 11, paragraph 4 of the Constitution provides for two grounds for unconstitutionality of the political parties. First, parties which are based on ethnic, race or religious ground are unconstitutional. Second and alternative ground for unconstitutionality concerns parties which aim at violent assent to power.

*899.* The limitations to the freedom of association in NGOs are set by Article 44, paragraph 2. According to this article, associations whose activity is directed against the sovereignty, the territorial integrity and the unity of the nation, towards inciting racial, ethnic, religious or national hatred, towards violation of the rights and freedoms of the citizens and organizations which establish secret or paramilitary structures or aim at violent achievement of their goals are prohibited.

*900.* Hence there is partial overlapping of the grounds for unconstitutionality of the political parties and the other organizations. The most obvious case concerns parties and organizations aiming at violent achievement of their goals. In contrast to the political parties, the other organizations can be based on racial, religious or ethnic grounds, but they cannot proclaim hatred related to these identity criteria.

*C. Remedies for Violations of Rights and Liberties*

*901.* The Bulgarian constitutional law provides for several remedies for violation of human rights and liberties which can be also defined as institutional safeguards and instruments for human rights protection. These are the judicial protection against human rights violations caused by the citizen (civil and criminal justice) or by the state administration (administrative justice), the ombudsman as an institution for prevention and detection of human rights violations accomplished by the state administration or the ombudsman and the Supreme Bar Council as institutions which may approach the Constitutional Court with claims for constitutional rights violations caused by an act of Parliament.

*902.* In contrast to the civil, criminal or administrative courts, the Constitutional Court and the ombudsman cannot directly remedy the violations of the rights and liberties of concrete persons. The Constitutional Court may declare an act of Parliament or its provisions unconstitutional but cannot directly deliver concrete remedy to the person whose rights are violated. The ombudsman may approach the competent institutions and can demand discontinuation of human rights infringement. But the ombudsman cannot directly impose sanctions or provide remedies for the concrete persons.

*903.* That is why the main remedy to human rights violations in Bulgaria remains the justice delivered by the courts. The Bulgarian law, however, provides also for one remedy which has been introduced in Bulgaria during the communist period. The Bulgarian state prosecutors have rather intense competences to safeguard human rights by issuing orders for discontinuation of human rights violations. This is a result of the general control for legality function ascribed to the state prosecutors' office by 1991 Constitution and inherited by the previous constitutional model. In addition, the state prosecutors have important competences for control of the legality of the execution of criminal sanctions and compulsory administrative and medical measures in the detention facilities thus safeguarding human rights of the imprisoned or detained persons.

*904.* The Liability of the State and the Municipalities for Damages Act provides some remedies against human rights infringements accomplished by the state or the municipal administration. These infringements must have occurred as a result of illegal acts of the state institutions or civil servants adopted or undertaken in the course of their professional activity. The Liability of the State and the Municipalities for Damages Act provides also for cases in which the state is liable and should grant remedies for human rights violations accomplished by the courts, the state prosecutors and the institutions for criminal investigation as well as by the Commission for Confiscation of Illegally Acquired Property.

*905.* Apart from the national there are also supranational safeguards for human rights infringement available to the Bulgarian citizens and under certain conditions also to the foreigners in Bulgaria. The most important of them is the jurisdiction of the ECtHR. Human rights may be defended also in front of the ECJ under the conditions provided by the EU law.

## VI. The Main Principles of the Constitutional Status of the Man and Citizen

### A. *Universality and Equality*

*906.* The universality of human rights and freedoms is proclaimed by Article 6 of the 1991 Constitution. According to this article, all people are born free and equal in dignity and rights. All citizens are equal in front of the law. No restrictions to the rights and no privileges based on race, ethnic or social origin, sex, religion, education, convictions, political affiliation, personal standing or social position or economic status should be allowed.

*907.* The Constitutional Court has added further elements and clarifications to this important constitutional provision which enshrines some of the key principles of the status of the people and the citizen under the 1991 Constitution. According to Decision No. 14 of 1992 of the Constitutional Court, the equality of all citizens in front of the law provided by Article 6, paragraph 2 of the Constitution means equality in front of all normative acts and not only in front of the acts of the Parliament. The Constitutional Court provides that the equality is general principle for the whole Bulgarian legal order which is the basis for the interpretation and application of the Constitution and for the legislative activity of the Parliament and the norm-setting activity of the other state institutions.

*908.* Furthermore, according to Decision No 14 of 1992 of the Constitutional Court, privileges based on any of the criteria enshrined in Article 6, paragraph 2 are infringing the principle of equality of all citizens in front of the law and are thus unconstitutional. However, Decision No. 3 of 2006 of the Constitutional Court declares that the equality provided by Article 6, paragraph 2 of the Constitution concerns only the assurance of equality in front of the law and cannot be extended to social equality related to equality in wealth and property.

*909.* Decision No. 14 of 1992 provides that the criteria for non-discrimination provided by Article 6 of the Constitution constitute an exhaustive list. The thesis of the exhaustive character of the constitutional list with the criteria for non-discrimination has been launched also in subsequent decisions of the Constitutional Court. These are Decision No. 1 of 1997 in which the Court admits that the Parliament can introduce additional criteria for non-discrimination by virtue of ordinary legislation, Decision No. 12 of 2001, Decision No. 1 of 2005 and Decision No. 1 of 2008. However, several years later the Constitutional Court has changed its opinion on the exhaustive nature of the list with criteria for non-discrimination provided by Article 6, paragraph 2. Thus the Constitutional Court in Decision No. 11

of 2010 implicitly admits the non-exhaustive character of the catalogue of criteria for non-discrimination provided by Article 6, paragraph 2 of the Constitution.

*910.* The universality and equality as key principles of the civic status are proclaimed not only by the general provision of Article 6 of the Constitution, but they are also enshrined in other constitutional provisions related to human rights. Thus the universality and equality are provided with regard to the electoral rights of the citizen (Article 10), the safeguarding of all constitutional rights to all Bulgarian citizens both in Bulgaria and abroad (Article 26, paragraph 1), the granting of all constitutional rights to all foreigners except for the rights explicitly reserved for Bulgarian citizens (Article 26, paragraph 2), the universality and equality of the civil rights (Articles 28–39), the universality and equality of most of the political rights, and the universality and equality of the people in front of the institutions of the judicial power as part of the right to fair trial and due process of law.

### *B. Irrevocability*

*911.* Article 57 of the Constitution proclaims the irrevocability of the constitutionally enshrined human rights. The wording of the text mentions only the irrevocability of the 'basic rights of the citizen' thus creating two ambiguities. The first ambiguity is, what is meant under 'basic rights'? The question is whether these are only constitutional rights or also human rights which are not provided by the 1991 Constitution but by other sources of law, e.g., EU law, international law or acts of Parliament.

*912.* It seems that the constitutional legislator subsumes under the category 'basic rights' only the constitutional rights. This is due to the fact that the same term – 'basic rights' – is used in the title of Chapter II of the 1991 Constitution devoted to the constitutional rights. Moreover, it is clear that the Bulgarian Constitution cannot safeguard the irrevocability of human rights enshrined in EU law and international treaties. Finally, the 'basic rights' cannot be used as an all-encompassing term which includes human rights provided also by the acts of the Parliament and the acts of government. Such an approach will lead to improper broadening of their scope in accordance with the discretionary judgement of the ordinary and not of the constitutional legislator.

*913.* The second ambiguity is related to the issue whether the irrevocability of human rights is provided only for the rights of the Bulgarian citizen or is it related also to the rights of the foreigners. A clear answer in that case is difficult to be given. On the one hand, the 1991 Constitution frequently proclaims universal human rights as citizens' rights and thus has to be interpreted extensively since it seems that the intent of the VII Grand National Assembly was not to limit the personal scope of application of these rights. Moreover, the interpretation that the irrevocability of the 'basic rights' is granted also to the rights belonging to foreigners is much more in compliance with the concept of the open statehood which has been partially provided by the 1991 Constitution especially in the course of introduction of its

EU-related amendments. On the other hand, an argument can be raised that the irrevocability of human rights is a matter of sovereignty and thus should be limited to the citizens' rights. Indeed the first interpretation seems more reasonable, but the ambiguity still remains.

*914.* Important safeguard for the irrevocability of human rights is the fact that it can be amended or abolished only by the Grand National Assembly. However, the inclusion of the amendment of the irrevocability of human rights in the catalogue with competences of the Grand National Assembly enlisted in Article 158 of the Constitution itself proves that the 1991 Constitution provides not for absolute but for relative irrevocability of the constitutional rights. This is because the 1991 Constitution does not provide for any unamendable clauses but only for the entrenched clause of Article 158 comprising the constitutional provisions which can be amended only by the very difficult procedure resulting in the summoning of Grand National Assembly.

*915.* Moreover, according to Article 57, paragraph 3 of the Constitution, in case of war, state of siege or state of emergency, the National Assembly may temporarily limit some of the constitutional rights via act of Parliament. Thus in these extraordinary circumstances human rights are not revoked, but they are limited. Moreover, there is no constitutional prohibition for limitations also of the constitutional rights' core in the just-mentioned extraordinary situations. However, no limitations are allowed regarding the right to life, the prohibition of torture, inhuman or degrading treatment, the prohibition for medical and scientific experiments without explicit written consent, the right to fair trial and due process of law, the privacy rights related to the protection of personal and family life, the protection of honour and human dignity and the freedom of conscience, thought and religion.

## §2. Civil Rights

*916.* The 1991 Constitution grants all classical civil rights which are provided by most of the European constitutions and international human rights treaties. The system of civil rights enshrined in the 1991 Constitution includes: the right to life (Article 28), the prohibition of torture, cruel, inhuman or degrading treatment (Article 29), the prohibition of compulsory assimilation (Article 29), the prohibition of medical or other scientific experiments on humans without their previous knowledge and written consent (Article 29), the inviolability of personal freedom and integrity (Article 30) and the protection of privacy and private life (Article 32), the right to defence, including defence by an attorney-at-law (Articles 32, 56 and 122), the prohibition of illegal criminal procedure activities (Article 31), the due process of law, the inviolability of home and correspondence (Articles 33 and 34), the free movement on the Bulgarian territory (Article 35), the freedom to choose residence and to leave and return to the country (Article 35) and the freedom of conscience, thought and religion (Article 37).

*917.* The 1991 Constitution provides also for the right to private property tackled in its dual nature – as civil right and precondition for personal freedom and as economic right serving as a basis for the development of capitalist market economy. Comparable duality can be detected also with a view to the information and communication rights provided by Articles 39 to 41 because these rights and freedoms can be tackled as both civil and political rights.

*918.* This catalogue of civil rights demonstrates that the Bulgarian Constitution groups them around several key protected phenomena serving as organizing pillars. These key phenomena are the life, the physical and mental integrity, the intellectual autonomy of the person, its physical and social autonomy and the integrity of its fundamental social bonds. Thus the civil rights proclaimed by the 1991 Constitution protect the humans in some of their most important dimensions – physical and mental. They are safeguards also of some of the elements of its social dimension. The other aspects of the human personality – its political dimension and the remaining elements of its social dimension – are protected by the political and social, economic and cultural rights.

## §3. Political Rights

*919.* The 1991 Constitution provides for a fully-fledged system of political rights serving as a legal background for the active status of the citizen[91] and as instrument for promotion of their positive freedom.[92] The political rights provided by the 1991 Constitution institutionalize the forms of direct, participatory and deliberative democracy as well as some of the key pillars of the representative democracy in Bulgaria. The constitutional design of the political rights enshrined in the 1991 Constitution is inspired by the Western prototypes that have been followed in the course of its elaboration and adoption, by the international human rights standards at the beginning of the 1990s as well as by the Bulgarian constitutional tradition.

*920.* All Bulgarian constitutions provided for wide-ranging system of human rights, including the political rights. However, the key problem under the previous three Bulgarian constitutions has been how to safeguard human rights and especially the political rights from their infringement by the institutions of the constituted powers and how to make them really applicable. This is the reason why the 1991 Constitution not only continues the Bulgarian tradition in the sphere of political rights but also tries to provide remedies for its deficiencies exposed and developed throughout the history of the modern Bulgarian state. An example of the reflexivity and the reactivity of the 1991 Constitution towards the previous Bulgarian constitutions in the domain of human rights is the explicit provision of the political pluralism as well as the prohibition for proclaiming of specific party political ideology as official ideology of the state.

91. *See* Georg Jellinek, *supra* n. 86, 211 et seq.
92. *See* Isaiah Berlin, *supra* n. 88.

*921.* The 1991 Constitution provides for the following political rights: right to association in political parties (Article 11), freedom of opinion (Article 39), freedom of press and prohibition of censorship (Article 40), right to information (Article 41), electoral rights (Article 42), freedom of assembly (Article 43), freedom of association (Article 44) and right to file petitions, propositions and complaints (Article 45).

*922.* The Bulgarian constitutional law provides for both active and passive as well as for positive and negative aspects of these political rights. The active aspect safeguards the right of the people to express opinion, disseminate information, vote for candidates in elections, join political parties or other organizations, participate in assemblies and file petitions, propositions and complaints. The passive aspect concerns some of the rights and freedoms, e.g., the electoral rights and the right to information. It finds expression in the right to stand as a candidate for elections and in the right to receive information. The positive aspect of the political rights and freedoms safeguards the ability to engage and participate on the basis of these opportunities for political activism provided by the constitutional law whereas the negative aspect is a guarantee for the opposite choice namely not to make use of them. Thus no compulsory membership in political parties or other organizations and no compulsory requirement for any other engagement in the political life are provided by the Bulgarian constitutional law.

*923.* The only exception has been the compulsory voting in elections enshrined in in the Bulgarian Election Code of 2015. In fact, this novelty did not contain a real sanction, but it could be perceived as hidden and indirect requirement for active registration of the voters. However, even this quasi-sanction has been proclaimed unconstitutional by the Constitutional Court due to the fact that the 1991 Constitution provides only for electoral rights but not for electoral duties. Hence the introduction of compulsory voting in Bulgaria can be accomplished only by constitutional amendment.

*924.* Articles 39 to 41 of the Constitution provide for information and communication rights which are the legal basis of the deliberative democracy in Bulgaria. The freedom of opinion, the freedom of press and the right to information are universal human rights which are not limited to Bulgarian citizens. Moreover, their content and protective scope is not limited also to the political sphere. This is because they protect also the exchange of information, the formation of opinion and the publications related to all possible information content – political, economic, trade, cultural etc. Despite that fact, the political aspect of these rights and freedoms has specific prominence because it is most frequently supposed to be endangered by the activity of the institutions of public power.

*925.* Article 39 of the Constitution protects all forms of the freedom of expression not only with regard to its content but also with a view to the material source of information. Thus the Constitution safeguards the dissemination of information and the expression of opinion orally or in written, by virtue of sound, image or through any other means.

*926.* Article 40 of the Constitution protects not only the freedom of press but also the freedom of all other media. The Internet-based social media are not explicitly proclaimed as an object of protection. However, they must also enjoy such constitutional protection because they can be subsumed under the category 'means for mass information' used by the constitutional legislator. The censorship is prohibited apart from the constitutionally enshrined limitations to the freedom of the press and the media which have already been discussed above. If such a ground for limitation of the freedom of media is available, then the suppression and the confiscation of the media is allowed only on the basis of permission granted by the institutions of the judicial power. In case the media is not confiscated within 24 hours, then the suppression should be discontinued.

*927.* The 1991 Constitution provides also for the freedom of assembly, freedom of association and right to file petitions, propositions and complaints as political rights which serve as a basis for the establishment and the development of the participatory democracy in Bulgaria. The right to form and join political party and to vote and stand as a candidate for elections which are both instruments of participatory and direct democracy respectively and necessary components of the representative democracy are also constitutionally enshrined.

*928.* The 1991 Constitution provides also for some forms of direct democracy. Besides the elections, the Constitution provides also for local referenda, internal territorial plebiscites for administrative–territorial reform of the municipalities and for general assembly of the population. However, it remains unclear whether different types of national referenda and people's initiatives and especially constitutional referenda and people's initiatives are constitutionally permitted.

*929.* The legal basis of the freedom of assembly is set by Article 43 of the Constitution and by the Assemblies, Rallies and Manifestations Act. The Bulgarian constitutional legislation differentiates between indoor assemblies, outdoor assemblies (denominated also as rallies) and manifestations. The manifestations are assemblies in which the participants move on the territory of the place where they are accomplished.

*930.* According to Article 43, paragraph 3 of the Constitution, no permission is required for the organization of indoor assemblies. According to Articles 8 and 11 of the Assemblies, Rallies and Manifestations Act, the organizers of outdoor assemblies must inform the mayor of the municipality at least 48 hours in advance (24 hours in urgent cases). The term for informing the mayor of the municipality in case of organization of manifestation is 72 hours (reduced to 48 hours in urgent cases). The Assemblies, Rallies and Manifestations Act determines the territorial, personal and temporal conditions and limitations for organizing these forms of participatory democracy. It provides for the competences of the state institutions and the rights and the obligations of the organizers in that respect.

§4. SOCIAL, ECONOMIC AND CULTURAL RIGHTS

*931.* The provision of social, economic and cultural rights is part of the Bulgarian constitutional tradition. The Tarnovo Constitution re-established modern Bulgaria as a liberal and not as a welfare state. However, it provided for free first grade school education thus continuing the traditions of the Bulgarian educational communities which existed even before the Liberation from Ottoman rule in 1878. The 1947 and the 1971 communist constitutions provided for vast catalogues with social, economic and cultural rights. This has been a natural result of the official Marxist ideology underlying the regime.

*932.* The 1991 Constitution continued with the tradition established by the previous Bulgarian constitutions by providing wide-ranging social, economic and cultural human rights. This time the granting of such rights has been done not in the context of planned socialist economy based on Marxist ideology but as a consequence of the principle of welfare state and marked economy provided by the 1991 Constitution.

*933.* The provision of social, economic and cultural rights by the 1991 Constitution is a result not only of the Bulgarian constitutional tradition but also of its engagement with important international treaties enshrining such human rights. Special attention is due to the ICESCR and the conventions of the ILO and UNESCO.

*934.* The system of social and economic rights provided by the 1991 Constitution is structured around three main pillars. These are the property, the labour and the education. Most of the social and economic rights provided by the 1991 Constitution are based on them, derived from them or are supposed to serve as their safeguards.

*935.* At the same time, the cultural rights have an independent and specific place which is not connected with property, labour and education. Exceptions are the intellectual and industrial property rights. They are proclaimed in Article 54, paragraph 3 in conjunction with cultural rights such as the right to use the national and universal cultural heritage and the freedom of the scientific, cultural and technical creativity. However, the intellectual and industrial property rights are also systematically intertwined with the right to private property being its specific and logical continuation.[93]

*936.* The 1991 Constitution safeguards the private property in all its aspects and forms. It should be mentioned again that the private property is safeguarded in both its qualities as civil and as economic rights. Systematically the private property is constitutionally enshrined not in Chapter II devoted to human rights but in Chapter I encompassing the basic principles of the constitutional order. It is proclaimed as

93. This thesis is launched in the Bulgarian theory by Pavel Sarafov.

a part of the fundamental social institutions and national strategic resources such as the labour, the family, the land and the economic resources of Bulgaria.

*937.* The 1991 Constitution provides for the right to private property and the right to inheritance of private property (Article 17, paragraph 1), pronounces the private property as inviolable (Article 17, paragraph 3) and declares that the compulsory alienation of private property for state or municipal needs may be accomplished only if these needs cannot be otherwise satisfied and after equal compensation is given in advance.

*938.* The labour is proclaimed by Article 16 as part of the fundamental initial provisions of the 1991 Constitution. Article 16 of the Constitution stipulates that the labour is protected and safeguarded by the law. Furthermore, Article 48, paragraph 1 of the Constitution proclaims the right to labour and provides that the state should create conditions for its practical realization.

*939.* The subsequent paragraphs of Article 48 of the Constitution provide for the obligation of the state to promote conditions for the right to labour of mentally or physically disabled persons, to safeguard healthy and safe work environment, proclaim the right to free choice of profession and working place and prohibit forced labour. Last but not least, they grant the right to rest and leave, the right to a minimal wage and the right to pay that is proportional to the accomplished work. The right to association in trade unions (Article 49), the right to strike (Article 50), the social and health assurance rights as well as the right to social aid and assistance (Article s 51 and 52) are also directly or indirectly related to labour as key constitutional phenomenon.

*940.* The third central constitutional phenomenon and pillar for structuring the social and economic rights by the 1991 Constitution is education. The right to education is proclaimed in Article 53 as universal constitutional right. According to Article 53, paragraph 2, the education is compulsory until the age of 16 years. Moreover, according to Article 53, paragraph 3 the basic and high school education in the state and municipal schools is free of charge.

*941.* The academic autonomy of the universities as a right that is derivative but separate from the right to education is proclaimed in Article 53, paragraph 4 of the Constitution. Furthermore, the 1991 Constitution provides for the conditions for the establishment of schools and universities and for the freedom of the scientific, technical and cultural creativity (Article 54, paragraph 2).

*942.* The cultural rights provided by the 1991 Constitution include the right to use the national and universal cultural values and heritage and to develop its own culture in accordance with its ethnical origin (Article 54, paragraph 1). Moreover, the Constitution proclaims also an ecological right. This is the right to healthy environment (Article 55 of the Constitution).

## Chapter 3. Judicial Control of Administrative Action

### §1. System and Competence of the Administrative Courts in Bulgaria as Institutions for Judicial Control of Administrative Action

*943.* The 1991 Constitution provides for administrative justice as well as for a distinct Supreme Administrative Court. It does not contain explicit provisions for first instance administrative courts. However, it allows for the creation of specialized courts' systems and thus permits also the establishment of distinct system of the administrative courts. The post-totalitarian impetus after 1989 was that human rights must be guaranteed and the protection of the individual against the state should be assured. Hence the political climate was very appropriate for the re-establishment of the administrative justice in Bulgaria. The Supreme Administrative Court was established, however, in 1996, five years after the adoption of the 1991 Constitution.

*944.* For a ten-year period from 1996 to 2006, the administrative justice was delivered by the Supreme Administrative Court and twenty-eight administrative divisions at the district courts. Thus the system of the administrative justice was partially intertwined with the ordinary courts system. Hence the functional specialization of the judges was in place although the first level of the administrative justice was not institutionally independent from the ordinary courts. The establishment of separate first instance administrative courts was postponed with the argument that it will be expensive and will induce organizational difficulties. Moreover, Bulgaria has a modest tradition of specialized courts not only in administrative but also in civil matters.

*945.* However, in 2006, by virtue of a legal reform resulting in the adoption of the Code of Administrative Procedure, the twenty-eight administrative divisions at the district courts were replaced by twenty-eight independent administrative courts. That is why since 2006 Bulgaria has a fully-fledged system of specialized administrative courts which is separate from the ordinary courts system.

*946.* The justices of the Supreme Administrative Court form its general assembly. The Supreme Administrative Court is administered by the general assembly as well as by its Chairman and two Vice Chairmen. The justices of the Supreme Administrative Court are divided into two departments that are subdivided into eight divisions. The administrative courts are structured in general assemblies and divisions. They also have Chairman and Vice Chairmen.

*947.* The Supreme Administrative Court delivers justice through chambers composed of three or five judges. The three-member chamber is used in most cases whereas the five-judge chamber is competent when resolving cases against the decision of a three-member chamber of the Supreme Administrative Court. The administrative courts deliver justice through a single judge.

*948.* The Bulgarian law provides for two instances of administrative procedure. First instance in the administrative procedure in Bulgaria are the administrative courts and in some cases the three-member chamber of the Supreme Administrative Court. If the administrative court has been the first instance, then the Supreme Administrative Court is a cassation instance acting in a three-member chamber. If a three-member chamber of the Supreme Administrative Court is the first instance, then a five-member chamber of the Supreme Administrative Court is the cassation instance.

*949.* The following issues fall into the competence of the administrative courts:

- disputes pertaining to issuance, amendment, abolition and declaration of nullity of administrative acts;
- nullification and dissolution of administrative agreements;
- protection against unlawful actions and inactions of the administration;
- protection against unlawful compulsory execution of duties by the administration;
- remedies for damages induced by unlawful actions and inactions of the administration;
- proclamation of the untruthfulness of administrative acts.

*950.* The list of issues falling into the competence of the Supreme Administrative Court comprises:

- contestation of administrative normative acts such as the acts of the Council of Ministers, the Prime Minister, the Deputy Prime Ministers and the Ministers, except for the acts of the municipal councils. According to Decision No. 8 of 2018 of the Constitutional Court, the Supreme Administrative Court is obliged to pronounce as first instance on the legality of administrative acts issued by the Council of Ministers and the Ministers as a result of the accomplishment of their functions for state governance provided by the Constitution;
- contestation of the acts of the Supreme Judicial Council and the Bulgarian National Bank;
- appeals of cassation against First Instance Courts' decisions;
- appeals for the abolition of decisions that have already entered into force.

## §2. Judicial Review of Administrative Acts

*951.* The Bulgarian law provides for two-instance judicial review of the individual administrative acts. The First Instance Courts are usually the administrative courts which resolve the case with a single judge. The most important cases are decided as first instance by a three-member chamber of the Supreme Administrative Court.

*952.* The administrative acts may be appealed to the court only with regard to their supposed illegality and not with a claim for substantial inappropriateness. The individual administrative acts may be appealed in court as a whole or with regard to some of their parts. The individual administrative acts may be appealed directly to the court without being subjected to the internal administrative review procedure according to the choice of the interested parties. There is a fourteen-day term for launching the appeal to the court. The silent refusal or the silent agreement of the administrative body may be appealed during the month after the elapse of the term in which it was obliged to issue the act.

*953.* The object of judicial review in the first instance can be:

- the initial individual administrative act and the refusal for issuing of such act;
- the act of the superior administrative organ with which the initial act has been amended or abolished;
- the decisions on demands for issuing of documents that predetermine the recognition, practice or termination of rights or duties.

*954.* The grounds on which the individual administrative acts can be appealed in the administrative Courts of First Instance are:

- lack of competence of the administrative organ that has issued the act;
- non-observation of the required form;
- substantial infringement of the administrative procedure;
- contravention of the individual administrative act to the law;
- discrepancy between the individual administrative act and the aims and goals of the respective legal provisions regulating the subject matter.

*955.* The process in the First Instance Court begins with verification of the legitimation of the parties and of the regularity and admissibility of the complaint. If the complaint is admissible, then the court resolves the case on the basis of the theses defended by the parties, their arguments and the evidence presented to the court.

*956.* The court plays an active role in the Bulgarian administrative process. It guides the parties in their attempts to prove their statements. The administrative process is devoted to the revealing of the objective truth. The court is not limited to discussion of the grounds pointed out by the plaintiff but is obliged to check the lawfulness of the individual administrative act on all five grounds that were just presented above. The court must proclaim the nullity of the individual administrative act even if there is no demand by the parties for such a declaration. In its first instance decision, the court may declare the nullity of the individual administrative act, abolish the individual administrative act as a whole or abolish some of its parts, amend the individual administrative act or reject the complaint.

*957.* If the parties to the first instance case are not satisfied with the court's decision, they may appeal it as a whole or in some of its parts through a cassation complaint. If the first instance decision has been pronounced by the administrative court, then the cassation case is considered by a chamber of the Supreme Administrative Court composed of three judges. If the first instance decision has been pronounced by a three-judge chamber of the Supreme Administrative Court, then the cassation case is considered by a chamber of the Supreme Administrative Court composed of five judges. The cassation case is considered in a public session with the compulsory participation of a state prosecutor.

*958.* The cassation grounds on which the parties to the first instance case can develop their cassation complaint are:

- nullity of the first instance decision;
- inadmissibility of the first instance decision;
- incorrectness of the first instance decision due to infringement of the law, substantial infringement of the procedure or groundlessness.

*959.* The Supreme Administrative Court discusses only the cassation grounds that have been indicated in the cassation complaint. The validity, admissibility and infringement of the law are taken *ex officio* into account by the Supreme Administrative Court. The cassation ground may be proven only with written evidence. In the cassation instance, no new facts can be established. Hence the Supreme Administrative Court pronounces its decision on the basis of the facts that have been proven in the first instance case.

*960.* The Supreme Administrative Court pronounces its cassation decision within a month. The cassation decision can uphold the first instance decision or abolish it in the disputed part if it is incorrect. If the first instance decision is inadmissible, then the Supreme Administrative Court annuls its contested part and either terminates the case or returns it for a new trial to the First Instance Court, or sends the case to the competent body. If the first instance decision is null, the Supreme Administrative Court declares its nullity, and if the case has not to be terminated, then it is sent back to the First Instance Court for reconsideration.

*961.* When the first instance decision is abolished, the Supreme Administrative Court resolves the case with a decision. The cassation decision of the Supreme Administrative Court is final.

## §3. Claims for Damages Against the State and the Civil Servants

*962.* Article 7 of the 1991 Constitution provides that the state is responsible for damages which are caused by illegal acts or activities of state institutions or civil servants. Even before the adoption of the 1991 Constitution at the end of the communist regime, the National Assembly had adopted in 1988 the Liability of the State and the Municipalities for Damages Act. This act had been part of the reforming attempts of the late communist state to adopt some standards related to rule of law in the course of the 'Perestroika' process that run in the communist states since the mid-1980s. Since the adoption of the new Constitution, this act has been amended several times and has been adjusted to the new post-communist reality. The National

Assembly has interpreted extensively Article 7 of the 1991 Constitution by tackling the concept of state institution in a broader sense as including also the municipal institutions.

*963.* The procedure for raising claims against the illegal acts or activities of the state and municipal institutions is provided not by the Liability of the State and the Municipalities for Damages Act but by the Code of Administrative Procedure. This procedure has already been described above. The Liability of the State and the Municipalities for Damages Act enlists the types of institutions against which a claim for damages can be raised, the types of damages that should be remedied and the different activities which might serve as a ground for such claims.

*964.* There are also few procedural rules provided by the Liability of the State and the Municipalities for Damages Act. They concern the obligation of the state or municipal institutions to explain to the citizen the procedure through which they can claim compensation for damages caused by state or municipal office holders or civil servants, the jurisdiction of the court in front of which the claim for compensation of damages should be raised, the applicable law and the taxes and expenditures related to the procedure. It should be mentioned that according to Article 10 of the Liability of the State and the Municipalities for Damages Act, the participation of a state prosecutor in the cases for compensation of damages caused by state or municipal office holders or civil servants is compulsory.

# Chapter 4. Rights and Status of Foreigners

## §1. Constitutional Rights and Protections

### I. Equal Protection

*965.* The Foreigners in the Republic of Bulgaria Act determines the persons who should be defined as foreigners. According to its Article 2, foreigners are persons who do not possess Bulgarian citizenship. This category includes also the *apatrides*. Hence the Bulgarian citizens with dual citizenship are not foreigners.

*966.* Pertaining to Article 26, paragraph 2 of the Bulgarian Constitution and Article 3 of the Foreigners in the Republic of Bulgaria Act, the foreigners residing in Bulgaria are in possession of the same constitutional rights and duties except for those for which Bulgarian citizenship is required. In addition, all foreigners enjoy the same safeguards for their constitutional rights and freedoms as the Bulgarian citizen. They can approach the general and specialized courts as well as supranational courts such as the ECtHR. They can file petitions to the ombudsman and to the state agencies safeguarding different categories of human rights. The foreigners have the same safeguards for the due process of law and the fair trial as the Bulgarian citizens.

*967.* It has to be mentioned that not only some rights are reserved for the Bulgarian citizens but also there are constitutional duties which are attributed exclusively to that category of subjects. These are the duty to defend the Republic of Bulgaria, the duty to cooperate with the state in case of disasters and the duty to learn the Bulgarian language. However, according to Articles 58 and 60 of the Constitution and Article 4 of the Foreigners in the Republic of Bulgaria Act, the foreigners are obliged to respect the Bulgarian Constitution and legislation, to pay taxes, to be loyal to the Bulgarian state and to respect the dignity of the Bulgarian people. Furthermore, according to Article 5 of the Foreigners in the Republic of Bulgaria Act, the foreigners on Bulgarian territory may be subject to civil, administrative and criminal responsibility as the Bulgarian citizens except in the cases provided by the Bulgarian legislation, the international treaties and the international customary law.

### II. Restrictions

*968.* The restrictions of human rights of foreigners have already been analysed above. They concern the reservation of some political and social rights to the Bulgarian citizens. It has already been discussed that there are four circles of constitutional rights granted to four categories of subjects. The widest one is the circle of human rights provided for the Bulgarian citizens without dual citizenship, followed by the rights granted to the Bulgarian citizens with dual citizenship, to the EU citizens and to the foreigners who are in possession neither of Bulgarian nor of European citizenship.

§2. IMMIGRATION, ASYLUM, EXTRADITION AND EUROPEAN ARREST WARRANT

## I. Immigration and Asylum

*969.* The Asylum and Refugees Act provides for the types of protection granted to the foreigners in Bulgaria, the conditions and procedures for refusal, termination and deprivation of such protection as well as for suspension and termination of such procedure and the rights and obligations of the foreigners who look for protection in Bulgaria. Moreover, it establishes the status of the State Agency for Refugees which is the state institution accomplishing the most important functions in that policy domain.

*970.* There are three main types of protection provided by the Asylum and Refugees Act. These are the asylum, the international protection and the temporary protection. The international protection is granted on the basis of the 1951 Convention for the Status of Refugees, the 1967 Protocol on the Status of Refugees and the Asylum and Refugees Act. The international protection includes the status of a refugee and the humanitarian status. Temporary protection is provided in case of massive entering of foreigners into the territory of the Republic of Bulgaria who are forced to leave their country of origin because of armed conflict, civil war, foreign aggression, human rights violations or high-scale violence on the territory of their state or on some of its regions due to which they are not able to return.

*971.* According to Articles 27, paragraphs 2 and 3 and 98, point 10 of the Constitution and Article 2 of the Asylum and Refugees Act, asylum is granted by the President of the Republic via presidential decree to foreigners who are persecuted for their convictions or activities for protection of internationally recognized human rights. Temporary protection is granted by the Council of Ministers on the basis of a decision of the Council of the EU. The duration of the temporary protection is determined by the Council of the EU. The Chairman of the State Agency for Refugees grants international protection. The Bulgarian institutions work in close cooperation with the Supreme Commissioner of the UN for Refugees via his or her representative in Bulgaria.

*972.* Article 8 of the Asylum and Refugees Act provides that refugee status is granted to foreigners who cannot or do not wish to return to their country of origin due to reasonable fear of persecution based on race, religion, nationality, political opinion or belongingness to a social group. Furthermore, the Asylum and Refugees Act determines the subjects that accomplish the persecution and thus create reasonable fear serving as a basis for applying for the refugee status, the activities they perform and defines the concept of persecution. Refugee status is granted also to foreigners on the territory of the Republic of Bulgaria who are recognized as refugees by the Supreme Commissioner of the UN for Refugees.

*973.* The humanitarian status is granted in accordance with Article 9 of the Asylum and Refugees Act. Pertaining to it, humanitarian status is granted to foreigners who do not fulfil the requirements for granting refugee status and who cannot or does not wish to receive protection from his or her state of origin because they can be exposed to real threat related to death penalty or execution, torture, inhuman or degrading treatment or severe threats for their life and personality as civilians in the context of an armed conflict.

## II. Extradition and European Arrest Warrant

*974.* Until 2005, the 1991 Constitution prohibited the extradition of Bulgarian citizens. However, in 2005, in the course of the preparation for EU integration, an amendment in Article 25, paragraph 4 was introduced. According to the current version of Article 25, paragraph 4 of the Constitution, Bulgarian citizens cannot be extradited to another state or to an international court for the purpose of criminal prosecution, except if an international treaty which is ratified, published and entered into force for the Republic of Bulgaria provides so. Currently Bulgarian citizens can be extradited to the International Criminal Court in The Hague as well as can be surrendered to other EU Member States on the basis of European Arrest Warrant. With regard to foreigners, Article 27, paragraph 1 of the Constitution provides that if they reside legally on the territory of Bulgaria, they cannot be expulsed or extradited except in the cases and under the conditions and procedure provided by an act of Parliament.

*975.* There is a special act of Parliament in Bulgaria which regulates the extradition and the European arrest warrant. This is the Extradition and European Arrest Warrant Act. It defines the extradition and the European arrest warrant as legal institutions, provides for the conditions for extradition and for refusal of extradition, determines the procedure for and the consequences of extradition as well as the procedure, modalities, conditions and consequences of the European arrest warrant.

*976.* The extradition and the European arrest warrant are defined in Articles 2 and 3 of the act. According to Article 5 of the Extradition and European Arrest Warrant Act, extradition is allowed if the criminal act for which it is required constitutes criminal offence according to both the Bulgarian criminal law and the criminal law of the state which issues the demand for extradition. Moreover, the sanction that may be imposed after a criminal trial should be either imprisonment for more than one year or other more serious sanctions. Extradition is permitted also in case of already-imposed sanction consisting in at least four months of imprisonment or other forms of detention.

*977.* Article 6 of the Extradition and European Arrest Warrant Act prohibits extradition of several categories of persons. These categories comprise: first, Bulgarian citizens, except of extradition that is explicitly provided for in an international treaty, ratified and entered into force for the Republic of Bulgaria; second, persons who are granted asylum in Bulgaria; third, foreigners who enjoy immunity from criminal prosecution in Bulgaria; fourth, persons who are not criminally responsible according to the Bulgarian legislation.

*978.* Furthermore, Articles 7 and 8 of the Extradition and European Arrest Warrant Act provide for ground for compulsory or facultative (discretionary) refusal for extradition. Article 7 enlists the circumstances in which the Bulgarian authorities must refuse extradition. These circumstances include: prosecution for political crimes or crimes related to them; prosecution for military criminal offence which is not a criminal offence according to the general criminal law; prosecution by extraordinary courts or imposition of a verdict pronounced by such courts; prosecution for crime based on race, religion, citizenship, ethnicity, sex, civic status or political convictions; risk of violence, cruel, inhuman or degrading treatment or lack of safeguards for human rights of the prosecuted person; prosecution for amnestied criminal offence or for criminal offence which is void by prescription; implementation of penalty for a crime for which there is already a criminal sentence which has entered into force in Bulgaria; risk of imposition of death penalty.

*979.* Article 8 of the Extradition and European Arrest Warrant Act provides for grounds on which the Bulgarian authorities may refuse a motion for extradition. Thus extradition may be rejected if: the criminal offence is under the jurisdiction of the Bulgarian courts; the criminal prosecution for the same criminal offence is terminated in Bulgaria; there is a pending criminal procedure in front of a Bulgarian court for the same criminal offence; the criminal sentence is pronounced in absentia without the knowledge of the sentenced person and there are no safeguards for the right to defence in a new trial; the criminal offence is accomplished outside of the territory of the state which demands the extradition and the Bulgarian legislation does not permit the accomplishment of criminal procedure for such crime.

*980.* The Extradition and European Arrest Warrant Act provides for the conditions, procedure, formal requirements and content of the European arrest warrant. It enlists the grounds on which the execution of a European arrest warrant must or may be rejected. Last but not least, the Extradition and European Arrest Warrant Act determines the procedure for issuing of European arrest warrants by the Bulgarian institutions.

# Part V. Specific Issues

## Chapter 1. War, Treaty and Foreign Affairs Powers

### §1. National Defence and the Police Services

*981.* The 1991 Constitution provides for the constitutional status of the armed forces and establishes a model for the distribution of competences between the President, the National Assembly and the Council of Ministers in the field of national defence. This model is partially further developed by the Constitutional Court. The Bulgarian Constitution does not provide for the status of either the Minister of Defence or the Minister of Interior. The only Minister who is mentioned by the 1991 Constitution is the Minister of Justice.

*982.* Furthermore, the 1991 Constitution does not contain any provisions regarding the police. Hence the police do not have any constitutional standing and thus will not be analysed here. However, the Constitution proclaims in its Article 9 the armed forces as a general category which encompasses both the army and the police to be safeguard for sovereignty, security, independence and territorial integrity of the state. In addition, Article 59 of the Constitution proclaims that the defence of the fatherland is a duty and honour for every Bulgarian citizen. The state treason is the heaviest criminal offence, and it should be persecuted by law.

*983.* The 1991 Constitution provides that both the status and the structure of the armed forces and the modes for defence of the fatherland by the Bulgarian citizens should be regulated by an act of Parliament. Several acts of Parliament determine that subject matter – the most important of which are the Defense and the Armed Forces Act and the Ministry of Interior Act.

*984.* The declaration of war and peace as the key and existential issues in the sphere of national security and defence is constitutionally reserved for the National Assembly. Moreover, the National Assembly declares state of siege and state of emergency on the whole territory of the state or on part of it on a proposal of the President or the Council of Ministers.

*985.* Article 64, paragraph 2 of the constitutions provides that in case of war, state of siege or state of emergency, the term of office of the Parliament is prolonged until the end of these events. This provision safeguards the ultimate control of the National Assembly over the crucial decisions in the national security in the context of extraordinary circumstances.

*986.* Furthermore, Article 84, point 11 declares that the National Assembly permits the sending or use of Bulgarian military troops abroad and the stay or crossing of foreign military troops through the Bulgarian territory. There are three important Constitutional Court's decisions related to this issue. These are Decision No. 23 of 1995, Decision No. 6 of 1999 and Decision No. 1 of 2003.

*987.* According to Decision No. 23 of 1995 of the Constitutional Court, the issuance of permission to such military deployments belongs to the exclusive competence of the National Assembly when it is accomplished with military or military–political aim. The National Assembly cannot permit the sending of Bulgarian military troops abroad without explicitly defining the mode of their use, the duration and the concrete place or places of their use and deployment. The decision of the National Assembly must also provide for the type of the armed forces and their strength.

*988.* Furthermore, according to Decision No. 6 of 1999 of the Constitutional Court, the National Assembly has an exclusive competence to ratify a via act of Parliament the international treaties which have political or military character. These treaties may provide for the aims, the procedure, the conditions and the time for dislocation or transition of foreign military troops through the Bulgarian territory as a result of national security operations or implementation of the international obligations of the Republic of Bulgaria. According to the Constitutional Court, there is no need for further decisions of the National Assembly for concrete and specific deployments or transitions of military troops if the National Assembly has ratified an international treaty which sets the just-mentioned framework for the deployment or transition of foreign military troops on Bulgarian territory.

*989.* Finally, Decision No. 1 of 2003 of the Constitutional Court declares that the military troops of political or military union in which Bulgaria participates, of Member States of such union or of states with which Bulgaria has concluded military–political alliance via international treaty ratified via act of Parliament are not foreign troops in the sense of Article 84 of the Constitution if their allocation on or transition through Bulgarian territory is related to the implementation of obligations stemming out of such treaty. Furthermore, no decision of the National Assembly is needed for the sending or use of Bulgarian military troops abroad or for the deployment or transition of foreign military troops in Bulgaria when such activities are accomplished for the implementation of alliance obligations stemming out of international treaty which is ratified by an act of Parliament, published and entered into force. Last but not least, decisions of the Parliament are not required for each concrete case if an act of Parliament determines exhaustively, fully and in advance the aims, procedure and conditions for the implementation of the duties for the Republic of Bulgaria stemming out of an international treaty.

*990.* Article 100 of the Constitution provides that the President is the supreme commander-in-chief of the armed forces of the Republic of Bulgaria. According to Decision No. 23 of 1998 of the Constitutional Court, the President is supreme commander-in-chief of the armed forces of the Republic of Bulgaria in both war and peace.

*991.* The President appoints and dismisses the supreme commando staff of the armed forces and assigns military ranks on a proposal of the Council of Ministers. The President is competent to declare general or partial mobilization of the population on a proposal of the government and in conformity with the law. The President declares state of siege, state of emergency or even war in case of military attack against Bulgaria or in case of necessity for immediate fulfilment of international obligations when the National Assembly is not in session. However, in such cases, the National Assembly must be immediately summoned in order to pronounce on the presidential decision.

*992.* The President presides over the Consultative Council for National Security. According to Decision No. 23 of 1998 of the Constitutional Court, the President in his or her role as head of state, supreme commander-in-chief of the armed forces and chairing person of the Consultative Council for National Security can require from all state institutions or private persons all necessary information related to the national security and the defence.

*993.* The Council of Ministers has central and very important competences in the sphere of national security and defence both as a collective institution and with regard to some of its members – the Prime Minister, the Minister of Defence and the Minister of Interior. However, the 1991 Constitution provides only for the competences of the government as a whole. According to its Article 105, paragraph 1, the Council of Ministers guides and implements the external and internal policy. The national security is a central part of both of these two policies. Furthermore, according to Article 105, paragraph 2 of the Constitution, the Council of Ministers assures the public order and the national security as well as accomplishes the general direction of the armed forces of the Republic of Bulgaria.

§2. Foreign Relations

## I. Introduction

*994.* This paragraph will set an outline of the external power which is the state power related to the participation of the state through its institutions in the international relations and in supranational regimes.[94] The external power comprises the competences of the state institutions that enable them to serve as veto players in the international and supranational context in which the state is set. There are several main groups of competences related to the external power which concern mainly the representation of the state, the preparation, negotiation and conclusion of international treaties, the implementation of the international treaties and the legislative, budgetary and other safeguarding of the observation of the international obligations of the state. Separate group of issues is related to the participation of the state in supranational regimes such as the EU.

## II. The Treaty-Making Power

*995.* The treaty-making power has already been analysed in Chapter II, section 1 of the monograph which is devoted to the international treaties. It will not be presented again here due to space constraints.

## III. Diplomatic Representation and Representation in International and Supranational Organizations

*996.* There are several institutions which are competent to represent the Republic of Bulgaria in the international relations and in the international organizations. The most important of them are the President of the Republic, the Prime Minister and the Minister of Foreign Affairs. These institutions have broad and general representative competence in the international relations.

*997.* The President of the Republic represents the state at the highest level in front of other states and in international organizations. He or she participates in international forums and conferences, visits foreign states and meets with foreign leaders during their official visits to Bulgaria. The President accepts the credential letters of the foreign diplomats in Bulgaria. He or she appoints and dismisses the Bulgarian diplomats abroad on a proposal of the Council of Ministers.

---

94. For more about the external power, *see* John Locke, *Two Treatises of Government*, 324–328 (Gal-Iko, 1996) (in Bulgarian); Martin Belov, *Separation of Powers Reconsidered: a Proposal for a New Theoretical Model at the Beginning of the 21st Century*, in *Law, Politics and the Constitution. New Perspectives from Legal and Political Theory*, 55–56 (Antonia Geisler, Michael Hein and Siri Hummel eds., Peter Lang, 2014).

*998.* The Vice President does not have representative competences in the international relations. According to the Bulgarian Constitution, the Vice President may possess only four competences – pardoning for criminal sentences, granting of asylum, granting of Bulgarian citizenship and appointing of civil servants in the presidential administration – if they are delegated to him or her by the President. Hence the Vice President cannot accomplish any tasks or missions in the foreign relations even if they are assigned to him or her by the President. Indeed in the political practice, the Vice Presidents of Bulgaria do accomplish representative missions abroad. These missions, however, are typically not related to official representation in front of other states or international and supranational organizations. They usually concern visits related to cultural and educational events, e.g., visits to the Bulgarian communities and diaspora living abroad.

*999.* The central figures in the external power of the state are the Prime Minister and the Minister of Foreign Affairs. The Prime Minister is the key veto player in the Bulgarian constitutional model and political system. He or she determines the strategy and the tactics of the external policy of the state. The Prime Minister is the institution which is competent to negotiate the most important political decisions related to the international relations, to set the international policy guidelines of the government. Informally and through political means, the Prime Minister can also assure the support of the National Assembly for the international policy of the government. This support typically consists in the ratification of international treaties, adoption of legislation and assurance of financial support for the external policy of the Council of Ministers.

*1000.* The Minister of Foreign Affairs is the most important specialized state institution in the external power domain. He or she is competent to represent the state in different international forums and in visits to other states and to international organizations. The Minister of Foreign Affairs conducts negotiations for the conclusion of international treaties and can sign in some of them. The distribution of the competence for signing international treaties among the President, the Prime Minister, the Minister of Foreign Affairs and other Ministers and state officials is provided by the International Treaties Act.

*1001.* The Minister of Foreign Affairs is the chief of the sector administration of the Ministry of Foreign Affairs. Due to the resort (department) principle of the organization of the activity of the government, he or she possesses the competence to determine the external policy of Bulgaria on the basis of the Constitution, the legislation, the decisions of the National Assembly and the general external policy of the Council of Ministers.

*1002.* The Minister of Foreign Affairs is the proactive veto player of both the substantial and the personal external policy of Bulgaria. He or she is the person that makes the initial proposal for the appointment or dismissal of the Bulgarian diplomats to the Council of Ministers which then proposes them to the President of the Republic.

*1003.* The Prime Minister represents the Republic of Bulgaria in the European Council. This is because Bulgaria is a parliamentary republic. The President represents the state in the European Council only in the case of a caretaker government. The reason is that in such a situation, for some of the months, the President is the only permanent political institution in Bulgaria because the National Assembly is dissolved and the Council of Ministers is appointed by the President. Hence the President has stronger democratic legitimacy to represent Bulgaria in the European Council than the caretaker Prime Minister who is appointed by the head of state. Such a situation has occurred in the term of office of two Bulgarian Presidents – Rosen Plevneliev and Rumen Radev.

*1004.* The Ministers represent Bulgaria in the Council of the EU in accordance with their governmental departments. They represent the state in accordance with the policy guidelines set by the Prime Minister and the Council of Ministers and eventually with the guidelines that the National Assembly may adopt.

*1005.* Last but not least, the Republic of Bulgaria is represented also by the Chairman of the National Assembly who can participate in different international and supranational deliberative and decision-making forums, conferences or institutions. The Chairman of the National Assembly represents both the Parliament and the state.

## IV. Parliamentary Involvement in Developing European Law

*1006.* The National Assembly participates in developing the EU law by implementing EU directives. Most of the EU directives are implemented via acts of Parliament instead of governmental decrees. In most of the cases, the National Assembly swiftly implements the EU directives without extensive debates on the adjustment of their provisions to the Bulgarian context. Thus the National Assembly frequently reproduces uncritically the provisions of the EU directives in acts of Parliament. Literal translation of terms provided by the EU directives and direct transplantation of concepts provided by the EU law in the Bulgarian legal system are not so much an indicator of the full harmonization and compliance of the Bulgarian legislation with the standards set by the EU law. They are sometimes evidence of uncritical and fast adoption of legal transplants. Hence the Bulgarian Parliament is not capable of at least partially remedying the de-parliamentarization stemming out of the EU integration which is a common problem to most of the EU Member States but is quite evident in the Southern and Eastern European Member States.

*1007.* The Bulgarian Parliament refrains also from issuing either binding mandates or at least policy frameworks for the activity of the Ministers to the Council of Ministers of the EU. The parliamentary control accomplished by the National Assembly on the Prime Minister and the Ministers with regard to their participation in the decision-making and legislative procedures on EU level is also rather pale.

# Chapter 2. Taxing and Spending Power

## §1. The National Level

### I. Constitutional Principles

*1008.* The 1991 Constitution provides for several principles of the public finances. The principle of legality and the principle of correspondence of taxation to the incomes and the property are provided by Article 60 of the Constitution. They jointly provide that the citizens are obliged to pay taxes and fees which are established by an act of Parliament in accordance with their incomes and property. Tax concessions and drags can be established only via an act of Parliament. Hence the principle of legality as provided by the Constitution consists specifically in the constitutionality of the taxation and of its correspondence with the acts of the Parliament. This is a limitation to the government to establish or modify taxes without explicit parliamentary approval via an act of Parliament.

*1009.* It is questionable whether the principle of correspondence of taxation to the incomes and the property should be interpreted narrowly thus being reduced to the principle of proportionality of taxation or it provides for the requirement of broader adequacy of the taxation to the property status of the person. In the former case, only proportional taxation system should be deemed constitutional whereas in the latter case also flat rate taxation system can be perceived as in compliance with the constitution.

*1010.* Since 2008, there is a 10% flat rate for the personal incomes in Bulgaria. Until 2017, no institution has officially questioned its constitutionality by approaching the Constitutional Court. If this is the correct interpretation of Article 60 of the Constitution, then it seems that the principle of correspondence of taxation to the incomes and the property has to be interpreted in the latter broader sense. In that case, however, its proper meaning and importance is doubtful since the flat rate taxation does not really provide for any connection between the degree of wealth and the amount of taxation.

*1011.* The principle of universality of taxation is not explicitly provided as such by the 1991 Constitution. It can be derived from the general equality clause (Article 6 of the Constitution), from the general principles of universality of the rights and duties (Article 26 of the Constitution) and from the principle that the law provides for equal conditions for economic activity of all natural and legal persons (Article 19, paragraph 2).

*1012.* The principle of the annual and public nature of the state budget and the other budgets is an important element of the principle of representative democracy and cornerstone element of the parliamentarism in Bulgaria. All types of budgets in Bulgaria – the state budget, the budget of the National Assembly, the budget of the judiciary, the budget of the National Assurance Institute, the budget of the National Health Insurance Fund, the municipal budgets etc. are public and annual. The annual and public nature of the state budget as well as of the budgets of the different national institutions is a safeguard for the competence of the National Assembly to serve as an ultimate check on the legality and the efficiency of the public finance management in Bulgaria.

## II. Constitutional Distribution of the Competences in the Financial Power on National Level

*1013.* The distribution of the competences in the financial power in Bulgaria has already been discussed in the chapters devoted to the state institutions and especially in the chapters analysing the competences of the National Assembly and the Council of Ministers. That is why here only a brief outline will be provided with a special emphasis on the taxing and the spending power.

*1014.* The financial power comprises the functions and the competences of the state institutions related to the public finance management.[95] The most important of them concern the adoption, implementation and control of the state budget and of the other public budgets, the taxing and spending powers, the control over the implementation of national and EU funding and the conclusion and ratification of international financial treaties.

*1015.* The taxing power has two main aspects – the power to determine the taxation and the power to implement the taxation. From an institutional point of view, the National Assembly possesses almost full monopoly of the power to determine the taxation in Bulgaria, especially on national level. It is the only institution that can adopt the state budget and the tax laws and thus impose taxation to the citizens, the foreigners and the companies. Neither the Council of Ministers nor the President, nor any other state institution can create new taxes or modify the existing ones.

*1016.* Indeed the Council of Ministers is the driving force behind the power to determine the taxation. This is because it is monopolist of the right to initiate the state budget. Moreover, it is the power unit composed of the government and its parliamentary majority and topped by the Prime Minister, who determines not only the general policy but also the taxation and financial policy of the state. However, from an institutional perspective, it is the National Assembly and not the Council of Ministers or the parliamentary majority which is formally competent to adopt and amend the state budget and the tax laws in Bulgaria.

*1017.* Since 2007, the municipal councils can determine the amount of the local taxes. However, they can do that only with regard to the amount of the tax and not with a view to its type. The municipal councils can determine the local taxes only in the framework set by the National Assembly via an act of Parliament.

95. *See* Martin Belov, *supra* n. 94, 56–57.

*1018.* The power to implement the taxation as well as the spending power is dispersed among several actors. The most important among them are the Council of Ministers, the Minister of Finance and the Tax Administration. The Minister of Finance governs the implementation of the state budget and the financial and tax laws under the guidance and supervision and in the policy framework determined by the Council of Ministers. The Minister of Finance and the Council of Ministers accomplish control over the implementation of both taxing and spending powers related to public finance spending and to the collecting of financial and tax revenues.

*1019.* However, all budgetary state institutions on national, regional and local level are participants in the procedures related to spending of public finance. Thus they are also included in the general scheme of the tax spending power. *Special* role in collecting public finance revenues and in the control over the implementation of tax laws is played by the tax administration topped by the National Revenues Agency.

## §2. The Financial Power and Financial Autonomy of the Municipalities

*1020.* The constitutional aspects of the financial power on local level concerning the distribution of the functions and competences between the local self-government and local government institutions in the sphere of public finance management, the structure of municipal finances and the financial autonomy of the municipalities are regulated by the 1991 Constitution and the Local Self-Government and Self-Administration Act. Some constitutionally relevant provisions are contained also in finance and economy law acts of Parliament such as the Local Taxes and Fees Act, the Municipal Debt Act and the Municipal Property Act.

*1021.* Article 141, paragraphs 1 and 2 of the Constitution is devoted especially to the budgetary and financial autonomy of the municipalities. It provides that the municipalities have their own budgets. The permanent financial revenues of the municipalities should be determined by an act of Parliament.

*1022.* According to Article 141, paragraph 5 of the Constitution, the state supports the proper functioning of the municipalities through finances provided by the state budget and by other proper means. Furthermore, Article 20 of the Constitution provides that the state creates conditions for balanced development of the different regions of the country and supports the activity of the territorial institutions and activities via the financial, credit and investment policy.

*1023.* These two constitutional provisions serve as elements of the principle of financial solidarity between the state and the municipalities and between the different municipalities and regions of Bulgaria. Hence the state is allowed to intervene in support of financially weaker municipalities and regions of the state. In fact, it is not only permitted but is actually required to remedy financial and economic disproportions, which may impede the balanced development of all parts of the country.

*1024.* The principles of financial solidarity and of balanced development of the territory and its administrative–territorial units has been confirmed and further developed by Decision No. 9 of 2000 of the Constitutional Court. According to this decision, the constitutionally provided competences of the institutions of the local self-government will be impeded and even made redundant if they are deprived from financial means for their accomplishment. That is why Article 141 of the Constitution structures the model for financing of the municipalities in accordance with the principle of proportionality between the tasks and competences assigned to the local self-government institutions and the financial resources they possess.

*1025.* The Constitutional Court underlines also the state's task to protect the financially weaker municipalities. According to the Constitutional Court the main instruments for achieving these principles are the existence of municipal budgets which are independent from the state budget, the provision of own financial revenue sources for the municipalities and, more precisely, the provision of local taxes and fees.

*1026.* In this decision from 2000, the Constitutional Court provides that according to the 1991 Constitution, the municipalities are prohibited from determining the local taxes and fees. However, in 2007, a constitutional reform was introduced. According to the new paragraphs 3 and 4 of Article 141 of the Constitution, the municipal council determines the amount (but not the type) of the local taxes under conditions, procedure and in a framework established by an act of Parliament. With regard to the local fees, the act of Parliament may provide only for the procedure but cannot determine the conditions and the framework for their imposition. Hence the 2007 constitutional amendment has increased the financial and tax autonomy of the municipalities while at the same time reducing the direct influence of the state in municipal tax matters.

*1027.* Many municipalities made use of these new constitutional provisions in order to increase and adjust their taxation policies. However, this constitutional amendment did not limit the principle of financial solidarity due to the fact that the state can still continue to engage in removing and remedying financial and economic disproportionalities by virtue of different means, such as the subsidies and subventions provided by the state budget. Moreover, the state still determines the structure and types of municipal taxes and fees as well as the structure, instruments and modalities of the municipal debt as prescribed by the Local Taxes and Fees Act and the Municipal Debt Act.

*1028.* The constitutional logic of limited but, since 2007, increased financial autonomy of the municipalities combined with state obligation to maintain a degree of financial symmetry and equilibrium between the different regions is further developed also on legislative level. Article 17 of the Local Self-Government and

Local Administration Act provides that the local self-government consists in the right and the real capability of the citizens and the elected institutions to decide upon all issues of local importance which the law has granted as a part of their sphere of competence. This article includes among these activities and issues the administration and management of municipal property, municipal enterprises and municipal finances, taxes and fees. In fact, the provision of Article 17 of the Local Self-Government and Local Administration Act is inspired by Article 3 of the European Charter of Local Self-Government.

*1029.* In compliance with the 1991 Constitution, the Local Self-Government and Local Administration Act distributes the competences for public finance management among the municipal institutions and more precisely among the municipal council and the mayors of the municipality, rayon and mayorship. According to Article 21 of the Local Self-Government and Local Administration Act, the municipal council is competent to adopt and amend the annual budget of the municipality, to approve the report for its accomplishment as well as to control the implementation of the municipal budget. The municipal council determines the amount of the local taxes and fees and adopts decisions for taking bank loans and credits, for issuing of municipal debt, for granting loans without interest and for granting municipal financial guarantees.

*1030.* According to Article 44, paragraph 1 of the Local Self-Government and Local Administration Act, the municipal mayor is competent to organize the implementation of the municipal budget. Article 46, paragraph 1, point 1 of the Local Self-Government and Local Administration Act provides for the competence of the mayors of rayons and mayorships to implement the municipal budget related to their rayon or mayorship.

*1031.* Article 52, paragraph 1 of the Local Self-Government and Local Administration Act provides that the municipal budget is outside of the state budget. The municipal budget revenues consist of the financial revenues of the municipality itself and of subsidies granted by the state. Articles 1 and 6 of the Local Taxes and Fees Act enlist the type of the local taxes and the local fees accordingly.

*1032.* Article 52, paragraph 4 of the Local Self-Government and Local Administration Act provides that the municipality is competent to issue bonds. The conditions for issuing of such bonds are enlisted in Chapter VII of the Municipal Debt Act which is devoted to the municipal securities. Furthermore, according to Articles 3 and 13 of the Municipal Debt Act, municipal debt can be issued by a decision of the municipal council on a proposal of the municipal mayor. The permitted forms of municipal debt are determined by Article 4 of the Municipal Debt Act regarding the long-term debt and Article 5 of the Municipal Debt Act regarding the short-term debt. Article 54 of the Local Self-Government and Local Administration Act provides that municipal expenditures can be accomplished for financing local needs as well as for activities related to the execution of outsourced state functions. However, the latter should be financed by the state budget.

## Chapter 3. Emergency Laws

*1033*. The 1991 Constitution does not allow the adoption of emergency laws. This is due to its reactivity with regard to the Tarnovo Constitution. According to Article 47 of the Tarnovo Constitution, the monarch under the responsibility of the Ministers can issue decree laws – normative acts with the force of an act of Parliament – in case of external or internal threat to the state and the society. These decree laws must be approved by the National Assembly once summoned.

*1034*. All Bulgarian monarchs frequently misused this competence. This is especially true for the last years of the rule of Tzar Boris III who dissolved the Parliament, prohibited the political parties and governed by decree laws although there was no immediate threat to the state.

*1035*. The VII Grand National Assembly having in mind that practice and the risks for the establishment of authoritarian rule, which the existence of emergency laws create, has refrained from providing not only of emergency law but also of delegated legislation. Thus in case of war, state of siege or state of emergency, only the regular Bulgarian legislation applies. Moreover, only the National Assembly can adopt primary legislation in the form of act of Parliament. Neither the President nor the government, nor any other state institutions can seize the competence of the National Assembly to adopt legislation.

# Chapter 4. The Constitutional Relationship Between Church and State

## §1. Introduction

*1036.* The freedom of religion and the relationship between the religious institutions and denominations and the state are regulated by the 1991 Constitution and the Religious Denominations Act. The 1991 Constitution provides for three main groups of issues of the relationship between state, church and religion. The first concerns the constitutional status of the religious denomination, the granting of special status to the Christian Orthodoxy and the legal and formal equality of all religious institutions. The second group of issues is structured around the freedom of religion as a constitutional right. The 1991 Constitution provides for the positive and negative freedom of religion, the modalities of the freedom of religion and the constitutionally permissible limitations to it. The third group of issues is related to the religion as an element of the principle of equality and to the safeguarding of the non-discrimination on the basis of religion. This issue is actually interrelated with the neutral attitude of the secular state towards the religious beliefs and serves as a safeguard to the freedom of religion.

*1037.* The 1991 Constitution and the Religious Denominations Act provide for equality of all religions in Bulgaria and for equal treatment of all believers as well as atheists. The Religious Denominations Act provides for registration regime of the religious denominations. This means that the religious denominations must be registered with the public register of the Sofia District Court if they fulfil the legally provided requirements. Consequently, they do not need the permission of any state institution for their establishment if they comply with the law.

*1038.* The Religious Denominations Act provides for the different aspects of the freedom of religion and the different forms by virtue of which it can be accomplished. It grants the religious denominations the status of legal person and allows them to accomplish cultural, educational and healthcare activities under some conditions. Moreover, the Religious Denominations Act provides for the procedure for the establishment and termination of the religious denominations and for their property and finance. The supervision over the activity of the religious denominations is accomplished by the Directorate of the Religious Denominations at the Council of Ministers.

## §2. Freedom of Religion

*1039.* Article 6 of the 1991 Constitution proclaims the principle of equality and prohibits discrimination on the basis of several criteria among which is also the religion. The freedom of thought, conscious, religious and atheistic beliefs are provided for in Article 37, paragraph 1 of the Constitution according to which they are inviolable. Moreover, this article assigns to the state the task to foster the toleration between the believers from the different religious denominations as well as between the believers and non-believers.

*1040.* The Religious Denominations Act provides for the positive and the negative freedom of religion and defines and safeguards the specific forms for practicing religious beliefs. According to Article 2 of the Religious Denominations Act, the freedom of religion is a basic, absolute, subjective, personal and inviolable human right. It includes the freedom to form, choose and change the religious beliefs and to practice them individually or collectively, in public or in private, via education, rituals or different religious practices.

*1041.* The 1991 Constitution and the Religious Denominations Act contain also limitations to the freedom of religion. According to Article 37, paragraph 2 of the 1991 Constitution, the freedom of religion cannot be directed against the national security, the public order, the public health, the public moral or the rights and freedoms of other persons. Moreover, Article 44, paragraph 2 of the 1991 Constitution prohibits organizations which are directed, among others, against the violation of human rights of citizens, including the freedom of religion. It prohibits also organizations aiming at instigation of religious hatred. Last but not least, Article 58, paragraph 2 of the 1991 Constitution declares that the religious beliefs are not valid ground for refusal to fulfil the legal duties set by the Constitution and the legislation.

## §3. Official Recognition of a Religion and Its Effects

*1042.* Bulgaria traditionally applies the liberal–republican and not the multicultural model for structuring its public sphere in general and for organization of the relations between the state and the religious institutions in particular. All Bulgarian constitutions provide for the principle of secular state and the separation between the state and the religion. According to Article 78 of the 1947 Constitution and Article 53, paragraph 2, Article 13, paragraph 2 of the 1991 Constitution, the religious institutions and denominations are distinct and separate from the state.

*1043.* The Tarnovo Constitution is the only Bulgarian Constitution which devotes wider attention to the relationship between the church and the state. It implicitly provides for the secular character of the Bulgarian state but contains provisions regarding the religion of the monarch and his heirs to the throne. Moreover, it specifies the relationship between the Bulgarian state and the Bulgarian church. This is due to the fact that the state of Bulgaria and its territory were only part of the much wider jurisdiction of the Bulgarian Orthodox Church (the Bulgarian Exarchate), the latter including also territories which remained part of the Ottoman Empire until the beginning of the twentieth century.

*1044.* It must be noted that the constitutional status of the religion and more precisely of the Bulgarian Orthodox Church and the Orthodox religion has passed through different phases. The Tarnovo Constitution treated them as cornerstones of the Bulgarian identity and safeguarded them a special and dominant status. The 1947 and the 1971 constitutions at least formally safeguarded the freedom of religion but did not provide for any constitutional status of either the Bulgarian Orthodox Church or the Orthodox religion. The 1991 Constitution grants special status of the Orthodox religion as traditional denomination but without any concrete legal consequences and without substantial sociolegal impact.

*1045.* Article 13 of the 1991 Constitution defines the constitutional status of the religious denominations in Bulgaria. It proclaims Christian Orthodoxy to be the traditional religion in Bulgaria, declares the separation between the state and the church in parallel to the freedom and equality of the religions and prohibits the use of the religious communities, institutions or beliefs for political purposes.

*1046.* The qualification of the Christian Orthodoxy has been changed from 'dominant' religion as defined by the Tarnovo Constitution into 'traditional' religion by the 1991 Constitution. Thus neither the Bulgarian Christian Orthodox Church is supposed to have primacy among the religious institutions nor the Christian Orthodoxy has supremacy among the religious denominations in Bulgaria. The idea of the constitutional legislator has been to revive the Christian routes of the Bulgarian society, which have been deliberately mitigated during the communist regime, and to preserve the Christian values as a part of the Bulgarian identity. The 'specific and traditional role of the Bulgarian Orthodox Church in the history of Bulgaria for forming and development of its culture' has been emphasized also by the preamble of the Religious Denominations Act. It also proclaims 'the respect for the Christianity, Islam, Judaism and all other religions'.

# Selected Bibliography

Belov, M. Българската конституционна идентичност [*The Bulgarian Constitutional Identity*]. Sofia: Sibi, 2017.

Belov, M. 'Establishment of the Modern Constitutional Principles in Bulgaria. The Tarnovo Constitution of 1879'. In *Konflikt und Koexistenz. Die Rechtsordnungen Südosteuropas im 19. und 20. Jahrhundert. Band 1: Rumänien, Bulgarien, Griechenland*, edited by M. Stolleis. Frankfurt am Main: Vittorio Klostermann Verlag, 2015.

Belov, M. 'Executive Power Metamorphoses in the History of the Balkan Constitutionalism: Between the Imperatives of the Constitutional Teleology and the Potentialities of the Political Reality' .*Romanian Journal of Comparative Law* 5, no. 2 (2014): 299–360.

Belov, M. 'The idea of "Europe" as a factor in the Building of the Bulgarian Legal Identity'. *Romanian Journal of Comparative Law*, 8, no. 1 (2017): 39–61.

Belov, M. The Opening of the Constitutional Order of Democracy in Transition Towards Supranational Constitutionalism: The Bulgarian Case. In *Central and Eastern European Socio-Political and Legal Transition Revisited*, edited by B. Fekete and F. Gardos-Orosz. Frankfurt am Main: Peter Lang, 2017

Belov, M. 'Finding Ways through the Clouds of Uncertainty, Searching for Paths in the Desert of Sorrow. The Functioning of Constitutional Justice in a Non-Consolidated Democracy'. In *Constitutional Review and Democracy*, edited by M. Jovanovich. Hague: Eleven International Publishing, 2015.

Belov, M. 'The Institutional Infrastructure of the Rule of Law in Bulgaria and the European Convention for the Protection of Human Rights and Fundamental Freedoms'. In *The European Convention of Human Rights and Fundamental Freedoms in Central and Eastern Europe*, edited by F. Emmert & L. Hammer. Hague: Eleven International Publishing and Boom Uitgevers, 2012.

Belov, M. & M. Fartunova. 'Bulgaria'. In *The Charter of Fundamental Rights as Apprehended by Judges in Europe*, edited by L. Burgorgue-Larsen. Paris: Pedone, 2017.

Belov, M. 'Rule of Law in Space of Flows'. In *Rule of Law at the Beginning of the Twenty-First Century*, edited by M. Belov. The Hague: Eleven publishing, 2018, Belov, M. *Финансов конституционализъм* [Financial Constitutionalism]. Sofia: Sibi, 2015.

Belov, M. The Preamble of the Constitution in the European Constitutionalism, 20 Revista General de Derecho Romano, (2013) Iustel

## Selected Bibliography


Belov M. **Функции на конституционния преамбюл** Functions of the Constitutional Preamble]. In *Law, Governance and Media in XXI Century*. Blagoevgrad: South-Western University „Neofit Rilski" Press, 2012

Bliznashki, G. ***Парламентарно право*** [*Parliamentary Law*]. Sofia: 'St. Kliment Ohridski' University Press, 2015.

Bliznashki, G. ***Парламентарното управление в България*** [*The Parliamentary Government in Bulgaria*]. Sofia: 'St. Kliment Ohridski' University Press, 2009.

Drumeva, E. ***Конституционно право*** [*Constitutional Law*]. Sofia: Ciela, 2013.

Kirov, P. ***Конституиране на представителното управление в България***[*Establishment of the Representative Government in Bulgaria*]. Sofia: Ciela, 2015.

Kirov, P. ***Президентът в българския конституционен модел*** [*The President in the Bulgarian Constitutional Model*]. Sofia: Sibi, 2004.

Penev, P. ***Съдебната власт в България** 1989–2014 **г.*** [*The Judicial Power in Bulgaria 1989–2014*]. Sofia: Sibi, 2014.

Tanchev, E. & M. Belov. 'The Governmental System of the Republic of Bulgaria'. In *Governmental Systems of Central and Eastern European States*, edited by N. Chronowski, T. Drinoczi, T. Takacs. Warsaw: Oficyna, 2011.

Tanchev, E. & M. Belov. 'The Republic of Bulgaria'. In *Constitutional Law of the EU Member States*, edited by L. Besselink, P. Bovend'Eert, H. Broeksteeg, R. de Lange, W. Voermans. Deventer: Kluwer, 2014.

# Index

*(The numbers here refer to paragraph numbers.)*

## Index

# Index

www.ingramcontent.com/pod-product-compliance
Ingram Content Group UK Ltd.
Pitfield, Milton Keynes, MK11 3LW, UK
UKHW020137290926
15471UKWH00003B/550

9 789403 517353